Making Digital Videos

MAKING DIGITAL VIDEOS

BEN LONG

FIREWALL MEDIA

(An Imprint of Laxmi Publications Pvt. Ltd.)

BANGALORE • CHENNAI • COCHIN • GUWAHATI • HYDERABAD
JALANDHAR • KOLKATA • LUCKNOW • MUMBAI • RANCHI
NEW DELHI • BOSTON, USA

Published by :

FIREWALL MEDIA

(An Imprint of Laxmi Publications Pvt. Ltd.)

113, Golden House, Daryaganj,

New Delhi-110002

Phone : 011-43 53 25 00

Fax : 011-43 53 25 28

www.laxmipublications.com

info@laxmipublications.com

Economy Edition Price : **Rs. 295.00** *Only.* *Edition* : 2008

OFFICES

India

✆ **Bangalore**	080-26 61 15 61
✆ **Chennai**	044-24 34 47 26
✆ **Cochin**	0484-239 70 04
✆ **Guwahati**	0361-254 36 69, 251 38 81
✆ **Hyderabad**	040-24 65 23 33
✆ **Jalandhar**	0181-222 12 72
✆ **Kolkata**	033-22 27 37 73, 22 27 52 47
✆ **Lucknow**	0522-220 95 78
✆ **Mumbai**	022-24 91 54 15, 24 92 78 69
✆ **Ranchi**	0651-230 77 64

USA

Boston

11, Leavitt Street, Hingham,
MA 02043, USA

FMA-2756-295-MAKING DIGITAL VIDEOS

ISBN: 81-7008-621-3

C—14848/07/10

Printed at : Sanjeev Offset Press, Delhi.

Contents

CHAPTER

1

Introduction

IN THIS CHAPTER

- What to Do First
- Film School on a Disk
- Analog and Digital

Let's cut to the chase: you want to make a movie, right?

Perhaps it's a full-length epic movie, or maybe it's a short. Or could it be a music video of your best friend's band? Or maybe you don't know yet. Perhaps you just have an inkling of an idea—or no specific idea at all—but you know that you like movies and you want to try making one yourself. After all, it looks like a lot of fun, doesn't it? Who wouldn't want to make a movie?!

Well, you're in luck, because this book is going to tell you how to do so.

The fact is, no matter what type of project you have in mind—feature length or short, musical or a straight story—you still need to learn the same things: what makes a good story, how to translate that story into images, how to capture those images, and how to turn those images into a finished piece. This book covers all of those questions; everything from writing your script, to planning your shoot, to using your gear, to delivering your movie to your friends on tape, CD, DVD, e-mail, or the Web.

So, what do you need to get started? These days, not much. In addition to a computer and a camera, you'll need some software, microphones, lights, and one or two other accessories. You'll learn about these in Chapter 2, "What You Need."

Obviously, you'll need a script or storyline to get started, so you'll spend a lot of time in Chapter 3, "Writing," learning about screenwriting. In Chapters 4, 5, and 6, you'll learn everything you need to know about shooting your project. These chapters cover all the details of capturing your scenes on tape, from using your camera, to planning your shots, to working with a crew and recording your audio. Once you've shot your movie, it will be time to start editing and adding any titles and effects. These tasks are covered in Chapters 7, 8, and 9.

When you're finished, you'll want to screen your masterpiece, either by showing it on TV or by broadcasting it over the Web. Outputting your movie to videotape, DVD, VideoCD or the Web is covered in Chapter 10, "Output."

Finally, you'll want to sit back and wait for the rave reviews to start rolling in, along with the inevitable telephone call from a high-powered Hollywood movie producer. We don't actually cover this part of the process, but you'll probably be able to wing it with no trouble. (If you *do* get invited to an expensive Hollywood gala in your honor—you know, one of those huge parties packed with fine food and beautiful movie stars—and you're a little nervous about what to do, don't hesitate to invite me along. I'd certainly be glad to help out, another example of how *this* book goes above and beyond to help you make the best movie you can!)

What Should You Do First?

There's one thing you should accept right now: making a movie is hard, and making a *good* movie is even harder. Consequently, if you want to pull this off, you're going to have to do some studying, a lot of thinking, and a good amount of basic hard work. The good news is that most of this work is pretty fun and, whether or not you end up with the movie you want, you'll certainly end up with some good stories to tell your friends.

Although you can use this book as a reference for times when you get stuck, you'll get the most out of it by reading it through from start to finish. In addition to learning how to do a number of things, you'll get a good idea of how your movie-making production will progress. Some chapters (Chapters 3 and 5,) include special troubleshooting sections that you can turn to during your production when you're having specific problems.

On the companion CD-ROM that's bound to the inside back cover, you'll find a demo of Adobe Premiere that you can use to follow along with the book's tutorials. When you get serious you'll need to invest in a full version of an editing program but for the projects here, this works fine.

In some chapters, you'll be asked to go watch one of the QuickTime movies included on the CD-ROM. These movies are grouped by chapter and are located in the Movies folder. They provide real-world examples and commentary on many of the topics covered in the book.

Because hands-on experience is often the best way to learn something, there will be a number of times when we'll ask you to create a particular type of short or video project. The book's CD-ROM includes a number of samples for each project, as well as other videos that will help better explain some concepts and lessons.

Film School on a Disk

If you're like me, you probably watch a lot of movies. And, if you're like me, you probably like some of these movies more than others. Since you're obviously interested in movie making, you've probably given some thought as to why some movies work and others don't. Asking yourself such questions is one of the best ways to learn how to make good movies.

Fortunately for us, there have been quite a few genius filmmakers who've crafted brilliant movies during the last 100 years of movie history. Looking at why those movies work can be a great way to learn how to tell your own story. Similarly, there have been many filmmaking simpletons over the last century. Although they might have wasted your time and money, or insulted your intelligence with their movies, they have also offered you the opportunity to learn what *not* to do when telling your own story.

On the *Making Digital Videos* CD-ROM in the Filmschool folder are a number of essays that examine a number of great films. Careful study of these essays and films (all of which are available at your local video store) will help you make better movies. You might also find that learning how to critique and dissect a movie makes movie-going a lot more fun.

Whenever appropriate, this book will prompt you to read a particular essay from the Filmschool folder. Since most of the essays center on a particular movie, you'll need to rent the movie and watch it. Although watching other people's movies might seem like it has very little to do with making a movie of your own, bear in mind that you can't always be writing or shooting or editing. Relaxing with a little film study is a good way to step away from your project, kick back, get a new perspective, and learn something at the same time.

Hard Work

Finally, there's one thing that we can't include in this book: hard work is something you have to come up with yourself. By hard work, we mean the hard work of writing your script, then rewriting your script, then throwing it out and starting over. By hard work we mean trying to talk your friends into showing up on time, wearing silly costumes, remaining patient while you set up your gear, and not getting bored when you demand take after take. By hard work we mean trying to talk someone into letting you use their house for a location, or their cool antique car as a prop.

Hard work also means sticking with your project through all of the days, weeks, or months it might take to complete. For example, just when your shoot is over and you think you're past the worst of your production, you might find that the audio in your favorite scene is bad and can't be used. At this point, you'll have to start the hard work of trying to find a solution.

This talk isn't meant to discourage you. In fact, solving the preceding problems is usually the fun part of movie making. However, to get through these issues you have to be committed to doing the work that has to be done. This commitment includes lots of thinking and planning, lots of research, and a good amount of study.

To be a good filmmaker, you need to know the technical details of using your gear, while managing to keep a vision of what your finished product should look like. And, while doing all of that, you'll need to be organizing and marshalling your cast, crew, and all of the other people that even a small video production requires.

Yeah, yeah…you've heard it before, right? Good. Then let's get started with the first order of business.

ANALOG AND DIGITAL

Although this book centers on the latest *digital video* technology, it's important to understand that digital video gear is still partly analog.

Your eyes and ears (as well as your nose and skin, for that matter) are *analog* devices. Take your ears as an example.

Sound is caused by vibrations in the air. These vibrations reach your ear in the form of continuous *waves*. Your ear, in turn, senses these waves and translates that information into your sense of sound.

Just like a wave on the ocean, a wave in the air has a peak. The *frequency* of a wave is simply a measurement of how many peaks occur over a given length of wave. A wave with more peaks is said to have a higher frequency. Your ear hears a wave with more peaks (that is, a wave with a higher frequency) as a higher-pitched sound (Figure 1.1).

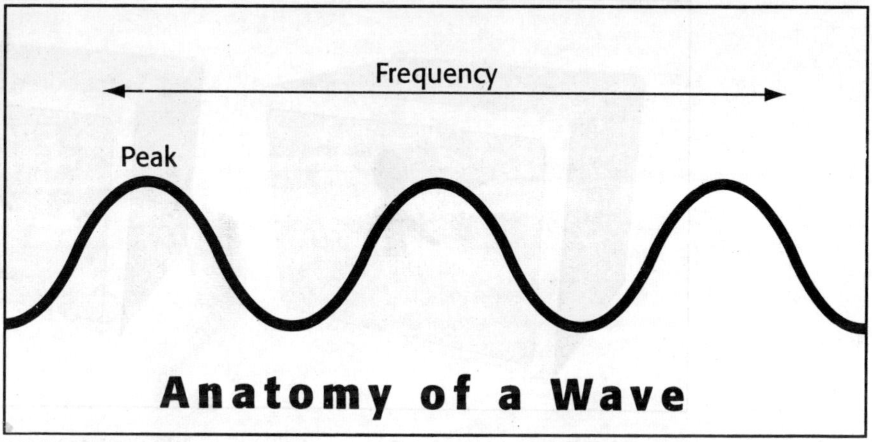

FIGURE 1.1 Sound and light waves have peaks and troughs. The number of peaks that occur over a given length of time is referred to as the wave's *frequency*. When peaks occur more frequently, the wave is said to have a higher frequency. In the case of a sound wave, a higher frequency means a higher-pitched sound. In the case of a light wave, different frequencies mean different colors.

An analog recording system records a representation of a sound wave. In the case of a record player, sound waves are recorded by scraping a groove with tiny variations into the surface of a vinyl disk. When you play back the recording, the analog signal stored on the record is amplified and then sent to a pair of speakers. Big cloth or paper cones inside the speaker vibrate to recreate the waves of sound that were originally recorded.

Light works in a similar fashion. Waves of photons are received by your eyes and converted into your sense of sight. In the case of light, higher-frequency light waves have a different color than lower-frequency light waves. The best example of light frequencies occurs in a rainbow, when rain droplets split sunlight into all of its separate frequencies ranging from low-frequency red and orange, to high-frequency indigo and violet.

Analog video cameras use special tubes or computer chips to store a representation of light waves on a magnetic tape. Later, those waves can be read off of the tape, and passed to a television where specially colored *electron guns* paint a colored image on the inside of a picture tube (Figure 1.2).

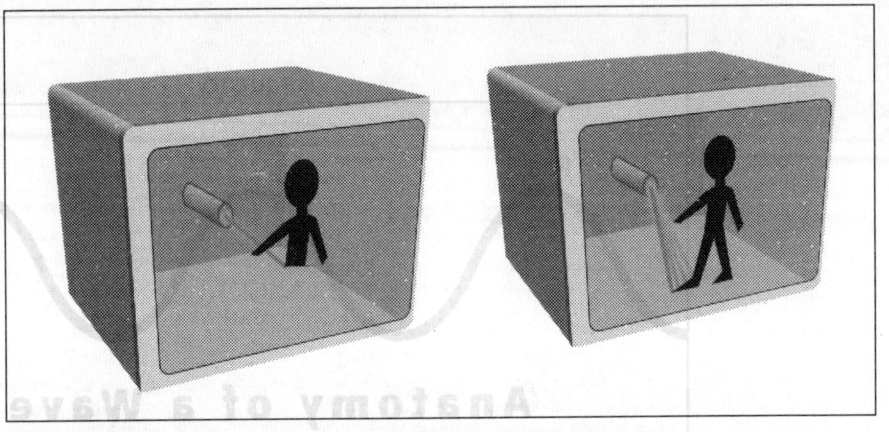

FIGURE 1.2 Inside every TV is an electron gun that paints an image onto the screen every 30th of a second. Actually, there are three guns, one that paints red, one green, and one blue. Your TV combines all three of these colors to create every other color.

Digital: Working by the Numbers

Unlike your eyes and ears, your computer cannot think in terms of waves. The only thing it can understand is numbers, or digits. So, before you can put any data into your computer, the data must be converted to digits, or *digitized* (Figure 1.3).

When you're finally ready for playback, the numbers in your digital file are converted back into analog waves, which are sent to your TV monitor and speakers. Once your images and sounds are back in the analog world, your eyes and ears can detect them.

Why do you need to know all this? Because your video and computer gear uses *both* analog and digital connectors for different functions, that's why. You can't send analog data over a digital connection (or digital data

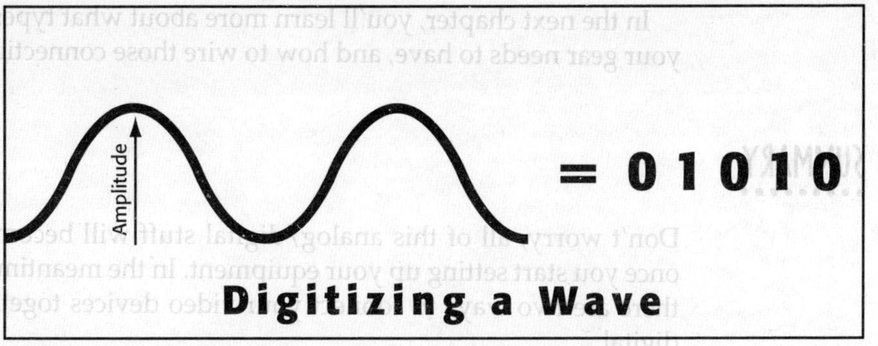

FIGURE 1.3 An analog wave can be converted into digits by assigning numerical values to different amplitude values. In the example shown here, if we say that a trough equals 0 and a peak equals 1, then we can represent this wave as a series of numbers. In other words, we can convert the wave to digits, or *digitize* it.

over an analog connection), so you need to understand what types of connections are used for different functions.

For example, you connect your camera or VCR to your TV using an analog connection (similarly, you connect your computer to its monitor using an analog connection), but to connect your digital camera to your computer, you'll use a digital connection.

FILM SCHOOL: KNOW YOUR HISTORY

If this were the year 1903 and you wanted to shoot a color movie, you would have to color each frame *by hand*. Sounds awful, doesn't it? But that's what Thomas Edison had to do to create the world's first color movie.

This history of film and cinema is pretty interesting and it's a great way to learn how to make your own movies much better. After all, it's always good to know what foolish things people have done before, so that you can avoid them (or come up with your own, original, foolish things to do in the future).

ON THE CD

Check out the "Brief History of the Cinema" in the Filmschool> Chapter 1 folder of the companion CD-ROM. This PDF document gives you a quick overview of the 100-year history of film technology and filmmaking and provides you with a cool list of really great movies to watch and learn from.

In the next chapter, you'll learn more about what types of connections your gear needs to have, and how to wire those connections together.

SUMMARY

Don't worry, all of this analog/digital stuff will become much clearer once you start setting up your equipment. In the meantime, be aware that there are two ways to connect your video devices together: analog and digital.

Now you're ready to start selecting your equipment and preparing for your shoot! Chapter 2 covers all of your equipment questions, and Chapter 3 gets you started on writing and planning.

CHAPTER

2

What You Need

IN THIS CHAPTER

- Your Camera
- Dealing with Microphones
- All That Other Gear

Check this out: in a typical Hollywood movie (shot on 35mm film), the film stock alone costs an average of $100,000. That's just for the film! That doesn't include the processing of the film or the rental of a camera package. Most Hollywood movies use special cameras that you can't even buy; you have to rent them at a cost of approximately $800 per day. Oh, and that doesn't include lenses, that's just the camera body and various accessories. Lenses typically run an extra $500 a day. And, they don't shoot movies without equipment to light the scenes. Large lighting packages (that come in trucks) normally cost about $2,000 per day.

After eight weeks, or so, of shooting with all this expensive gear, a Hollywood filmmaker has a single film negative (just as when you shoot a roll of film with a 35mm still camera you have a single negative). Before they can look at it, they have to develop the negative (which costs money) and make a print of the negative (which costs more money). To edit, they take their print and cut it together to create an edited print.

By this point, they've spent maybe $200,000 just for film and camera rentals, and all they have is a single edited print! They now have to give that print to a negative cutter who will cut apart the original negative and put it back together so that it matches the edited print (a process called *conforming*). Now they can strike prints from this edited negative to distribute to movie theaters.

Bear in mind that these numbers cover *just* the cost of film, and camera rentals. Film processing, actors, crew, editors, lights, props, sets, special effects, writers, directors, trucks to carry everything around, coffee, donuts . . . all that costs extra. They don't call it the movie "business" for nothing!

Maybe now you can understand why people are excited by the idea of digital video cameras that cost $700 and computer-based editing systems that cost $1000.

To make your digital movie—no matter what kind of movie it is—you're going to need a lot of gear, ranging from a camera and computer to lights, microphones, cables, and disk drives. In this chapter, you'll learn the details about all the equipment you'll need to have to produce your digital movie. Even if you already have a lot of this equipment, it's worth taking a look at this chapter to better understand what you have, what you might need, and how you'll get it all to work together.

First, though, you need to make a big decision.

DIGITAL OR ANALOG

There are two types of video cameras: digital and analog. Which type you choose (or which type you already have) will affect all of your other equipment choices, as well as your software choices and your post-production work.

Digitizing

In an analog video camera, the analog image that the camera shoots is written to tape as is; that is, as an analog signal, the type of signal that your TV needs. However, remember that before your computer can work with a piece of video, that video has to be converted to numbers, or *digitized*, a process that requires your computer to have special hardware.

If your computer has an analog digitizing card, you can plug the video and audio outs of your camera into the card—just as if you were connecting your camera to a TV or to another video deck. Then, using special software you can "dub" the video into your computer.

A digital camera works quite a bit differently. Rather than storing an analog signal on tape, a digital camera digitizes the video *while you shoot* and stores a digital file on tape. This means you don't have to have any special digitizing hardware in your computer. When you're ready to put your video into your computer for editing, you simply connect the camera to your computer using a high-speed interface of some kind, usually FireWire (fancy, high-end cameras use an interface called SDI).

When you're ready to edit, your computer copies the digital information from the tape into your computer. It's really just like copying a file from one hard drive to another.

Compression

The problem with video is that, information-wise, it's really big. It simply takes a lot of data to store a video image. Take a look at the numbers (Figure 2.1).

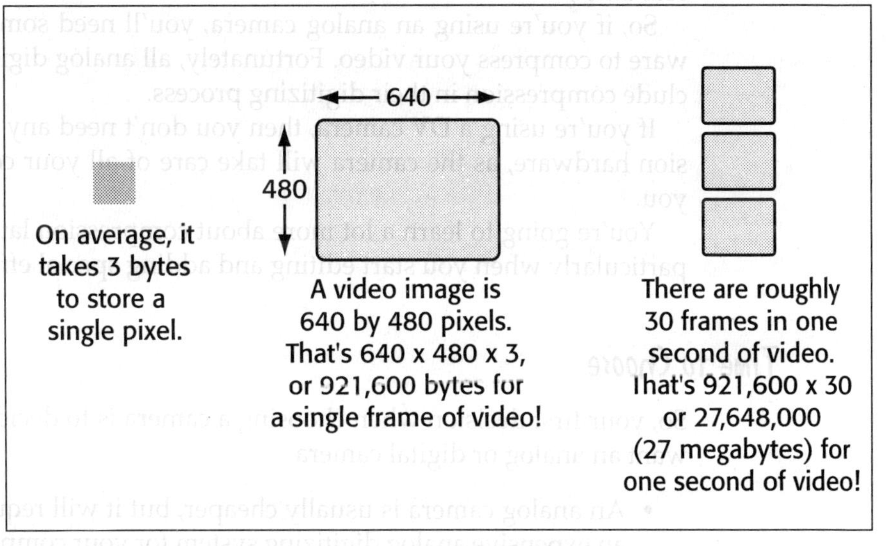

FIGURE 2.1 Video—even a single frame—takes up a lot of space.

Obviously, 20 megabytes per second is not really practical if you only have a 20-gigabyte hard drive—you'd use up the entire drive on 20 seconds of video! What's more, even today's fastest desktop computers are too slow to move that much data around quickly enough to play video back at full speed.

To avoid these problems, your video must be compressed before you can edit or manipulate it on your computer. If you've ever saved a picture as a JPEG file, or converted a CD into MP3 files, then you've engaged in a form of compression. Video compression is very similar. Using complex algorithms and a bunch of gnarly math, your video is crunched down into a much smaller space. There is a tiny bit of quality loss when this happens, but it's usually not perceptible and, if you're careful, you can manage this loss of quality as you work.

Analog cameras don't compress their video because they don't deal with digital data. Digital cameras, on the other hand, compress their data as they record using a special compressor called the *DV compressor* (clever, those video guys, huh?). What's really amazing about video compression is that, although it can take a *long* time to compress a piece of video, it can be decompressed in real time, while the video plays. (DV cameras have special hardware that allows them to compress video in real time.)

So, if you're using an analog camera, you'll need some special hardware to compress your video. Fortunately, all analog digitizing cards include compression in their digitizing process.

If you're using a DV camera, then you don't need any extra compression hardware, as the camera will take care of all your compression for you.

You're going to learn a lot more about compression later in this book, particularly when you start editing and adding special effects.

Time to Choose

So, your first decision when choosing a camera is to decide whether you want an analog or digital camera.

- An analog camera is usually cheaper, but it will require you to buy an expensive analog digitizing system for your computer. However, with an analog digitizing system, you can use any camera from VHS to Hi8 and beyond.
- With a digital camera, you can use any computer that has a FireWire interface. Therefore, although digital cameras are often more expensive than analog cameras, in the long run they usually end up being a bit cheaper because you don't have to add expensive digitizing gear to your computer. On the downside, you can't use any tapes you might already have, such as tapes from an old VHS camera.

WHAT IF YOU ALREADY HAVE A CAMERA?

If you already have a camera, then that's just one less decision you have to make right now. However, you do need to figure out if you have an analog or digital camera, because this will affect some of your hardware and software decisions when you select a computer.

It's usually pretty easy to tell if you have an analog or digital video camera. Digital video cameras typically say "Digital Video" somewhere on the side in big, flashy letters. If you can't find anything like that, then look at the tape format the camera uses. Analog and digital cameras use formats specifically designed for analog or digital recording. Look at the tape format your camera uses and then compare it to the table in Figure 2.2.

	Analog	Digital
VHS	•	
VHS-C	•	
Beta	•	
8mm	•	
Hi8	•	
Digital-8		•
DV		•
MiniDV		•
DVCam		•
DVCPro		•

FIGURE 2.2 If you're unsure if your video camera is analog or digital, just look at the type of tape it uses.

LOAD IT WITH OPTIONS

Once you've chosen analog or digital, you're ready to start looking for a camera. As you might have already discovered, there are a lot of cameras out there. Fortunately, choosing one isn't too hard if you know what features you want.

CHOOSING A CAMERA

Picking a video camera is pretty easy if you know what you're looking for. This book isn't going to cover any specific cameras, but it will show you how to make an intelligent choice when buying a camera.

When shopping for a camera, your main concern is to balance price with features and quality. In this section, we walk through all of the features that you need to consider when camera-shopping.

Image Quality

Your main concern when buying a video camera should be image quality. You want the camera that will shoot the best image you can afford.

Quality-wise, cameras can be broken down into two categories: single-chip cameras and three-chip cameras. A single-chip camera uses a single imaging chip to grab a full-color image, while a three-chip camera uses separate imaging chips for red, green, and blue information. This information gets merged into a full-color file.

Three-chip cameras deliver better color in some circumstances and do a better job reproducing fine edge detail. However, three-chip cameras start at around $1700 and go up from there. If you can't afford a three-chip camera, don't worry about it: a single chip camera can still deliver a great image.

The best way to judge image quality is to go to the store and look at some different cameras. Many electronics stores have lots of cameras hooked up to monitors so you can see exactly what their image looks like.

When checking out a camera's image quality, consider the following:

- **How is the overall color?** Some cameras will have a color *cast*, a general color tone that covers the entire image. For example, Sony cameras tend to shoot very cool images with a strong bluish tone, while Canon cameras tend to shoot rather warm images with reddish tones. One is not better than the other, but you might find that you have a personal preference.
- **How does the camera perform in low light?** Although this can be a little difficult to do in a brightly lit electronics store, ask the salesperson if you can stick the camera under a cabinet or in a dark corner to get an idea for how well it performs in low light.
- **Does the camera sharpen too much?** Most digital cameras employ some type of digital sharpening process to sharpen up their image. Unfortunately, some cameras take this too far, resulting in severely oversharpened images that are full of weird artifacts and funky noise. Check out Figure 2.3 for an example. Ideally, you want a camera with a sharpening control that lets you change the degree of sharpening.

FIGURE 2.3 Some cameras have a tendency to oversharpen their images, resulting in weird artifacts like the ones shown here in the upper image.

- **Finally, how does the image look overall?** There are lots of ways to pick apart the quality of an image. In the end, though, it's best to trust your overall impression. You might not be able to explain why one image looks better, but that's okay. Go with that one.

Lens

The quality of a camera's image depends a lot on the quality of its lens. If you've considered the preceding image quality questions, then you've covered most of what you need to worry about, lens-wise. Now you can start looking at the controls and range of a particular lens.

Most digital video cameras today include big zoom lenses with zoom ratios of 8 to 10x. Any of these are going to be fine. However, you'll also meet many salespeople hyping the "digital zoom" feature of a camera. A camera with digital zoom simply digitally enlarges an image to make it look like you're zooming in closer—sometimes as much as 200x! Although this might sound cool, digital zooms don't work very well, and you shouldn't use them. In fact, one of the first things you should do when you get your camera is to turn off its digital zoom.

WATCHOUT!

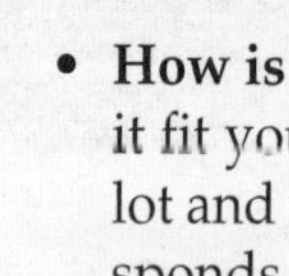

Don't let digital zoom be a factor in your buying decision! It's not a feature you need to worry about.

The only other lens issues you need to worry about have to do with controls. When looking at a camera, check the following:

- **How is the zoom control?** Is it easy to reach and comfortable? Does it fit your hand well? Zoom is something that you're going to use a lot and you need to have fine control over it. A really good zoom responds "proportionally"; in other words, the farther you push it, the faster (or slower) it zooms. You want that.
- **Is there a manual focus control?** This might not be a focus ring like you'd see on a film camera, but try to find out if the camera offers some type of manual focus control. It can be very handy.
- **How about manual iris and shutter speed?** Although you'll mostly depend on your camera's auto-exposure features, manual overrides can be essential for weird lighting situations and special effects.

Manual aperture controls also give you many extra composition and shooting possibilities, as you can see in Figure 2.4.

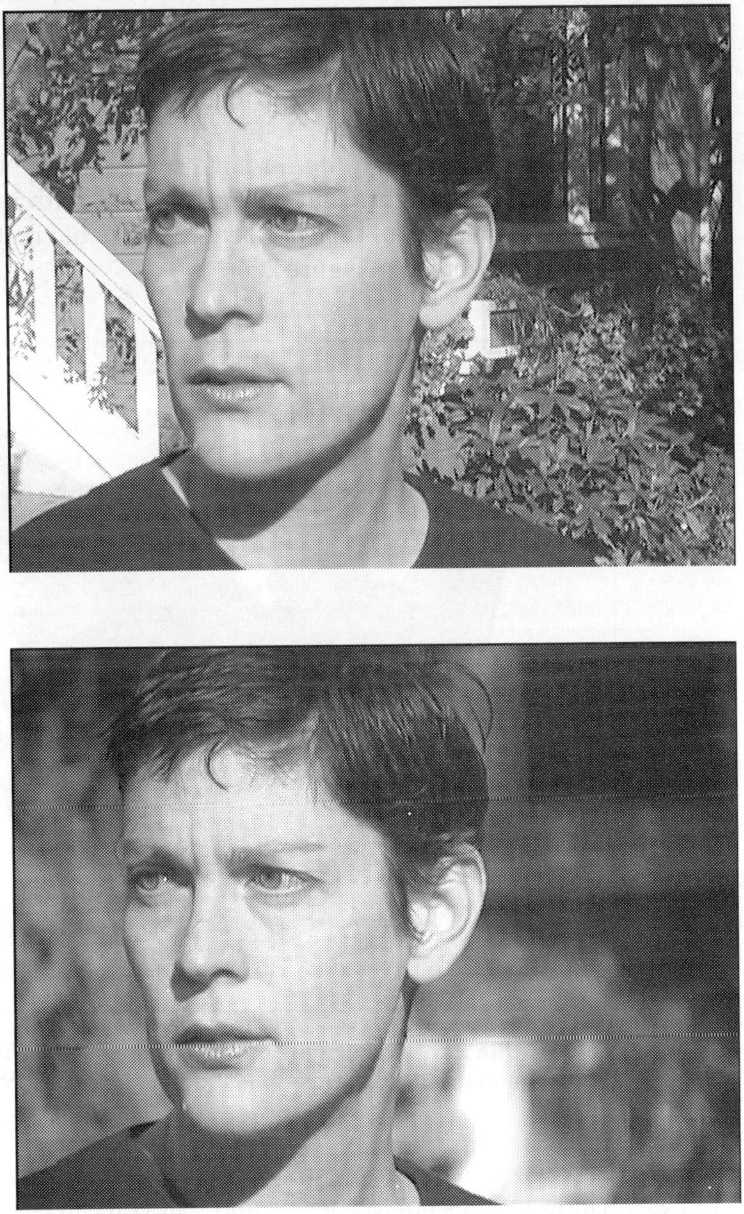

FIGURE 2.4 With manual aperture controls, you can do cool things like blur out the background in a shot to bring more focus to your foreground.

Camera Design

Cameras come in all shapes and sizes and you want to be sure you get one that's comfortable for you and fits your shooting needs. For example, if you plan on lots of "on-the-go" shooting of your friends, or you want to shoot documentary-style footage, then you might want a very tiny digital camera that can be easily carried around and won't be annoying or distracting to your subject.

On the other hand, if you have some very specific shots and scenes planned, you might want a larger camera with better controls. With a bigger camera, you'll have a better chance of creating smooth, complex camera movements (Figure 2.5).

FIGURE 2.5 The design of your camera not only affects how comfortable the camera is, but also what kinds of shots you can get.

When looking at a camera, make sure it feels comfortable in your hands, that it's not too heavy, and that you can easily reach and use all of its controls.

Some other things to consider:

- **How sturdy is the camera?** If you're tough on equipment, you might want to get a beefier camera.
- **Does the camera provide bigger, longer-life batteries?** Most cameras ship with wimpy little batteries. Make sure it's possible to get extra, longer-life batteries.
- **Can you change batteries while the camera is mounted on a tripod?** It can be really annoying and time consuming to have to take the camera off its tripod every time you want to change the battery.
- **Can you change the tape while the camera is mounted on a tripod?**

Audio

All cameras these days have built-in microphones. Unfortunately, these microphones are not usually the best quality (Figure 2.6).

On-camera mics are okay in a pinch, but for serious work you're going to want to attach an external microphone. Make sure that the camera has an external microphone jack and a headphone jack (for monitoring your

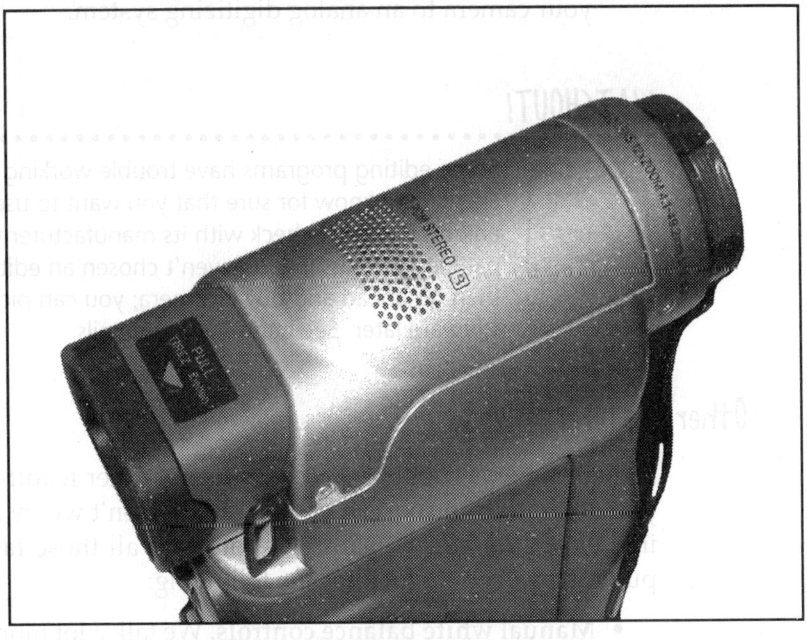

FIGURE 2.6 Almost all video cameras have a built-in microphone. Unfortunately, these microphones are usually bad and poorly positioned. It's far too easy to unintentionally bump a microphone like the one shown in this picture.

audio while recording). We talk more about microphones later in this chapter.

Ports and Connectivity

Having a fancy digital video camera doesn't do you any good if you can't connect it to your computer hardware for editing. Make sure that the camera provides all of the ports you need:

- **Digital.** If you're buying a digital camera and your computer has a FireWire port, make sure that the camera also provides a FireWire port. (You'll learn more about FireWire ports later in this chapter).
- **S-video.** Whether you're buying a digital or analog camera, you're going to want to hook it up to a monitor, and S-video is the best way to do this. If you're using an analog digitizing system, you can also use the S-video connector for digitizing.
- **Composite.** Many TVs don't have S-connections, but have composite connections instead. Make sure your camera provides composite video and audio outputs. These are also essential for connecting your camera to an analog digitizing system.

WATCHOUT!

Some editing programs have trouble working with some cameras. If you know for sure that you want to use a particular editing package, check with its manufacturer for a list of compatible cameras. If you haven't chosen an editing program, then go ahead and buy a camera; you can pick compatible software later. See page 159 for details.

Other Features

Digital cameras come packed with lots of other features, many of which you don't need to concern yourself with. Don't worry about titling, editing, or special effects features—you'll do all those tasks on your computer. However, do look for the following:

- **Manual white balance controls.** We talk a lot more about white balance in Chapter 5, "Preparing Your Camera."
- **Image stabilization.** Although no substitute for a tripod, image stabilization is a great way to improve the quality of your video. A

camera with image stabilization can automatically smooth out the small jitters and vibrations in your hand. Opt for a camera that provides optical image stabilization rather than digital image stabilization.

Making the Choice

Obviously, cost will play a large part in the camera that you buy and, although it would be nice to buy that fancy $5000 DV camera with all the cool features, it's probably just not going to happen. The following sections list features in order of priority. If you can afford a camera with all of these, great. If not, go for the items at the top of the list.

IF YOU'RE ON A SMALL BUDGET, BE SURE TO GET THESE FEATURES

- **Image quality.** Get the best you can afford.
- **Interface.** Get a camera with the type of interface your computer needs (usually FireWire).
- **External microphone jack.** This will allow you to record *much* better audio.

IF YOU HAVE MORE TO SPEND, TRY TO GET THESE FEATURES

- Image quality
- Interface
- External microphone jack
- Manual white balance
- Manual aperture and shutter speed controls
- Electronic image stabilization

CHOOSING A COMPUTER

In the old days (circa 1990), editing video required a room full of expensive video decks and edit controllers, as well as racks of fancy machines for color correcting, titling, and superimposing different pieces of video. Nowadays, you can do all of that—and much more—on your desktop computer. What's more, you can do a lot of it using software that's absolutely free!

Odds are, you already have a computer, but you might not have a computer that has all of the muscle you need for video editing and post-production. This section explains everything you need, computer-wise, to have a full-featured video post-production facility. If you don't have a computer, this section will help you choose one. If you do have a computer, this section will help you make sure that it has everything it needs.

If You Already Have a Computer

If you already have a computer, you'll want to assess its specs before you continue reading. Hopefully, your computer is already equipped to deal with the hardware and software that we discuss here. If it doesn't, you'll need to add or upgrade. In this section, we'll quickly run through the specifications that you need to check out if you already have a system.

IF YOU HAVE A MAC

If you have a Macintosh, you can answer most of your questions by running a simple application that's probably already installed on your computer. From the Finder, select "About this Mac" from the Apple menu. You should see one of the two dialog boxes shown in Figure 2.7, depending on whether your computer is running OS 9 or X. If your Mac says that it's running an operating system earlier than 9.0, you're going to have to upgrade your OS (and, odds are, you're going to have to upgrade your hardware as well, but we'll get to that in a minute).

If you're running OS 9, then go to the Apple menu and select Apple System Profiler. If you're running OS X, go to your Applications folder and, from there, into your Utilities folder. There you should find the Apple System Profiler (see Figure 7.1 on page 160).

In the Apple System Profiler, you can quickly see what type of processor your Mac has and how fast the processor is running. In addition, you can also determine your computer's built-in memory size and hard drive capacity.

The following are the minimum specs that you want to have if you're using a Mac:

- A PowerPC G3 or G4 processor running at a minimum of 300MHz.
- At least 128MB of RAM (virtual memory doesn't count).
- At least a 6GB hard drive (any less than this and you're going to be frustrated).
- At least one FireWire port.

FIGURE 2.7 On a Macintosh, you can easily find out how much RAM is available by choosing "about this Mac" from the Apple menu.

If your computer has a slower processor, then there's not much you can do but upgrade to a newer machine. If it has less RAM or storage then you need to look into buying more memory or a bigger hard drive.

If your computer lacks a FireWire port, you might have to upgrade to a newer machine. However, if your computer is a PowerBook that has a fast enough processor, but no FireWire port, you can add a PC Card FireWire port.

In general, if you have a PowerBook, iMac, G3 or G4 tower, or G4 Cube purchased after 1999, your Mac should be ready for handling DV. You'll need some editing software, of course, but we'll talk more about that in Chapter 7, "Preparing to Edit."

IF YOU HAVE A WINDOWS-BASED SYSTEM

Unless you bought a Windows system that was specifically designed for video editing, there's a good chance that your computer is not quite DV-ready. Fortunately, boosting it up to DV specs is not too difficult.

First, you need to determine your computer's RAM and disk sizes, as well as processor type and speed. To learn about your RAM and processor, choose Start>Settings>Control Panels, and click on System (see Figure 7.2 on page 162).

From the Properties tab of the Windows Settings dialog, you can determine most of the relevant specifications. Your specifications will vary depending on the software and hardware that you're using, but in general, it's safe to say that you need at least the following:

- A Pentium II or better processor running at 300 MHz or faster.
- At least 128MB of RAM.
- At least a 6GB hard drive; ideally, a 10 to 20 GB hard drive.
- A DirectX 6.0-compatible video card and sound card with enough video RAM to display at least 256 colors.

Finally, your computer will also need a FireWire interface. If your system was specifically configured as a DV workstation, then it probably already has a FireWire interface. However, FireWire is not yet prevalent on Windows computers, so odds are that you'll need to add a FireWire PCI card. These cards are usually pretty affordable—around $100 to $200—and can be quickly installed in any free PCI slot inside your computer. If you're not sure if your computer has a FireWire port, look on the back of your computer for a port like the one shown in Figure 7.4 on page 164.

Most FireWire cards also include video editing software, so you can kill two birds with one stone if you pick the right package. Pinnacle Systems' StudioDV package (www.pinnaclesys.com) is a great choice if you need to add a FireWire card to your system.

When you do pick a FireWire card, be sure to check its RAM and processor requirements, as well as compatibility with the other components in your system.

Choosing an Operating System

If you already have a computer, this choice has probably been made for you. If you don't have a computer, you'll need to decide if you want an Apple Macintosh or a Windows-compatible computer. There are advantages to both, ranging from ease of use, to flexibility, to cost. Which computer is right for you is a personal choice you'll have to make. Here are some of the advantages and disadvantages of each platform.

MACINTOSH

For digital video, Macs have a few advantages over Windows machines. Video and FireWire support is better-integrated into the Mac OS than it is in Windows. This means that hardware and software installation is quite a bit easier, and troubleshooting problems is pretty straightforward. Macs, in general, are easier to set up and maintain than Windows machines, so if you're striking out on your own—that is, if you don't have anyone you can turn to for technical help—then a Mac might be the best choice (Figure 2.8).

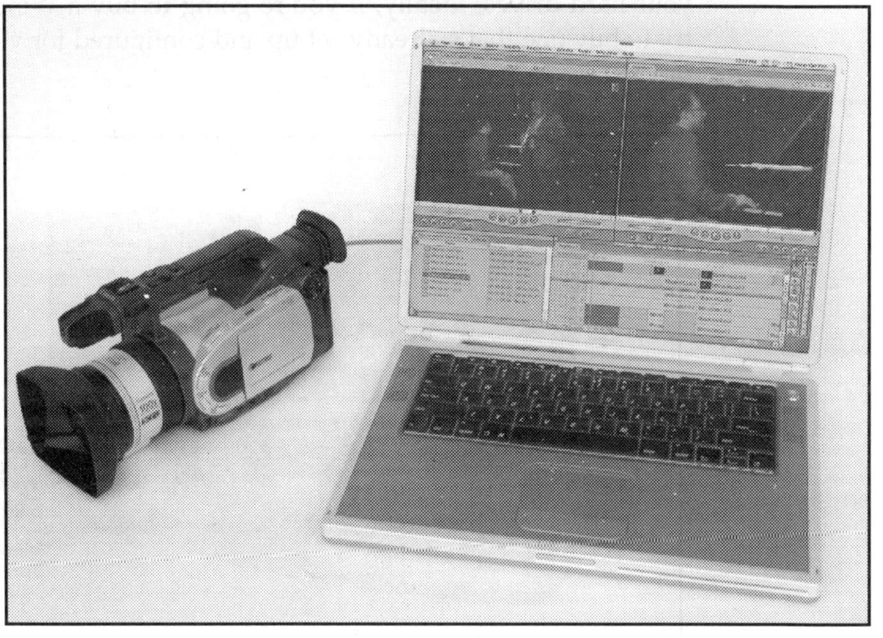

FIGURE 2.8 With a laptop like this Apple PowerBook, you can create a completely portable editing system.

Macs are also still the machine-of-choice in most of the movie and TV industry, so learning your Mac skills now might help later if you decide to look for a job in this field.

On the downside, Macs aren't as widely used as Windows machines, meaning that you might have trouble finding service and support if you live somewhere where there's not a huge Mac community.

WINDOWS

The main advantage of Windows machines is that they're *everywhere*, making it easy to get service, and affordable to buy replacement parts and upgrades. What's more, there's now a very good selection of shareware and commercial software for everything from editing to special effects.

On the downside, Windows machines are more difficult to set up and maintain than Macintoshes, and they don't necessarily have FireWire support built-in. You'll probably have to add a FireWire port by buying a third-party card, which means you'll have to do some research to find a FireWire card that you know is compatible with your computer and your hard drives. Ideally, if you're going to buy a Windows machine, try to buy one that's already set up and configured for video work (Figure 2.9).

FIGURE 2.9 If you're a Windows user, get a fast Pentium-class machine with a FireWire port, a good video card, and a sound board.

Your Computer's Processor

Working with video—whether analog or digital—can quickly bring even a powerful computer to its knees (computers don't actually have knees, of course, but you get the idea). You're going to need a pretty speedy computer for your video work. How speedy depends on the level of quality you hope to produce.

Your main concern when choosing a computer is to get a processor that is quick enough to capture video without missing, or "dropping," any frames. Dropped frames result in stuttery, jittery video. It's also nice to have a fast computer to speed up the many calculations that stack up when you start adding transitions and effects.

MACINTOSH PROCESSORS

If you're using a Macintosh, you need to be sure you have at least a 300MHz G3 processor. Although you might be able to get by with a 266, your chances of dropping frames will go way up. Any processor earlier than a G3 will be too slow.

Note that some analog digitizing systems pack so much processing horsepower that they'll work with a slower Mac. Check your system's specs for details.

In general, any new iMac, iBook, PowerBook, Cube, or PowerMac tower will have all of the processing power, video display, and FireWire connectivity you'll need.

WINDOWS PROCESSORS

If you're using a Windows computer, you'll want at least a 266MHz Pentium II processor. If you can swing a faster processor, go for it. For most software, you'll also need a DirectX 6.0-compatible video card with enough video RAM to display at least 256 colors. For better quality, you'll want a display card that can display thousands of colors, and for serious effects work, you'll want a display that can handle millions of colors.

Finally, you'll also want a DirectX-compatible sound card. In general, if you already have a powerfully configured gaming machine, you've probably got all of the processing and video power you need.

RAM

Ram is pretty easy: get as much as you can afford. Both Mac and Windows users should get at least 128MB of RAM, although you might be able to get by with 64MB depending on the software you're using. Going above 128 will make it easier and more comfortable to keep both an editing program and effects package open at the same time.

Disk Storage

Disk storage is like RAM: no one ever complains about having too much, so get as much as you can. If you're capturing footage from a DV camera through your computer's FireWire port, you'll need 13GB of storage for every hour of video. Of course, you also need space for your operating system and software, so you should aim for at least a 20GB drive.

"But I'm not planning on shooting an hour-long video!" you might be thinking. This might be true, but remember that even if you're only planning on a five-minute movie, you'll probably shoot at least 15 minutes of raw footage. As you'll see later, you always shoot more footage than you need, and you'll probably need to store this footage while editing.

If you're using an analog digitizing system, then you might need special fast hard drives like an array of SCSI drives. SCSI drives are much faster than the ATA and EIDE drives used in most Windows machines and Macs. Unfortunately, SCSI drives are also more expensive. If you're using an analog digitizer, check your system's manual for storage details.

Choosing a Video System

As mentioned earlier, there are two types of video cameras: digital and analog. Digital cameras digitize and compress video while you shoot, while analog cameras require separate digitizing and compression hardware.

IF YOU'RE SHOOTING WITH A DIGITAL VIDEO CAMERA

If you're shooting with a digital video camera, you need to make sure that your computer has a FireWire interface. If you're using a fairly new Mac, it will have a FireWire interface. An older iMac, or any pre-G3 machine will require the addition of a FireWire card. Because iMacs lack slots, you might not be able to add a FireWire connector, and so will need to start from scratch with a new computer.

If you're using a Windows computer, you'll need to buy a FireWire card of some kind. When shopping, be certain to get a card that is compatible with your processor, your drive controllers, and any other hardware you might have. If you're not sure if the card is compatible, be sure to buy from a vendor with a good return policy.

IF YOU'RE SHOOTING WITH AN ANALOG VIDEO CAMERA

An analog camera will require you to add an analog digitizing card to your computer. This is the card into which you will plug your camera when you're ready to pour your video into the computer for editing.

If your ultimate goal is smaller, lower-res videos for distribution over the Web, e-mail, or CD-ROM, then you can go with an inexpensive USB digitizer. These are small devices that plug into your computer's USB port. Simply plug your camera's video out port into the digitizer and you're ready to go (Figure 2.10).

FIGURE 2.10 If you don't have a digital video camera, or if you're only concerned about producing Web-resolution video, then an inexpensive, USB digitizer might be the best way to get video into your computer.

These devices are inexpensive, usually around $100, but they can only digitize small (320 × 240 or smaller) video at low frame rates (12 to 15 frames per second). They will *not* work if you want to create videos that you can show on your TV.

If you want TV-resolution video, you'll have to go with a more expensive digitizing system that will fit into one of the slots in your computer. These systems provide full-frame, full-frame rate video, but usually require fairly fast hard drives, and are usually pretty expensive.

Other Goodies

As long as you're shopping, there are certainly other handy computer goodies that are nice to have around. Although none of these are essential, they're certainly useful.

- **CD burner.** Once you start editing, you'll generate a *lot* of data. A CD burner is the most cost-effective way to back up your project files, raw footage, and special effects concoctions. Remember: your computer *will* crash. Be ready for it by backing up your data!
- **Drawing tablet.** If you plan to create a lot of special effects work, or do *rotoscoping*, or *painting* (all of which will be covered later), a pressure-sensitive drawing tablet can be a real life-saver.

TV or NTSC Monitor

Unfortunately, your computer monitor cannot display your video as it will really appear when it's finally shown on a TV. This is because your computer—no matter how fast—is not fast enough to decompress and play back video in real time. What's more, your computer can generate far more colors and a much bigger image than a TV can display.

Therefore, to get a truly accurate look at what your final video will look like, you need to have a TV hooked up to your editing system (you'll learn how to do this in Chapter 7). For now, though, plan on having access to a TV that you can install right next to your computer. This can be any TV with an S-video or Composite input, or it can be a fancy NTSC monitor like you'd find in a TV station (Figure 2.11).

Software

Finally, you'll need some special software for creating digital movies. In addition to editing software (which lets you pour video clips into your computer, edit them together, and then output them back to videotape, CD, the Web, or DVD), you also might want different types of special ef-

FIGURE 2.11 A typical DV editing system includes a computer, computer monitor, camera, and a TV monitor.

fects software ranging from titling software, to 3D animation, to compositing and rotoscoping programs. All of this software, as well as guidelines for choosing, are discussed in Chapter 7.

SOUND

Although your video camera probably has a microphone built into it, it's safe to assume that that microphone is not of the best quality. The trouble with on-board mics is that they produce audio that is very echo-y and boomy. What's more, because of their position on the camera, they tend to pick up noise from behind the camera as well as in front. Since *you* are usually the thing directly behind the camera, it's very easy for your camera's microphone to record your breathing and footsteps and murmurings.

What's more, it's easy to bump an on-camera mic with your fingers, and many on-camera mics are sensitive enough that they actually record the sounds of the camera itself.

For all these reasons, and more, you'll want to use an external microphone when shooting your video. Obviously, if you're just shooting candid, vacation-type footage, an external microphone is less of an option. Any time you're shooting an interview or a scripted scene, though, you're going to want to invest some time in miking your scene.

Types of Microphones

There are many different types of microphones, but the most common are handheld mics and lavalier, or *clip-on*, mics (Figure 2.12).

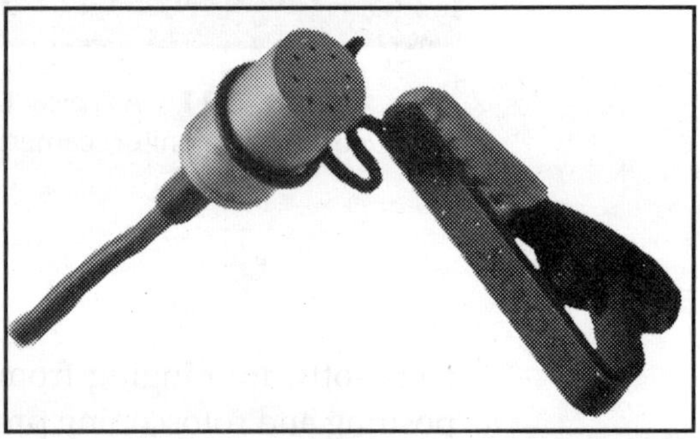

FIGURE 2.12 Mics fall mostly into two categories: handhelds and *lavaliers* (or clip-ons).

Lavalier mics are great for interviews because they're small, unobtrusive, and deliver very good quality. For recording an individual person's voice, they're really the best choice.

For recording a dialog, or conversation between several people, lavaliers are less practical, mostly because you need one for each person. In addition, if you have a separate mic for each person, you'll need a special *mixing* board to mix those mics together into a single audio signal that you can plug into your camera.

Handheld mics are a little more versatile. With a handheld mic, your subject can simply hold the mic while talking, or you can try to hide the mic somewhere on your set. For the greatest flexibility, you can mount the mic on the end of a pole, or *boom*, and have a *boom operator* move the mic from person to person as they speak. With the boom overhead, and out of frame, you don't have to worry about hiding the mic (Figure 2.13).

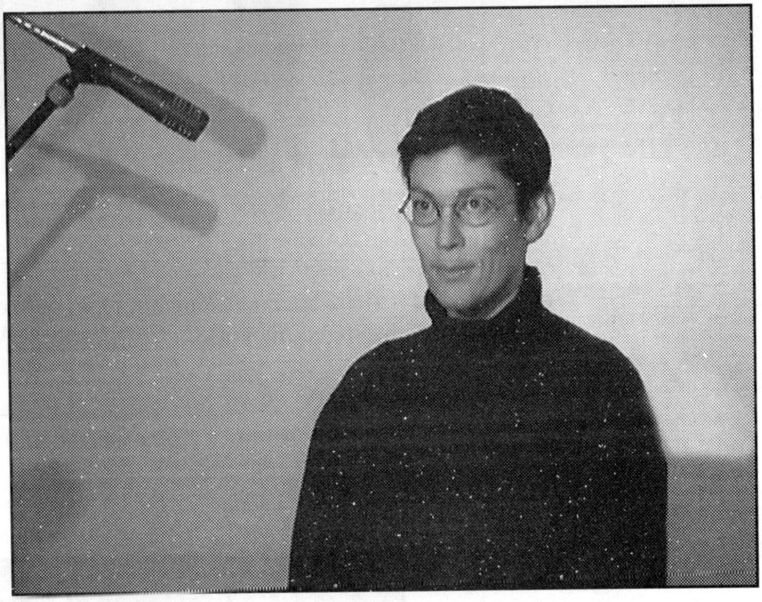

FIGURE 2.13 By sticking a handheld mic on a *boom* you can easily mic a group of people (normally, of course, you'd keep the mic out of the shot).

MIC DIRECTIONS

A microphone also has a *pickup pattern* that determines what direction the microphone can "hear" in. An *omnidirectional* mic picks up sounds from all directions, while a *directional* mic mostly picks up sound in a single direction. Directional mics can be really great for very noisy situations, but for the greatest flexibility, go for an omnidirectional mic.

In fact, if you can only choose one microphone, get an omnidirectional handheld mic.

MICROPHONE CONNECTIONS

Microphones can use many different kinds of plugs and sockets, as you can see in Figure 2.14.

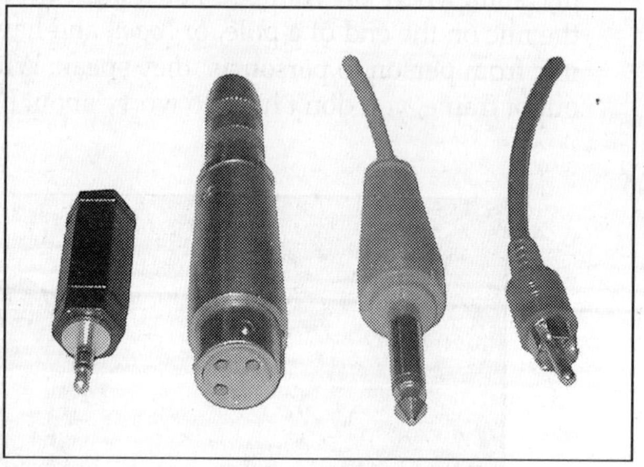

FIGURE 2.14 There are many different types of microphone plugs. From left to right: stereo-mini, BNC, 1/4" photo, RCA.

Your camera, though, probably has a stereo mini socket like the one shown in Figure 2.15.

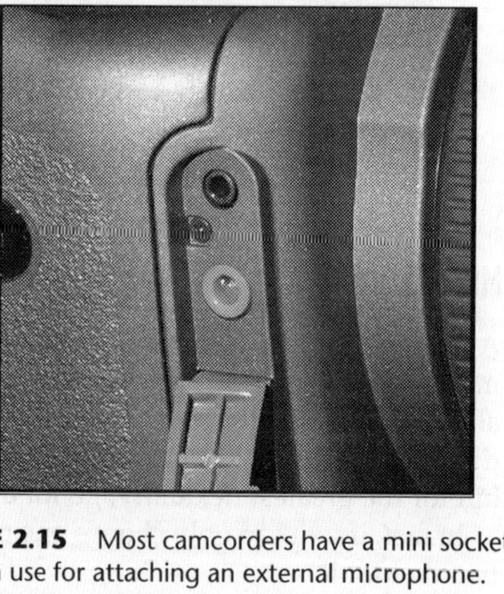

FIGURE 2.15 Most camcorders have a mini socket that you can use for attaching an external microphone.

When selecting a mic, make things easy on yourself and buy one that has a stereo mini plug. If you get this type of mic, you won't have to worry about buying extra adapters and converters to fit your mic into your camera. Try to get an *electret condensor* microphone.

WATCHOUT!

If you buy an electret mic, you'll be getting a mic that needs its own battery. Most battery-powered mics use a small watch battery for power. Be sure to buy a few extra batteries because you *never* know when your microphone battery will die.

Some microphones don't have batteries and need to get power from an external power source such as your camera. These types of microphones will require some extra adapters and special pieces of hardware. This is another reason to go with a mic that's ready to use with your camera.

Headphones

The problem with audio is that things can sound just fine to your ears while you're on the set, but sound really terrible to your camera while it's recording. Bear in mind that you can't necessarily tell by looking that the microphone is actually plugged in, its battery is still working, and it's not actually picking up the sound of that cement mixer across the street.

The easiest way to be sure that your camera is recording the sound that you want it to record is to plug a pair of headphones into your camera's headphone jack. Any old pair of headphones will do; you're not looking for great quality, just a way to tell that your camera is recording.

LIGHTS

First the good news: digital cameras are *great* at shooting in low light!

However (this is the bad news), if you don't take some time to consider the lighting in your scene, you might end up shooting some really ugly footage. Remember: if people can't see your video clearly, they'll have a very hard time following your story.

Lights might seem complicated at first because they involve a lot of gear and a lot of trial and error when setting up. However, it doesn't have to be this complicated. Even just a simple piece of white cardboard can make a huge difference in the quality of your video. We'll talk more about lighting in Chapter 6, "Shooting." For now, though, you might want to start trying to figure out what type of lighting gear you have access to.

Lighting Kits

If you're serious about lighting, you'll want to get a lighting kit like the one shown in Figure 2.16.

Don't worry, you don't have to *buy* a lighting kit, as most photo supply or film and video supply houses will rent you one for a very reasonable price. In Chapter 6, you'll learn more about what to look for in a lighting kit.

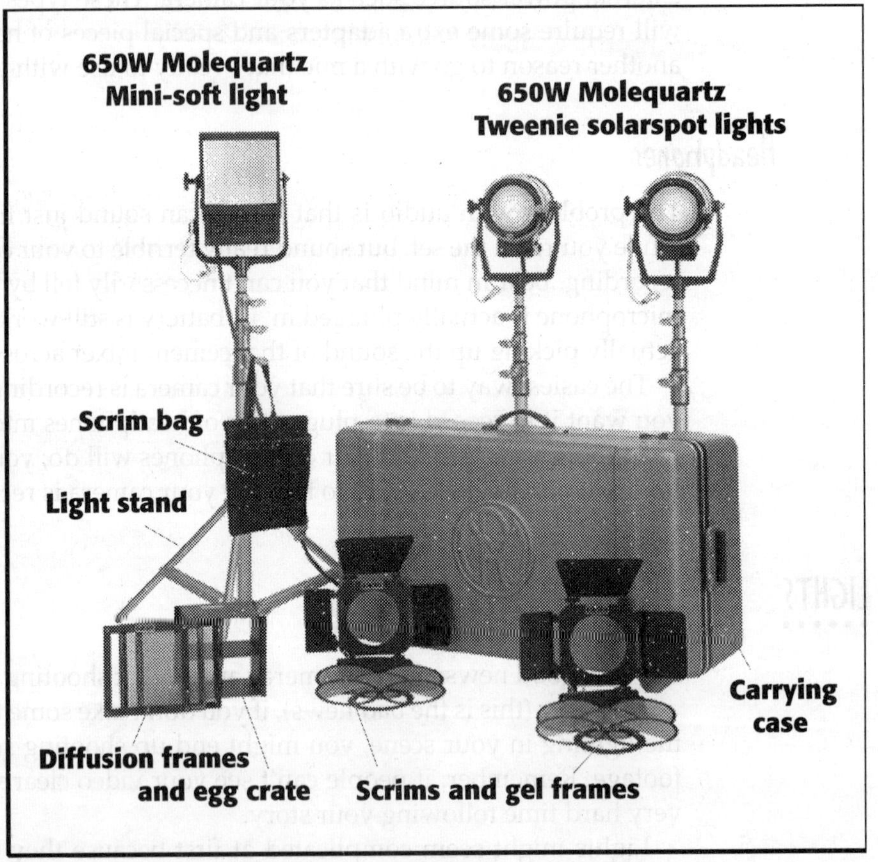

FIGURE 2.16 This lighting kit is a good example of the type of lighting kit you can rent.

Homemade Lights

If your lighting needs aren't too complex, you might be able to get away with using whatever light is available at your scene. If the available light isn't great, you can always supplement it with some simple homemade lights you might find at a hardware store.

Once you've read some more about lighting, you'll have a better idea of what types of lights you might need.

Reflectors and Bounce Cards

Although expensive lights might be beyond your needs or budget, there's no excuse not to make some simple reflectors and a bounce card. A single piece of white cardboard or poster board can be all you need to throw some much-needed light on your subject. You'll learn more about these in Chapter 6.

HINT

Reflectors and Jargon

For those of you with some photography experience: a simple white reflector can often brighten a person by as much as 1.5 to 2 stops! This can make the difference between a well-exposed subject and one that's too dark.

ALL THAT OTHER GEAR

As if all this weren't enough, there's still a lot of other gear that you'll need for your shoot. In addition to your props, costumes, and set pieces (which we'll discuss in Chapter 4, "Preproduction"), you'll also need a good assortment of other equipment.

Tripod

The one thing that can make the *biggest* improvement in the quality of your footage is to put your camera on a tripod before you shoot. There's nothing more annoying to watch than shaky, unstable footage. What's more, stable footage will make edits easier, and is essential for certain types of effects work.

Although there will be times when you choose to shoot handheld, most of the time you'll want to use a tripod. When shopping for a tripod, get one like the one shown in Figure 2.17.

FIGURE 2.17 A tripod is absolutely *essential* for shooting good video. Don't think you can always get away with shooting handheld. Even an inexpensive tripod will make a world of difference to your final product.

WATCHOUT!

Many tripods have a "pistol grip" head instead. These tripods are terrible for video because you can't move the camera on a single axis; that is, it's too hard to only pan or tilt the camera.

Videotape

Obviously, you'll need tape to shoot on. How much depends on how long your project is and what you think your *shooting ratio* will be. A typical dramatic movie has a shooting ratio of 3:1. That is, a typical filmmaker shoots three times as much footage as is actually needed. On a documentary, the shooting ratio is closer to 10:1 or 20:1. The fact is, you simply don't know what footage you might need once you start shooting, so it's best to shoot as much as you can.

Therefore, if you plan on shooting a 15-minute movie, count on needing at least an hour's worth of tape. To be safe, double that and buy two hours' worth of tape.

If you're really cautious, you'll want to make backups of your tapes (usually referred to as *safety copies*) so that you won't lose any footage if your camera eats one of your tapes while you're editing. In that case, you'll need twice again as much tape.

Tape, String, Glue, Clamps, Etc.

If you're shooting a scripted movie, you'll have a lot of work to do once you arrive at your location. From setting up props to setting up lights, you'll have a lot of makeshift "rigging" to do. Tape, clamps, string, and other fastening tools can be essential for setting a light or microphone. As you gain more shooting experience, you'll have a better idea of what sort of items you'll need once you're on location.

SUMMARY

Hopefully, by now you have a good idea of what kind of equipment and gear you'll need to start making movies. At this point, you should know:

- What type of computer you need, or how to modify your current computer to make it digital video-ready.
- The specs required for editing DV. For the Mac: a 300MHz G3 or better processor with at least 128MB of RAM, a 6GB hard drive, and a FireWire port. For Windows: a 300MHz Pentium II or better processor with at least 128MB of RAM, a 6GB hard drive, a FireWire port, a sound card, and a DirectX 6-compatible video card with enough video RAM to display at least 256 colors.
- The difference between a digital and analog video camera, and what type of computer gear you'll need to work with your camera of choice.
- What you might need in the way of lighting and sound equipment.

If you're confused about any of these topics, maybe you need to read a little further. Your camera needs should become clearer after you read Chapter 6. Digital and analog video will make a lot more sense after you read Chapter 7. Lighting and sound, meanwhile, will also be covered in Chapter 6.

ACTIVITY: WATCH SOME DIGITAL VIDEO

I'm sure you've seen lots of movies and lots of TV shows, but these don't necessarily give you an idea of what a movie shot on digital video will look like. Hollywood movies are usually shot on 35mm film, while broadcast television shows are usually shot on film, or on high-end video formats such as Betacam or Digital Betacam.

But what can you expect from a digital video camera? Glad you asked! To find out, you need go no further than your neighborhood video store, where you should rent the following movies:

Hands on a Hard Body. This documentary is one of the funniest movies you'll ever watch! Every year in Longview, Texas, the local Nissan dealer holds a contest to win a brand new Nissan Hardbody pickup truck. The contest is very simple: the contestants must stand with one hand on the truck. No kneeling, no leaning. Last one standing wins the truck. One previous winner won after standing for 87 hours! *Hilarious* interviews and great filmmaking make this a fantastic movie that you shouldn't miss! Shot entirely with a Hi8 analog camera.

The Buena Vista Social Club. This very good documentary tells the story of a group of Cuban musicians who, with the help of guitarist Ry Cooder, released a best-selling album in 1997 after decades of obscurity. Shot using a combination of Digital Betacam and MiniDV (using a Sony VX1000 MiniDV) camera, this masterfully shot movie shows how beautiful digital footage can be. See if you can spot which footage was shot on Betacam, and which was shot on MiniDV.

These two movies have one thing in common: after being shot and edited using digital video, the final movies were transferred to film for theatrical release.

CHAPTER

3

Writing

IN THIS CHAPTER

- Telling a Good Story
- Writing a Story
- Writing a Script

Have you heard this one?

> A guy goes into a bar, sits down, and orders a drink. He has barely taken a sip when he hears a polite voice say, "Hey, nice tie!"
>
> The guy looks around, but the only other person he can see is the bartender, who's at the other end of the bar. The man forgets about it, goes back to his drink, and almost immediately hears, "Hey! Nice shirt!"
>
> Again, the guy looks up, but again, there's no one around. Almost immediately, he hears the same voice say, "Hey! Nice suit!"
>
> Finally, he asks the bartender, "Did you just say something?"
>
> And the bartender replies, "Oh no, that's not me, it's the complimentary peanuts."

Okay, it's not a great joke, but bear with me for a minute, and try out this one:

Three boys were misbehaving at the zoo when the zookeeper came up and demanded to know who they were and what they were doing.

"My name is Tommy," said the first boy, "and I was trying to feed peanuts to the lions."

"My name is Billy," said the second boy, "and I was trying to feed peanuts to the lions."

"My name is Peanuts," said the third boy.

Alright, alright, that one's not so great either. However, these two jokes have something very interesting in common (besides the presence of peanuts): both follow the "rule of three." That is, both jokes provide three examples of something before they deliver the punch line. This is a very common format for jokes, and if you start paying attention when someone tells you a joke, you'll probably find that many jokes are structured just like these two.

Consider the second joke. If we remove Billy from the joke (leaving only Tommy and Peanuts), the joke doesn't make as much sense. If we add a fourth boy, then the joke is too long. In either case, the joke loses its "rhythm," or timing, and becomes less funny. Because of something inherent in human psychology, we need three examples for a joke like this to work. We need the first example to present an idea, the second example to clarify what the idea might be, and the third example to establish a pattern. The third example can also be the punch line, or can be presented right before the punch line.

The point of subjecting you to such poor humor is to point out that there is a science to joke writing. Experienced joke writers have a vast store of knowledge and theories about what makes a good joke. They understand that there are different joke structures ranging from one-liners to "shaggy-dog" stories, to "bait-and-switch" jokes. They also understand that just as some things are inherently sad, other things are inherently funny, and they usually have an arsenal of these inherently funny items that they can use to construct a joke.

Joke writing is more than just a science, of course. Knowing the rules doesn't insure that you can write a great joke, but it does improve your chances. Rules, of course, are made to be broken, and every so often, someone comes along who successfully bends, breaks, or changes the rules, or discovers an entirely new set of rules that create an entirely new type of joke.

Telling stories works the same way. If you know the rules of storytelling, you stand a much better chance of creating a story that is interesting, and that entices your audience to keep watching. And let's face it, whether you're planning on making a music video, or shooting a story from a script that you've written, or just editing together some footage you've shot of you and your friends, the last thing you want to do is to create a movie that's *boring*!

In this chapter, you're going to learn some simple rudiments of storytelling. These rules will not only help you create stories that are more interesting, they'll also make your storytelling process a bit easier, as you'll have a better idea of where to start and how to proceed.

TELLING A GOOD STORY

Consider the following story:

> Mary had decided to go for a walk, so she called her dog, Spot, got his leash, and went outside. She walked down the sidewalk and crossed the street in front of the small, neighborhood grocery store. She liked the store and was always happy to see the "regulars" buying their food. She kept walking until she got to the park. As always, the park was filled with dogs that were running, and jumping and catching Frisbees. Both she and Spot really liked it at the park.

Not much of a story, right? In fact, Mary's story isn't really a "story" at all; it's just a series of events. I could, in fact, continue that series of events for pages and pages, covering all of the events that happened during Mary's day. In the end, we would simply have a much longer, boring description of a bunch of events.

"Maybe Mary is just a boring person," you might be thinking. Certainly, subject matter has a lot to do with making a story interesting. If Mary was an international super-spy instead of a woman walking her dog, the story might automatically be more interesting. However, even with the seemingly boring events of Mary's life, it is possible to tell a more compelling story:

> Mary was going stir crazy. She'd been stuck in the house all day and it was starting to get to her. She called her dog, Spot, put on his leash, and went outside. She crossed the street in front of her neighborhood grocery store. She liked the store and always felt

> comfortable there. But now, when she looked in and saw the lines of people loaded down with heaps of cans and boxes she just felt more stir crazy. She walked on until she finally reached the park, and there, at last, she was able to relax.

Okay, so this story might not be Shakespeare caliber, but it does, at least, feel more like a story than a simple chain of events. However, both stories contain exactly the same series of events. Nothing new happens in the second story—it's still just a tale of a woman going for a walk with her dog. So, what's the difference between the two?

The main difference is that in the second story, Mary, our main character, has a goal: she's stir crazy and she needs to relax. This goal is stated in the very first sentence. By giving Mary a goal, we've also given the readers a goal: they want to find out if she'll solve her problem.

There's not a lot of detail in this story, of course. We really don't know much about Mary. By adding a few simple details, we can help the reader understand Mary and her problem a little more, and make the story a bit more compelling.

> Mary was going stir crazy. She'd been stuck in the house all day and it was starting to get to her. She felt like the walls were closing in on her and she kept imagining that she was breathing up all of the air. (The last time this happened, Mary flipped out and painted all of the furniture in the house pink, a redecoration that did not please any of her roommates.)
>
> "Get your leash, Spot, we're going for a walk."
>
> With her dog in tow (Spot didn't like walks), she scrambled out the door and down the street. She crossed the street in front of her neighborhood grocery store. She liked the store and always felt comfortable there. But this time, when she looked in and saw the lines of people loaded down with heaps of cans and boxes, she could only feel terror. She imagined the people returning to their houses and unloading their groceries, and she could again feel the walls closing in and the air vanishing.
>
> Spot tugged at his leash and Mary looked down at him.
>
> "Bark!" said Spot.
>
> "The park? Of course!" said Mary, suddenly realizing. "The park! Let's go, Spot."
>
> And so, Mary soon found herself in the park, relaxing under a tree, where there was plenty of air, and not a wall to be seen.

Structure

In the preceding example, we took a pretty boring chain of events and turned them into a story by giving our main character a goal. We did something else as well: we gave the story a structure. If you look at the second story, you'll see that it has a very definite beginning, middle, and end.

In the beginning, we learn that Mary has a problem: she's stir crazy. In the middle, we see her go to a store that is normally comforting, but this doesn't solve her problem. Perhaps her problem is worse than she realized. In the end, she finally finds a comfortable place to be and is no longer stir crazy.

More than anything else, learning this simple structure will help you tell better stories and make better movies. Not only will you be able to create movies that are more interesting to your audience, but by following this structure, you'll have an easier time finding your way through the writing, shooting, and editing of your movie.

HOLLYWOOD STRUCTURE

Hollywood movies all use a slightly more complex version of this same structure. In fact, many movies follow this structure so rigidly that you can often literally set your watch by the progression of the story.

Hollywood movies typically unfold in the following way:

Act I: The beginning. Wherein the main character is introduced, along with his or her nemesis, and the supporting cast. The main character's "problem" is also introduced. This is the problem that will be solved by the end of the movie. This section usually takes 20 to 30 minutes.

Act II: The middle. The main thing that happens in Act II is that the character's problem is complicated. This is the bulk of the movie, and any subplots are usually introduced and solved here. Very rarely are new characters introduced in this act. Halfway through the act—that is, in the exact middle of the movie—the main character's luck will change, and things will start working out in his or her favor. By the end of the third act, the solution to the problem will be clear. This act is usually 40 to 50 minutes long.

Act III: The End. In this act, the main character's problem is solved. This usually takes about 20 minutes.

Note that there is never a clear separation of acts presented in the movie. The actual change might be a simple cut from one scene to another, or the scene might just barrel on ahead into the new act. It's not important that the audience know *where* the act breaks are, but that doesn't mean that they aren't there.

You don't have to follow this structure, and many foreign movies don't. However, it is a fairly simple, effective way of ensuring a compelling story that "moves."

RAIDERS OF THE LOST ARK

Raiders of the Lost Ark follows the typical Hollywood structure very closely, and so provides a good example of how three-act structure works (if you haven't seen the movie, you'll need to for this explanation to work).

Act I ends right after the fight in Marion's bar. We have all of our main characters, and we have our problem: find the Ark before the Nazis do.

Act II ends when the Nazis show up to take the Ark off the ship. More specifically, it ends when Indy swims to the Nazi sub and climbs aboard. With him, the Nazis, the girl, and the Ark all on board, we're ready for the final confrontation.

Act III ends with the end of the movie. Indy got the Ark (never mind that it was taken away from him by the good guys, he still did what he was supposed to do).

FILM SCHOOL: LEARN MORE ABOUT STRUCTURE

ON THE CD

Located in the Film School>Chapter 3 folder of the companion CD-ROM is a document called *Structure.pdf*. This essay begins with a much more detailed analysis of the structure of *Raiders* as well as analyses of other movies, including *The Mummy, Butch Cassidy and the Sundance Kid, Return of the Jedi, Witness,* and *The Purple Rose of Cairo.*

If you're wondering why you should care about the storytelling structure of big Hollywood movies, there are two reasons: first,

Hollywood uses this structure because it works (and they've got the profits to prove it). What's more, this structure is so basic that you can easily apply it to other stories, including simple shorts, music videos, home movies, or whatever. Second, you might want to, some day, make a feature-length movie. If you do, then an understanding of this type of structure will be very helpful.

The story-telling structure discussed here has been used for thousands of years. The Greeks used it in their theater, Shakespeare used a longer, five-act version of the same structure, and Hollywood writers follow this structure *religiously*, often to their detriment. Three-act structure is not the best way to tell every story, but it is a good form for movie-making, and it makes a great starting point from which you can learn about other storytelling structures.

WRITING A STORY

There's no right or wrong way to write a story, but there are some ideas and practices that you can follow that will make it *easier* to write a story. And, if you're writing a story that you intend to turn into a movie—that is, if you're writing a *screenplay*—then there are a few rules you should follow that will make your planning and shooting process much easier.

Coming Up with an Idea

First, of course, you need an idea for a story. Hopefully, the previous example of Mary and her dog showed you that there are not necessarily any *bad* ideas, only bad tellings. So, if you've got an idea that strikes you as interesting, go for it! Start writing! If you're confused as to where to start, try to answer the following questions:

- **Who are your characters?** Try to figure out as much about your characters as you can. What do they look like? How do they spend their days? Are they nice or mean? Short-tempered, or generous? Any details that strike you are important details. In particular, you want to know a lot about your main character (sometimes called the *protagonist*).

- **What is the problem that your character will face?** This doesn't have to be a huge problem. In fact, you might not have been thinking that your character would face a problem. However, just as in Mary's story, if you can structure your story around a conflict of some type, your story will be more engaging. Bear in mind that the problem can often be another character (the *antagonist*). The problem might be more or less complicated than you realize, so it's good to find out now.
- **How will your character solve that problem?** This one may be more difficult to answer than you realize. If it's a big enough problem to confuse your main protagonist, it might also take you some time to find a way for them to solve it.

If you start with these questions, you'll immediately have a rough idea of your story's beginning, middle, and end.

WATCHOUT!

Ignore what you just read! Remember, there's no right or wrong way to create a story! The preceding suggestions are just suggestions. You might have a very clear idea of how your story will work. Great! Go with that and write it down. Once you're done, go back and look at it, and see if it has a good structure. You might find then that you need to add, remove, or rearrange some things. The most important thing is to follow the process that works for you!

What to Do if You Get Stuck

Writing is hard work and you'll often find yourself bogged down, or blocked. If you find yourself at a storytelling impasse, try the following:

- **Ask yourself: "What happens next?"** It's easy to get stuck by looking at the "big picture" of your story. By asking yourself the simple question "what happens next?"—a question you can usually answer—you might find that you're back into the "meat" of the story.
- **Interview your characters.** Sometimes, it's difficult to know what a character might do. If this happens, try to get to know them better. Imagine they're being interviewed on a talk show, and simply write down that interview. You might be surprised by what you discover.

- **Say "yes."** Don't try to control your characters and your story! Don't be afraid of where it seems to be going. Often, a story will go in a very different direction from where you originally thought or intended. If you think of something, accept it! Say yes to it and keep writing. It might not take you in the direction you thought, and you might end up going somewhere better or worse. But remember, you can always go back and rewrite later. And don't worry that your story is revealing something about you as a person. You have an imagination that can concoct lots of things that don't necessarily reflect any truth about who you are or what you believe.

GENRE

When a story conforms to a very specific set of characteristics, it is said to be part of a particular *genre*. For example, a story set in the 1800s in the American West is typically considered to be in the Western genre. There are many other genres, including science fiction, romantic comedy, film noir, and screwball comedy.

Genre can be helpful when you're writing a script. If you've been thinking of your script as fitting into a particular genre, and you get stuck in your writing, knowing some things about your genre of choice can help you get unstuck. Every genre has its own *trappings*, or specific characteristics. If you get stuck, you can turn to those trappings to try to come up with ideas.

Here's a list of some simple genre trappings:

- **Science fiction.** Set in a world where change—either progress or decline—has made something new possible. Change can be technological, political, magical, spiritual, or whatever.
- **Western.** You probably already have a pretty good idea of what westerns are. Usually set in the American West, sometime in the 18th century, westerns typically center on events on the American frontier. Examples of westerns that you should watch include *Rio Bravo* and *High Noon.* More recent westerns include *The Unforgiven.*
- **Film noir.** The term film *noir* was coined to describe certain films from the 1940s and 1950s that centered on stories of gritty detectives and seedy criminals. In film noir, both heroes and villains are usually cynical loners who are often betrayed by a double-crossing heroine. Film noir movies are usually black and white with extreme lighting and shadows. Examples of film noir include *The Maltese Falcon, Out of the Past,* and *Double Indemnity,* all great movies that are worth renting.

- **Documentary.** A factual film depicting real events and people. Documentaries come in many different styles, from simple narrated films like you'll see on *National Geographic* or *Nova*, to long, complex works such as Ken Burns' *Civil War*. Some excellent examples of documentaries include *Hands on a Hard Body*, *Genghis Blues* (both of which include DV footage), and Spike Lee's *Four Little Girls*.

Finally, genres can also be combined, so you might end up with a "comedy noir" or a science fiction western (the 1981 Sean Connery movie *Outland* was such a genre mix, and was often described as "*High Noon* in space").

Knowledge of genre can also be handy if you're out shooting random footage of you and your friends. Because this type of candid footage can often be boring to people who weren't involved, thinking about a particular genre can help you quickly add an interesting story to otherwise normal events, as you'll see in a moment.

TRUE CONFESSIONS

It turns out that I, myself, was a teenage video maker. Although at that time there wasn't all this cool digital stuff, I was fortunate enough to get a job in a video production/cable studio. Because we had access to so much equipment (as well as a studio in which to shoot), I shot lots of shorts and small videos with my friend and coworker Byron Baker.

He and I and some other friends also spent a lot of time having races through the studio in the rolling chairs that were used in the control room. One day, we decided to make a video of one of these races. Rather than just shoot a bunch of footage and try to edit it into something interesting, we went fully into the "sports programming" genre. The result was a video that had a more interesting structure for the audience.

ACTIVITY: WATCH A CHAIR RACE

Go, now, to the companion CD-ROM and open the Activities>Chapter 3 folder. Watch the Chair Race QuickTime movie. This movie is a slightly shorter version of the video mentioned previously. After you've watched the movie, read the Chair Race.pdf file that's included in the same folder. It offers a quick discussion of how the video was shot, how it is structured, and what its specific genre characteristics are (Figure 3.1).

FIGURE 3.1 The *Chair Race.mov* file on the companion CD-ROM shows an example of using genre to make an event more interesting to watch.

Writing Visually (or, "Show It, Don't Say It")

Most beginning screenwriters make a very simple mistake: they forget that movies are made up of *pictures*. Yes there's dialog and talking and music, and all that other stuff, but first and foremost: movies are a *visual* form of storytelling.

Let's go back to *Raiders of the Lost Ark* for a moment. Consider the beginning of the movie. In *Raiders*, 2 minutes and 7 seconds of the movie pass before the first line of dialog when one of Indy's assistants says "The Hovitos are near." In other words, the first 2 minutes are told completely in pictures. Sure, there's music and sound effects, but you can turn the sound down and the scene still makes sense.

JOHNNY THE PAPERBOY

Here's another example. Let's say we're going to make a movie about Johnny, a 15-year-old kid who has a paper route. A paper route is a pretty easy thing to show, so let's make things more complicated. Let's say that Johnny's father died a few years ago and that his mother has recently remarried. Let's also say that Johnny isn't too happy about his mother's new marriage (now our story has a problem to solve). Here's a first pass at this story. Try to imagine each scene as it is would look in a movie.

> Johnny, a friendly looking 15-year-old, is walking down the sidewalk of a tree-lined street. Around his shoulders is a bag full of folded newspapers. He walks with heavy feet and his head held low. Occasionally, he pulls out a paper and half-heartedly throws it toward a house.
>
> In front of one house, a kind-looking old man sees Johnny. The old man shakes his head in sympathy and walks over to Johnny. Placing his hand on the boy's shoulder, he says:
>
> "Hi Johnny, you don't look too happy."
>
> "Hi Mr. Johnson. No, I guess I'm not."
>
> "Are you still upset that your mother just remarried?"
>
> "Yes, I guess I am."
>
> "Ah. I suppose you still miss your father. It's only been three years since he died, hasn't it? And the fact that your new stepfather is vice principal of your school can't be easy, either."

Alright, that's enough of that.

Do you see the problem? Sure, there's some visual storytelling going on—Johnny walks around looking sad, and we know that he has a paper route. However, the dialog isn't believable. Mr. Johnson plainly *knows* that Johnny is upset, *and* he knows why. The only reason he's asking is because the screenwriter needed someone to explain things to *us*, not to Johnny.

Let's try the scene again.

> A car pulls into the driveway of a nice-looking house on a tree-lined street. An attractive woman in her 40s gets out of the car and goes in the front door of the house. Inside, she sets down her purse, takes off her sunglasses, and glances at the mail.
>
> "Hello? Anyone home?" she yells absent-mindedly.
>
> (Cut to a hallway. We see her walking toward us, still looking at the mail.)
>
> "Johnny, are you home?"
>
> She walks up to Johnny's room and looks through the open doorway. Inside is a typical teenage boy's room. Heaped on the bed are a pile of folded newspapers and a newspaper bag. The woman suddenly looks concerned and hurries down the hall.

In the kitchen, she sets down the mail and is reaching for the telephone as a man, sweaty in his running clothes, walks in the back door.

"Hi honey," he says, slightly out of breath.

"Hi dear. Have you seen Johnny?"

"No, but I've been out for the last hour."

The woman now looks more upset.

"I'm afraid he's skipped his paper route again," she says. "I don't get it, this just isn't like him!"

The man looks concerned. He takes the woman's hand.

"It's hard having a new father. It's going to take time for all of us to adjust. That's all."

The woman looks at him and nods.

On a basketball court, a nice-looking kid stands on the free-throw line. He takes a shot and makes it.

"Alright, Johnny!" yells another kid.

There are, obviously, many things that are different about this telling. First, we actually get to see all of the characters involved—Johnny, his mother, and his stepfather. What's most important, though, is that when they speak, they aren't speaking to tell *us* things, they're speaking to tell things to *each other*. In other words, their dialog is more realistic than in the first scene.

Two other things are important. First, the emotions that the characters are expressing are more complex. The woman exhibits contentment when she walks in the house, then confusion, then distress. Johnny is revealed to be upset, but then we see him confidently make a basketball shot. In other words, the emotions aren't the stilted "Gee Johnny, you're sad" emotions of the first telling.

Also important is that, in the second telling, the filmmaker has the opportunity to present much more information to the audience. We get to see the inside of Johnny's house. We get to see his mother and stepfather. We see that his stepfather is active and fit, and that his stepfather and mother seem to get along very well. Yes, we haven't learned yet that he's the vice principal of the school, but we can be shown that later.

Telling a story visually is hard because you have to come up with situations where you can let your characters realistically and believably act out what they are feeling and doing. Sometimes, it can be very difficult to think up such situations. The pay-off, though, is a movie with much more believable, natural, interesting scenes.

WRITING A SCRIPT

The writing examples presented in this chapter so far have been written as straight prose, both because it's somewhat easier to read, and often easier to write, than a script format.

Screenplays—particularly Hollywood screenplays—are written in a very particular format. If you're shooting your own material, you can obviously write your scripts in any way that you choose. However, standard screenplay formatting is a pretty good system that produces a script that's both easy to read and eases your production.

Screenplay Format

The "standard" screenplay format uses margins and line spacing like those shown in Figure 3.2.

If you follow the standard screenplay format, your scripts will usually work out to be about one minute of screen time per page. Therefore, if you write a 100-page screenplay, you can expect your finished product to come out around an hour-and-a-half, maybe more, maybe less. (Bear in mind that the one-page-per-minute theory is an *average*. Obviously, an epic space battle that takes up one page might actually consume five minutes of screen time, while a page of witty dialog might fly by in 30 seconds.)

There are other important conventions in the standard screenplay format. First, every scene begins with a *slugline* that tells whether the scene takes place indoors or outdoors, the location of the scene, and whether the scene takes place during the day or night. Therefore, you might have a scene with the slugline:

```
INT.  HIGH SCHOOL GYMNASIUM  - DAY
```

Sluglines are handy because they make it easy to see where scenes begin and end, and because they let you quickly assess whether a scene will be easy to shoot (an interior day scene) or more difficult (an exterior scene at night).

As you can see from Figure 3.1, all action in a screenplay is written in blocks of text with no left or right margins, while dialog and character names are indented. What's more, if a piece of dialog continues to the next page, "MORE" is printed at the bottom of the dialog. Similarly, if a scene continues onto the next page, "CONTINUED" is printed at the bottom of the page.

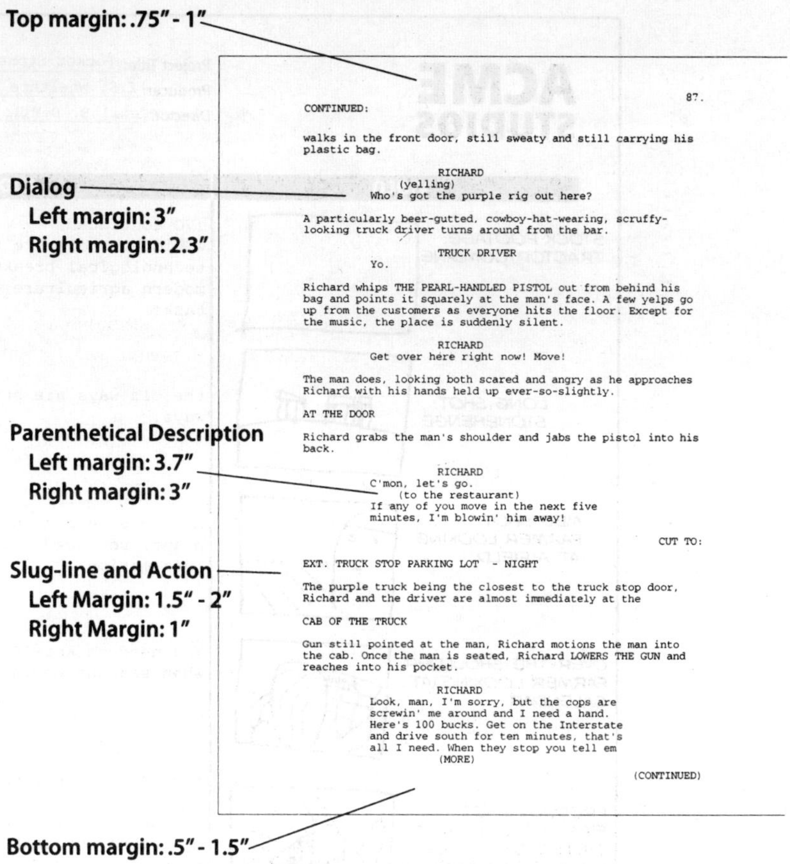

FIGURE 3.2 If you format your script using the measurements shown here, you'll have a script that fits the "standard" screenplay format.

When writing a screenplay, you don't have to worry about spelling out every camera angle and every shot—that's for the director to decide. All you need to do is write enough description that the reader can get a sense for how the movie will play out on-screen.

You'll see more examples of standard screenplay format later.

Two-Column (AV) Format

If you're shooting a music video, training video, or other types of "industrial" projects, you might want to use a two-column format like the one shown in Figure 3.3.

ACME STUDIOS

Project Title: Pocket Stonehenge Demo Video
Producer: I.S. Whelthie
Director: Cecil B. DeMilo **Date:** Aug 9, 1999

VIDEO	AUDIO
STOCK FOOTAGE: TRACTOR/COMBINE 	(VO continued) would ever dispute the incredible technological breakthroughs in modern agriculture. But for some tasks
LONG SHOT: STONEHENGE 	the old ways are still the best ways.
MED SHOT: FARMER LOOKING AT A FIELD 	When you're getting ready to plant, you need valuable, accurate information.
OVER-THE-SHOULDER: FARMER LOOKING AT CALENDAR 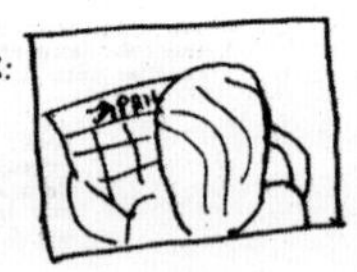	You need to know--with certainty--when seasons begin and end.
PRODUCT SHOT: FIRST STILL, IN PALM. THEN CLOSE-UP OF POCKET STONEHENGE BEING UNFOLDED AND DEPLOYED. 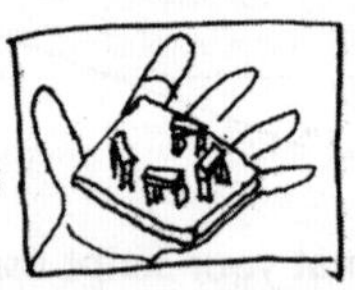	You need...the Pocket Stonehenge. Collapsible. Portable. And backed by technology that's stood the test of time. With the Pocket Stonehenge, you can be certain that you're getting accurate, up-to-the-minute solstice information with none of the expensive batteries or messy sacrifices required by other technologies.

Figure 3.3 Two-column scripts are usually used for commercials, music videos, or other types of "industrial" videos.

In this format, the left column is used to show a simple storyboard-like diagram of the shot that corresponds to the voice-over or dialog that's shown in the right column. For a shoot involving multiple cameras or other complex setups, this type of script is ideal.

Screenwriting Software

As a digital filmmaker, you cannot only use digital tools for editing and special effects, you can also use digital writing tools to help with the creation of your script. Screenwriting programs such as B.C. Software's *Final Draft* (Figure 3.4) take care of all of your formatting (including tricky MOREs and CONTINUEDs) and provide lots of other cool tools such as automatic character names and special organizational tools.

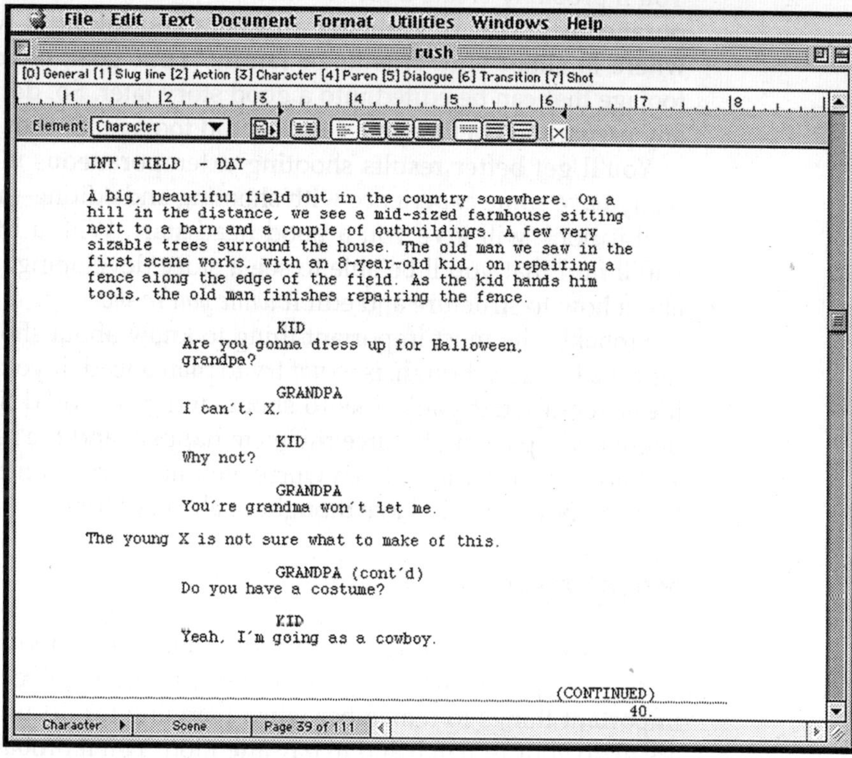

FIGURE 3.4 Screenwriting software such as B.C. Software's *Final Draft* will automatically format your screenplay while you type. It will also take care of page numbering, character names, and many other formatting problems.

Writing Movies That Don't Need Scripts

Not all of your video projects will be based on scripts or concrete story ideas. For example, if you and your friends are taking a road trip somewhere, and you've brought along a video camera with the hope of documenting your journey, you're not going to write a script ahead of time. Similarly, if you have an idea for a documentary-style project, you won't be writing a script ahead of time. Nevertheless, these types of projects still benefit from an understanding of story, and how to craft a compelling narrative.

EXTEMPORANEOUS SHOOTS

You'll probably create a lot of video projects by simply shooting extemporaneously; that is, grabbing a camera and taking it with you somewhere to shoot your friends or family. Your goal, of course, is to get footage that can be edited into a good story later. So, do you need to do any preparation before you shoot candid footage? Sort of.

You'll get better results shooting extemporaneous videos if you already have some experience with shooting and editing—reading the rest of this book will give you a good head-start. With a little experience, you'll find that you'll be able to see a story developing, and have ideas about how to structure and edit it *while you're shooting.*

Probably the most important thing to know about shooting extemporaneous footage, though, is to *not* try to plan ahead. If you have too many ideas about what you'd like to shoot, and how you'd like to edit, you might end up trying to force things to happen, and the resulting footage will not appear natural. Even worse, you might miss an even *better* story that you never would have thought of ahead of time.

DOCUMENTARIES

Whether you're shooting a short profile about an individual person, or a feature-length documentary about a much larger subject, the two most important things to remember when planning for documentary projects are to do your research and to pay attention. You'll probably need to do a fair amount of research to discover the best sources of information about your subject, whether they're books that you can read, or people whom you can interview.

Once you're on location shooting, keep your eyes open and pay attention to what's going on around you. Try to leave all preconceived notions at home, and stay open to what's available to be captured on camera.

When interviewing, it's important to have a prepared list of questions, but don't just read off each question and wait for an answer. *Listen* to what your subject says. See if their response triggers any more questions in you. *Discuss* your questions rather than simply ask them. The resulting interview will be more interesting, and you'll very likely discover some information that you wouldn't have found otherwise.

MUSIC VIDEOS

There are two types of music videos: simple "performance" videos that simply show a band playing, and narrative videos that try to tell a story of some kind. For a performance video, there's very little that you need to prepare, writing-wise. The real work on such a project takes place when you're shooting and editing. Narrative videos are a different story.

Narrative music videos don't usually have any dialog, but they often tell complex stories. Although it might sound strange, writing a script for such a music video is much like writing a silent movie, because if you want to tell a story in a music video, you have to do it without dialog. In the next activity, we're going to talk more about writing silent movies, so you'll get some good practice for writing and planning your music videos.

When you're writing a narrative video, you want to think about the same issues that we discussed earlier in this chapter: what is the beginning, middle, and end of the story you want to tell in your video? How will you show those elements visually? And so on.

Fortunately, with a music video you already have a starting point: the song. Spend some time thinking about both the music and the lyrics (if there are any) for the song you'll be shooting. There's a good chance that it already has a narrative (a beginning, middle, and end). Use this as a starting point for your writing.

You'll also want to think, of course, about the "feel" of the song. A fast paced, up-beat song will suggest a far different story than a lyrical ballad. It might also suggest a different storytelling style; for example, fast cutting between different scenes as opposed to long, serene shots.

ACTIVITY: WRITE A SCRIPT

Okay, now it's time to put all this theory into practice and write a script. However, for this exercise, you're not going to write just *any* script. As explained earlier, one of the hardest things for beginning screenwriters to understand is that movies are *visual*. Fortunately, there's a very easy way to learn how to work visually, and that's to make a silent movie.

Silent moves are, of course, how movies began and, if you've ever seen great silent movies such as Buster Keaton's *The General*, then you know how good a silent movie can be. The advantage to working silently is that, without dialog, you'll be *forced* to tell your story in pictures.

Your first step in writing any movie—even a silent one—is to write a script. So, grab your pen and pencil or your favorite word processor and get started. Although you can feel free to use any type of format, you might want to try writing using standard screenplay format. Try to keep your final project under five minutes.

Your script can be based on any idea you choose. If you're stuck for an idea, though, consider writing a script based on the following assignment:

Write a story that features an appliance in your house.

Finally, just to show you that I'm a good sport, and to provide some material for later work, I'm going to do this assignment as well. After poking around my house in search of an interesting appliance, I came across a broken "universal" remote control. This sparked an idea for a script that I've titled *Consumer Electronics.*

ON THE CD-ROM

Included in the Activities>Chapter Three on the companion CD-ROM is my finished script based on this assignment. Included with the script is a brief discussion of how the script is structured and how it was written. Feel free to read it now, or wait until you've written your own script. Later in this chapter, we'll explore this script some more.

Rewriting

Now the bad news: no one ever gets it right on the first draft. Sure, on a really short, simple piece, you might get it right on the first draft, but on a piece of any length, you're going to need to rewrite.

Rewriting can be hard sometimes. After all, you've just finished writing a script—you should be celebrating, right? Right! So go ahead. But then, get back to work and start writing your script again. Some writers actually throw out their first draft and start over from scratch, while others simply revise and rework their existing draft. Most of the time, it's best to let your first draft sit for a week or so before you start rewriting.

Your goal is to try to figure out your script's weaknesses – anything from bad dialog to bad structure to simple incoherence. Then, after you've finished your second draft, you can look forward to more re-writing! Odds are, once you let some friends read your script, they'll have suggestions, which will make you think of more changes. When you finally bring in some actors and start hearing your script read aloud, you'll probably realize that you need more changes. Don't worry, all this re-writing is *absolutely* normal.

WATCHOUT!

There's a very famous quote by William Faulkner: "All writers must be willing to murder their darlings." In other words, it doesn't matter how much you might like a particular scene, or character, or line of dialog—if something doesn't work, you *have* to get rid of it! It will feel awful, and you'll be certain that you'll never write anything that good again, but get rid of it anyway!

WATCH MORE MOVIES, WRITE MORE SCRIPTS

No matter how much experience you have, it always helps to watch movies. Now, though, you might want to watch them twice: once for your enjoyment, and then a second time to study the movie's structure and writing. See if you can figure out where the acts begin and end.

Finally, you can never get too much writing practice. Even if you don't think you have any ideas, start writing anyway. As you saw earlier, even a simple idea like a woman going for a walk can turn into a story. The most important thing for a writer to do is to write.

SUMMARY

Hopefully, you now feel more prepared to write (or, if you've already started, to rewrite) your script. After reading this chapter, you should have an understanding of:

- The need for structure in a story, and one type of structure (three-act structure).
- The need for a screenwriter to tell his or her story *visually*.

- Hopefully, you have some ideas about how to get yourself unstuck when you write yourself into a corner.
- You should have written a script for a short, silent movie. We'll be coming back to this script later. If you haven't read my silent script, do so now, as we'll be looking at it in the next chapter.
- Finally, you should be ready to rewrite and rewrite and rewrite.

You'll probably never feel like your script is *finished*, since you'll be constantly tweaking it throughout your production. However, there will come a point when you feel good enough about it that you want to start preparing to shoot. At that point, you're ready to think about *preproduction*, the subject of our next chapter.

CHAPTER

4

Preproduction

IN THIS CHAPTER

- Planning
- Scheduling
- Shots and Coverage
- Storyboarding

You'll probably never feel like your script is finished, since you'll be constantly tweaking it throughout your production. However, there will come a point where you feel good enough about it that you'll want to start preparing to shoot. Thus begins your preproduction stage, wherein you will make all of the decisions and preparations required to start rolling the camera.

How much preproduction you need depends on the type of movie you're planning to shoot. Obviously, if you're just going to go out and shoot some footage of your friends, then the only preparation you need to make is to be sure you have all the gear you need.

If, on the other hand, you're going to shoot something more complex, involving complicated camera setups and maybe some special effects, then you'll need to do more planning. The following guidelines, in other words, will vary from project to project.

PLANNING

It's difficult to stress just *how* important good planning is. Simply put: without careful preparation, you won't be able to make your movie. Good preproduction work will ensure that you arrive at your locations with everything you need, and that your cast and crew won't have to stand around bored and frustrated. What's more, if you're not properly prepared, you might find yourself with scenes that don't edit together well.

Fortunately, good preparation isn't too difficult. The process begins with a little list-making.

Making Lists

Once you have your script ready, it's time to start making lists of some of the things you'll need for your shoot. Read through your script very carefully, and list all of the following elements in your story:

- **Locations.** Any place that you'll need to shoot, whether inside or outside; locations can either be existing locations that you find, or sets that you build yourself.
- **Props.** Anything with which a character interacts.
- **Costumes.** What your characters will be wearing.
- **Set pieces.** Any special props that are needed on your set.

Spend some time visualizing what the overall look of your shoot will be. For example, if you're making a detective movie and you know that you want it to look like it's set in the 1940s, then you'll want to go back and refine your lists to make them more specific. For example, if your costume list includes a dress for the lead actress, you'll want to specify on your list that the dress look like it's from the 1940s.

Perhaps you simply want a general atmosphere for your movie. Maybe you envision everything looking beat up and grungy. Once you've decided on some of these overall *production design* questions, you can refine your location, prop, and costume lists to fit the overall "look" of your movie.

Location Scouting

Finding locations is one of the most difficult parts of preproduction. Although you might have a very clear image in your head of what a particular scene and location will look like, finding a location that matches that image can be difficult. Even if you have a particular location in mind, once you go look at the location you might find that you remembered it a little differently from it really is.

Location scouting is the process of finding all of the locations that you'll use during your shoot. Some locations will be indoors, some outdoors; some might even be on a pre-made set or stage.

Once you've found a potential location for a shot, ask yourself the following questions:

- **Can you shoot there?** Obviously, shooting on someone's private property might not be allowed, so be sure to ask the owners if its okay if you shoot on their location. Before you ask, it's best to have a rough idea of how long it will take to shoot, how many people will be involved, and when you were hoping to shoot.
- **Is the location too noisy?** Although the location might look great, if it sits on a busy street it might be too noisy to get good audio.
- **Can you get all of the different angles that you need?** For example: if you've found a great old building for your sword and sorcery epic, make sure that you can shoot all the different angles that you need without getting shots of modern things such as cars or power lines (Figure 4.1).
- **Is there enough space for your lighting?** If you're planning on setting up lights, make sure there's space (and power if you need it) for your lighting plan.

A B C

FIGURE 4.1 A) This Spanish-style mission might be just the location for some Western scenes... B) ...unfortunately, it sits on a very busy, four-lane thoroughfare, which will make shooting clean audio very difficult... C) ...also, across the street from the mission are very modern buildings with parking lots, which will make reverse angles difficult. (On the other hand, the location—San Francisco's Mission Dolores—was good enough for Hitchcock, who featured it prominently in *Vertigo*. Of course, it wasn't a period movie, and there was much less traffic in 1958.)

- **Does the location need to be modified?** Sometimes, you might need to cover up the sign on a building, or "dress" a building so that it looks older or different. Make sure that the owner of the building will let you make these changes, and that the changes can be easily added and removed.
- **Can a location be improved through the use of sound effects?** Sometimes, throwing in some subtle background sound can make a location seem much more realistic. Make sure you have access to, or can record, such sound effects.

As long as you're at your location, use your camera to shoot some video and stills of the site. These will be handy references for later, when you start storyboarding and planning your shots.

Finally, be creative when looking for your locations. Remember that you don't have to show *all* of a building or location; sometimes, just the doorway of a building is all you need to convey a particular mood. The audience has no idea what might be sitting just outside the frame, so it's easy to fool them.

Script Breakdown

One of the hardest things about being a movie director is managing all of the people, equipment, and locations that are needed to shoot your script. Hollywood directors have entire teams of people for each of these jobs—you're probably going to have to do most of it yourself. Fortunately, with a little bit of work, you should be able to get your project under control. *Script breakdown* is the first step in planning the actual shooting of your movie.

NUMBER YOUR SCENES

Before you go any further, take a copy of your script and number all of the scenes. If you wrote your script in standard screenplay format, then the scene breaks are easy to see—each slugline is the beginning of a new scene.

With your scenes numbered, you can now start breaking down your script to create a plan for who and what will be needed for each scene.

ACTIVITY: MAKING BREAKDOWN SHEETS

On the companion CD-ROM, in the Activities>Chapter 4 folder is a PDF file called "Script Breakdown Sheet." Open this file and print one copy for each scene in your script.

You'll want to fill in all of the appropriate information for each scene in your script. Figure 4.2 shows the breakdown sheet for scene 7 of my *Consumer Electronics* script. Of course, not all of your scenes will have special effects, sound effects, vehicles, or even cast members.

When all of your breakdown sheets are filled in, you'll have a set of very detailed lists for every shot in your movie.

SCRIPT BREAKDOWN

SCENE #: 7 SCENE NAME: Consumer becomes rich BREAKDOWN PAGE #: 7

DESCRIPTION: INT. OR EXT.: Int.

SCRIPT PAGE: DAY OR NIGHT: Day

CAST	CREW	EXTRAS
Rick	Director Camera Assistant	

PROPS	WARDROBE	MAKE-UP/HAIR
Remote Mona Lisa Wine glass	Suit	neater hair

VEHICLES	SPECIAL EQUIPMENT	SOUND FX/MUSIC
	Wall behind consumer will be rotoscoped red in post.	

FIGURE 4.2 This is a breakdown sheet for one scene from *Consumer Electronics*. You'll find a blank breakdown sheet on the companion CD-ROM.

SCHEDULING

Here's a sad fact that you should be prepared for as you start your movie-making process: everyone wants to be in a movie, but it's never as much fun as they think it's going to be.

Making a movie takes a lot of time and it's usually much more fun for the filmmakers than it is for the average amateur actor who thought that being in a movie was going to be very glamorous. The problem is that making a movie takes a *lot* of time. Unfortunately for the actors, most of that time is spent standing around while you and your crew set up cameras and lights.

Since your actors (and your crew, for that matter) will probably be working for free, it's important to make the most of their time by preparing good schedules for your shoot. A good schedule will help you get everyone to the right place at the right time, and ensure that you know what you're doing when you get there.

There are many different ways to make a schedule (and there are even programs available that will help you create Hollywood-style schedules), so feel free to use whatever works for you. Here's one method:

SCHEDULING YOUR SHOOT

The main problem with schedules is that they usually change from moment to moment as people become available or unavailable. Therefore, when scheduling, you want to use a method that will let you quickly and easily rearrange and reschedule the shooting of particular scenes.

In this tutorial, you'll create a preliminary schedule for your shoot. As an example, I'll be using the *Consumer Electronics* script from Chapter 3. You can either write out your schedule by hand, or use a spreadsheet program, as I'll be doing.

Step 1: Create a Grid

You're going to create your schedule on a big grid, with characters and crew listed on the rows, and scenes listed along the columns. Begin by creating a grid (either by hand, or using a spreadsheet or word processor) and filling in the names of your characters and crew positions as shown in Figure 4.3.

Step 2: Arrange Your Scenes

Next, you want to group all of your scenes together by location. For example, in *Consumer Electronics*, the main location is a couch in a living room. Each of the scenes that need to be shot in this location are listed in their own column, as shown in Figure 4.4.

Script: Consumer Electronics

CAST/CREW	
The Consumer Sitcom woman Sitcom man Newscaster Camera Grip Effects coordinator	

FIGURE 4.3 Begin your schedule by creating a grid with your character and crew names.

Script: Consumer Electronics

	Scene 1: Consumer entrance/opening	Scene 6: Consumer watching self	Scene 7: Rich consumer	Scene 8: Better-looking consumer	Scene 9: Smart consumer	Scene 10: Consumer gone bad	Scene 12: Consumer recovering	Scene 13: Consumer w/GPS	Scene 2: Watching newscast	Scene 3: Watching sitcom	Scene 4: Consumer in closet	Scene 5: Consumer videotaping self	Scene 11: Consumer cleaning tape	Scene 14: Consumer in desert
CAST/CREW The Consumer Sitcom woman Sitcom man Newscaster Camera Grip Effects Coordinator														

FIGURE 4.4 List each scene along the top of your grid, and then group your scenes together by location. For example, notice that scenes 2 and 3 sit between scenes 13 and 4. This is because they will be shot at the same time on a separate location.

The idea is that, when you get to a particular location, you want to shoot all the scenes that take place at that location so that you don't have to go traveling back and forth from one location to another.

Step 3: Mark Characters and Crew Needed

Now, put Xs on the grid to indicate which cast and crew members are required for each scene (Figure 4.5).

Script: Consumer Electronics

CAST/CREW	Scene 1: Consumer entrance/opening	Scene 6: Consumer watching self	Scene 7: Rich consumer	Scene 8: Better-looking consumer	Scene 9: Smart consumer	Scene 10: Consumer gone bad	Scene 12: Consumer recovering	Scene 13: Consumer w/GPS	END OF FIRST DAY	Scene 2: Watching newscast	Scene 3: Watching sitcom	END OF SECOND DAY	Scene 4: Consumer in closet	Scene 5: Consumer videotaping self	Scene 11: Consumer cleaning tape	END OF THIRD DAY	Scene 14: Consumer in desert
The Consumer	•	•	•	•	•	•	•	•					•	•	•		•
Sitcom woman											•						
Sitcom man											•						
Newscaster										•							
Camera	•	•	•	•	•	•	•	•		•	•		•	•	•		•
Grip	•	•	•	•	•	•	•	•		•	•		•	•	•		•
Effects Coordinator	•	•	•	•	•	•	•	•		•	•		•	•	•		•

FIGURE 4.5 Now you can easily mark off who will be needed to shoot which scene. You can also group your schedule to indicate which scenes will be shot on which day. In this schedule, we've planned for a three-day shoot.

Step 4: Rearrange as Needed

Now, as your scheduling needs change, you can simply re-order the columns. You can either cut your printed schedule into vertical strips, or rearrange the columns in your grid using your computer.

You need to try to estimate how long it will take to shoot each batch of scenes. You might not be able to shoot all of the scenes at a particular location in one trip, and so will need to schedule a couple of shoots at that location. Moreover, some scenes will take longer than others, even if they're at the same location. For example, a scene involving many different angles or special effects will take longer to shoot than a simple shot of a couple of actors. Similarly, a scene with lots of dialog might take longer because the actors might have a harder job in such a scene.

With more experience, you'll get better at estimating how long it will take to shoot a scene. For now, don't overextend yourself—schedule generously.

Budgeting

Hopefully, your script won't require a huge budget to shoot (ideally, it won't require any budget at all). However, even if you think your script can be shot cheap, it's worth checking out what's really required to shoot your movie. It's a real drag to get started and then realize you don't have enough money to finish.

Consider the following potential expenses:

- **Gear.** Hopefully, you have everything you need. If not, maybe you can borrow or rent what you're missing. Don't forget to budget for tapes.
- **Cast and crew.** Most likely, these will be your family, friends, or anyone else you can find who wants to be in a movie and is willing to work for free.
- **Props and sets.** Most of the time, between you and your friends, you can find all of the props you need. However, although you can probably scare up most of the props and set pieces you need, there will probably be one or two props that you'll need to invest some money in.
- **Costumes.** This is another one that you can hopefully borrow from your cast or friends. However, if you're shooting something unusual—a western, say—then you might need to find a costume shop that will rent you some costumes. Or, if you know someone at a local school or university, maybe you can borrow some costumes from their drama departments.
- **Locations.** Unfortunately, there might be times when you have to rent a location, or pay a fee for a location's use.
- **Travel.** If you need to drive or bus your cast and crew to somewhere, don't forget to budget in gas money or bus fare.

As you can see from the preceding list, you're going to try to get most of your expenses covered for free. This means you're going to do a lot of begging and borrowing, so get ready to turn on the charm and call in some favors. Remember that when someone loans you something, they're doing you a favor. Assure them that whatever they're loaning you will be taken care of, and be certain to return the stuff on time, and at their convenience. After all, you never know when you'll want to ask them again for something else!

ACTIVITY: SAMPLE BUDGET

In the Activities>Chapter 3 folder on the companion CD-ROM is a sample budget for the *Consumer Electronics* script that you read in the last chapter. Take a look at it now to get a better idea of some of the expenses you might encounter when shooting even a simple script.

SHOTS AND COVERAGE

Once you start shooting, your main concern will be to get all of the *coverage* that you will need when you're in the editing room. In other words, you want to make sure that you shoot plenty of takes and different angles so that when you're editing you'll have all of the footage you need to cover your scene. How much coverage is necessary? That all depends on your tastes, the needs of your script, and how much shooting you can reasonably manage to do.

It's important to realize that, although you may have written a very "visual" script, you probably didn't write out specific shots (in fact, you shouldn't have written out specific shots; it makes your script much less readable).

HINT

Shots? Scenes?

Before we go any further, let's define a *shot*. A shot is simply a single piece of footage—the video that you shoot between the time you start rolling and the time you finish. Shots, in turn, are edited together to create a *scene*.

In the first draft of the *Consumer Electronics* script that I wrote for the "Write a Script" activity on page 59, I originally had the following simple description of the first shot in the movie:

> The door opens and in walks The Consumer. Although not outright grungy, he is certainly a bit slovenly. Very casually dressed, and very eager, he happily plops down on the couch and opens a large shopping bag. Tossing the bag aside, he pulls out a big box festooned with photos and splashy graphics. The words *Universal Remote* are plainly visible on the front of the box.

This is a reasonably clear description of the action that will take place, but it tells nothing about how the scene will actually be shot and edited. Where will the camera go? What will it see? How many different shots might it take to show the action described in those few sentences? It's better to think about these questions during preproduction, If you wait until you get to your location, or onto your set, you'll end up making a lot of people stand around—bored—while you figure out what kind of shots you need.

HOW MANY SHOTS DOES IT TAKE TO MAKE A SCENE?

When a scene is well shot and expertly edited, you won't even be aware of one shot turning into the next. In fact, unless you actually choose to look at the number of shots, you might not ever have any idea of just how many shots it takes to create a scene.

Let's take a look at a real-world example. Perhaps you've seen the James Bond movie *Tomorrow Never Dies*. If you haven't, it's worth watching. Like all James Bond movies, this one begins with an action sequence that takes place before the main credits. One could describe this sequence as follows:

> On top of a snow-covered mountain, a group of terrorists have met to sell weapons. James Bond has managed to sneak in to the location and has set up a small video camera, which is relaying images back to headquarters where M and a number of generals are watching. After a lot of fighting and a daring air battle, Bond manages to escape with a nuke-laden airplane before a missile launched by the generals' strikes the mountain.

As you can see, it's your basic "excuse me, I have to save the world" sort of James Bond scene, and the whole thing lasts about nine minutes. However, take a look at this list of the first 19 shots in the scene:

1. Wide-shot—Terrorist arms bazaar. Pan down to reveal a video camera.
2. Reverse-angle of the video camera.
3. Shot of what the camera sees (called a "point-of-view," or POV shot).
4. Shot of the camera lens zooming.
5. Another POV shot. We zoom in to a group of terrorists.
6. Another shot of the video camera panning and zooming.
7. Another POV shot. This time, we see a fat, bearded man.
8. Another shot of the video camera.
9. Another POV shot. This time, some trucks.
10. Yet another shot of the video camera.
11. And yet another POV shot. Two terrorists making a deal.
12. Again, a shot of the video camera.
13. A POV shot of some guns.
14. Now, we see three big-screen monitors showing the videos we've just seen. The camera pans down to reveal a man speaking.
15. Medium shot of two men in military uniforms. They watch the screens.
16. The speaking man again.
17. Reverse shot showing the whole room, including the men and the big screens.
18. Close-up of a woman.
19. Two-shot of the woman and the speaking man.

There you have it, 19 shots, each completely different, and almost every one of them requiring a different camera setup—that is, the camera had to be moved and rearranged for *each* shot. What's really amazing, though, is that these 19 shots account for only *1 minute* of screen time! And this is a two-hour movie!

If we imagine what the terrorist arms bazaar set looked like, we can get a good idea of all of the different locations where they would have to put the camera to get those first 13 shots (Figure 4.6).

Two things are interesting about this scene: first, you can see that it can take a *lot* of different angles and setups to get the coverage you need to make the scene you want. Second, if you shoot and edit well, your audience won't necessarily even realize how many different shots they're seeing.

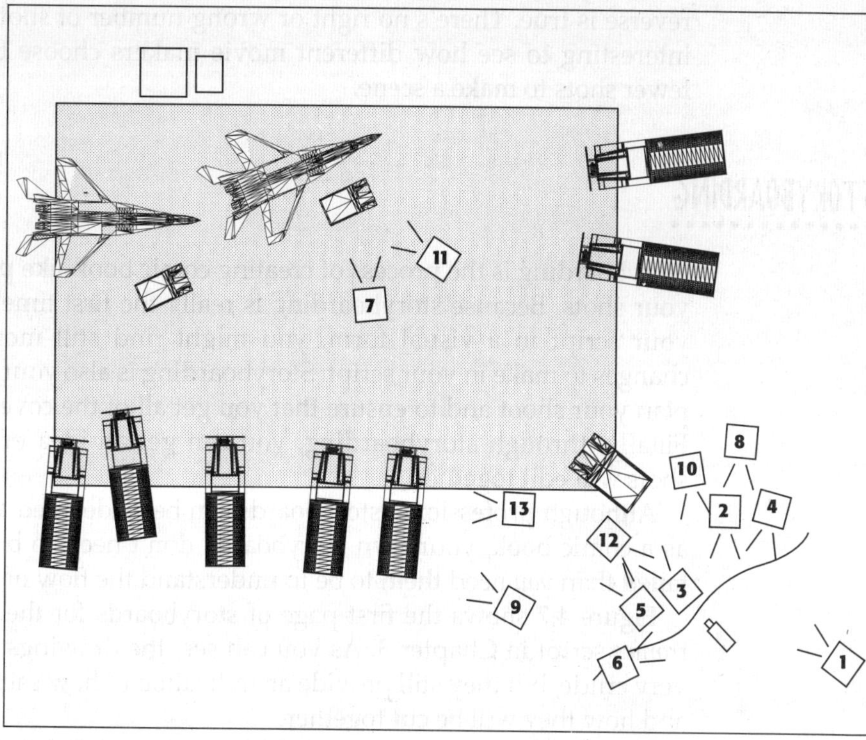

FIGURE 4.6 This map shows a rough approximation of the set for the first scene of the James Bond movie *Tomorrow Never Dies*, including camera positions and orientations for the first 13 shots. Note that these 13 shots take up only 40 seconds in the final scene! That's a lot of work for 40 seconds of finished film.

ACTIVITY: SHOT ANALYSIS

One of the best ways to learn how to break a scene down into shots is to look at how other people have done it. Think of a movie that you like that you've seen more than one time. Now think of the first scene of that movie and write a simple description of it (like the description on page 73).

Now go watch the movie and see how many shots it actually took to make that scene. Don't worry about what the shots are or how they're set up; just count them.

Now think of some different types of scenes in the same movie (action scenes, serious scenes, funny scenes). Count the number of shots in those scenes. Is there a difference? Sometimes, action or comedy scenes have lots of shots, while dramatic scenes have very few. At other times, the reverse is true. There's no right or wrong number of shots, but it can be interesting to see how different movie makers choose to use more or fewer shots to make a scene.

STORYBOARDING

Storyboarding is the process of creating comic book-like pictures of all of your shots. Because storyboarding is really the first time that you'll see your script in a visual form, you might find still more tweaks and changes to make in your script. Storyboarding is also your opportunity to plan your shoot and to ensure that you get all of the coverage you need. Finally, through storyboarding, you can get an idea of how different shots will edit together.

Although professional storyboards can be as detailed and compelling as a comic book, your own storyboards don't need to be any more detailed than *you* need them to be to understand the flow of your shoot.

Figure 4.7 shows the first page of storyboards for the *Consumer Electronics* script in Chapter 3. As you can see, the drawings themselves are very crude, but they still provide an indication of how each shot will look and how they will be cut together.

Below each picture, it's a good idea to include a brief description of that picture's action. The description doesn't have to be perfect, of course, because you'll typically refer to storyboards in conjunction with your script.

In addition to sample framings, you'll often want to give an indication of camera movements and other motion within the frame. The professionally drawn storyboard in Figure 4.8 shows how, through the use of arrows, you can indicate what the camera will be doing during a shot.

PHOTO STORYBOARDS

You can use the still feature on your digital camera to create photo-storyboards. Once you've found the locations for your shoot you can go to those locations and shoot stills that you can use as the backgrounds of your storyboards.

Shoot the stills so they're framed just as you want them in your final movie. Once you've dumped the photos into your computer, you can simply open them up in any paint or image editing program and draw over them.

FIGURE 4.7 Even if you can't draw well, you can probably draw well enough to create simple storyboards that will help you plan your shots and visualize how your shots will edit together.

DETAIL DOESN'T ALWAYS MATTER

Remember that the main purpose of a storyboard is to help you understand what shots you'll need to get, and what those shots will look like. Realistic detail is only important in a storyboard if you're trying to plan some kind of effects shot and you need your crew to be able to see what something should look like.

As you start storyboarding, you might discover things about your set and props—for example, maybe you need more or different props—and so will need to go back and update your breakdown sheets accordingly.

FIGURE 4.8 A picture can be worth a thousand words when drawn by a professional storyboard artist. Note the use of arrows to indicate camera movements.

ACTIVITY: CONSUMER ELECTRONICS PREPRODUCTION

Included in the Activities>Chapter 4 folder of the companion CD-ROM is the CEPreprod.pdf file, which includes most of the preproduction materials for the *Consumer Electronics* script from Chapter 3. Included in the file are: a copy of the script with numbered scenes; prop and location lists; breakdown sheets; a preliminary shooting schedule; budget; and a complete set of hand-drawn storyboards.

Note that this script is pretty dependent on special effects. We'll be getting into some special effects preproduction and production later in the book. These documents should provide both an example and a look at what it's going to take to actually shoot this script!

SUMMARY

After all this, you're probably getting pretty antsy to start shooting. Well, don't worry, that's about to happen. Fortunately, after working through this chapter you should be in a good position to roll your camera. You should now be comfortable with:

- Preproduction planning, including location scouting, scheduling, props and sets, and budgeting.
- What a shot is, and how many of them it takes to "cover" a scene.
- How to begin to visualize your movie in shots, and how to make storyboards to plan those shots.

In Chapter 6, you're going to learn more about what different types of shots and camera moves are called, and why you might choose one over another. After reading that chapter, you might want to rethink some of your storyboards. That's okay, constant revision is a normal part of the movie-making process.

First, though, it's time to learn how your camera works.

CHAPTER

5

Preparing Your Camera

IN THIS CHAPTER

- Your Camera
- Dealing with Microphones
- All That Other Gear
- Preparing a Camera Checklist

Whether you're shooting on the go or planning your shoot in fine detail, when the camera's actually rolling you've got to be able to move quickly to get the shots you want. The best way to do that is to learn all the details of your camera and equipment. Ideally, you want to be able to operate your camera without even looking at it, since you'll typically be looking through the viewfinder and won't have time to go searching for a control.

In this chapter, you're going to learn all of the video camera basics, as well as some simple lighting and audio techniques. Because this chapter won't cover specific models of cameras, you'll want to have your camera handy. If possible, you should also grab your camera's manual.

By the end of this chapter, you'll know what all of those buttons on your camera are and have a good idea of how to use them. After that, you'll be ready to start shooting!

YOUR CAMERA

Let's start with the basics: you need to know how to turn your camera on. This might seem like a very simple thing, but on some cameras it can actually be a bit complex, so let's take a quick look.

Figure 5.1 shows the power switch of a Canon Elura II.

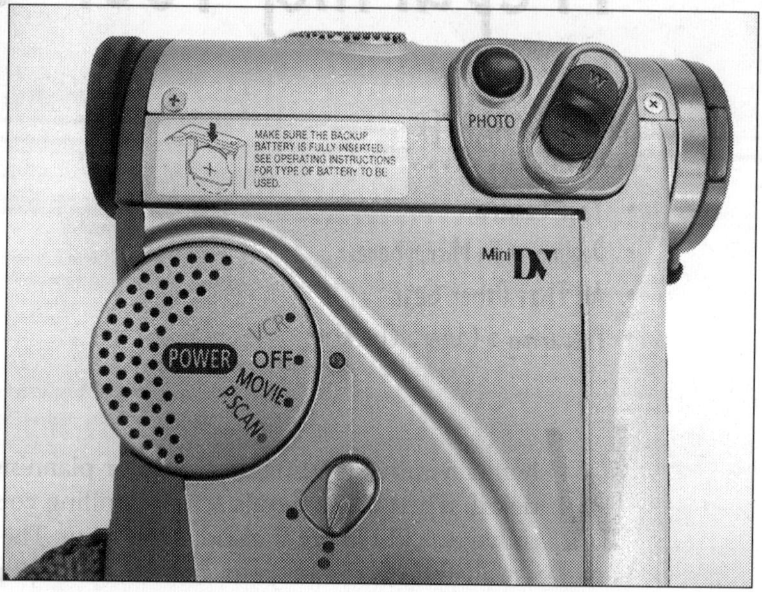

FIGURE 5.1 The power switch on this Canon Elura II is typical of most video camera power switches. It lets you select different modes, either shooting or playback.

Like most cameras, the Elura II can run in different modes: Movie mode, for shooting video; VCR mode for watching the tape; and P.SCAN mode, a special version of Movie mode that shoots a different type of video (not all cameras have this mode and we'll talk more about it later). Your camera will probably have some variation of these same modes. When you're ready to shoot, turn the camera on by selecting Movie mode. When you need to review your footage, dump footage into your computer, or cue up a tape, put the camera into VCR mode.

Before you can turn on your camera, however, it has to have power.

Power: Batteries and Plugs

You can power your camera with rechargeable batteries or an AC adapter that you plug into the wall. Obviously, when shooting in the field you'll use batteries. When you're editing at home, or if you're shooting near an electrical outlet, you should use your camera's AC adapter to save battery power. A battery charger should have been included with your camera.

Most cameras offer a choice of battery sizes that pack different capacities. Typically, a battery with a longer life will be much larger and heavier than a shorter-lived battery (Figure 5.2).

FIGURE 5.2 Batteries come in lots of different sizes and capacities. The battery that came with your camera is probably small and doesn't last very long. For extended field or location shooting, consider buying a larger, longer-lasting battery.

Batteries are a pretty simple thing: you charge them up, use them until they run down, and then charge them up again. Running out of battery power in the middle of a shoot is a real drag, though, so pay attention to these battery-saving tips:

- **Charge intelligently.** Look on your battery pack or check your camera's manual to find out what type of battery your camera uses. If it uses a Nickel-Cadmium (NiCAD) battery pack, then *always* make sure that the battery is completely dead before you put it back on the charger. NiCAD batteries can develop a "memory" if you only drain them part way. Once they have a memory, they can't be completely recharged.

If your camera uses Lithium-Ion (Li-ion) or Nickel-Metal Hydride (NiMH) batteries, you can recharge them at any time without giving the battery a memory. These types of batteries don't hold their charge for more than a month or so, so if they've been sitting for a while, stick them in the charger to "top them off" before you go shooting.

When you first get any type of new rechargeable battery, give it a good complete charge the first time you charge it.

- **Watch your battery meter.** Your camera's viewfinder should have a battery meter that tells how much charge you have left. After you've used the camera for a while, you should have a better idea of how accurate the meter is. If you see your power waning, you'll want to start taking some battery-saving measures, as detailed in the sidebar, *How to Save Battery Power*.
- **Don't use your battery if you don't have to.** If you're shooting indoors and there's an electrical outlet available, plug your camera into the wall. And, when you're back at home editing your video, don't run your camera off its batteries. This way, there will be a better chance of your batteries having a charge when you need them.

HOW TO SAVE BATTERY POWER

The last thing you want to have happen when you're in the middle of shooting is for your batteries to go dead. Lucky for you, your camera probably has a meter that will give you an idea of how much battery power you have left. If your meter starts running toward empty, then do the following to try to save as much power as possible:

- **Don't use your camera's LCD screen.** The LCD screen is your camera's biggest power drain. Don't use it when shooting or reviewing until you can plug into a wall or recharge your batteries.
- **Don't change tapes if you don't have to.** Ejecting and loading a tape takes some extra power. Don't do it if you don't need to.
- **Don't review your footage or search around on your tape.** Try to save your playback and searching around for when you get more power.

- **Turn the camera off when you're not using it.** If you need to pause between takes, or travel to a new location, turn your camera off or put it in standby mode (if it has a standby mode).
- **Keep your batteries warm.** If you're shooting in really cold weather, your battery life might shorten. If your battery finally dies, try taking it out of the camera and putting it in your pocket. Believe it or not, if you can warm it up a bit, you might coax some more power out of it.

Videotape

Although videotape is pretty straightforward—you load it into your camera and shoot on it—there are still one or two things to keep in mind:

- **Be careful when loading a DV tape.** Most digital video cameras use a tape transport mechanism like the one shown in Figure 5.3.

  Although this mechanism is pretty sturdy, you still need to *be careful* when loading a tape. Follow the directions marked on the camera.

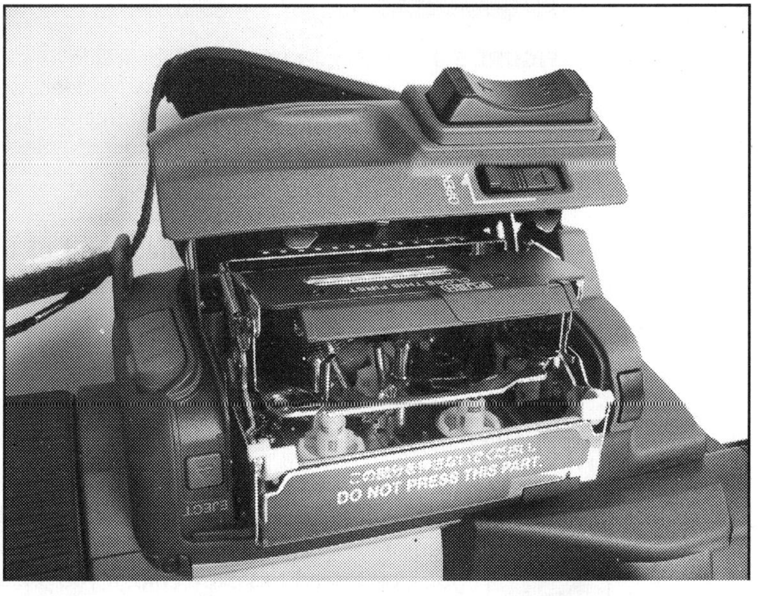

FIGURE 5.3 Most DV cameras feature a tape transport that looks something like this. Although this mechanism is sturdy, you *do* need to follow the camera's instructions on how to insert a tape.

- **Never touch the tape.** Touching the tape that's inside of a cassette can mess it up (Figure 5.4). If you're curious about what's inside a videocassette, then go ahead and take one apart. Just make sure it doesn't contain any video that you care about.

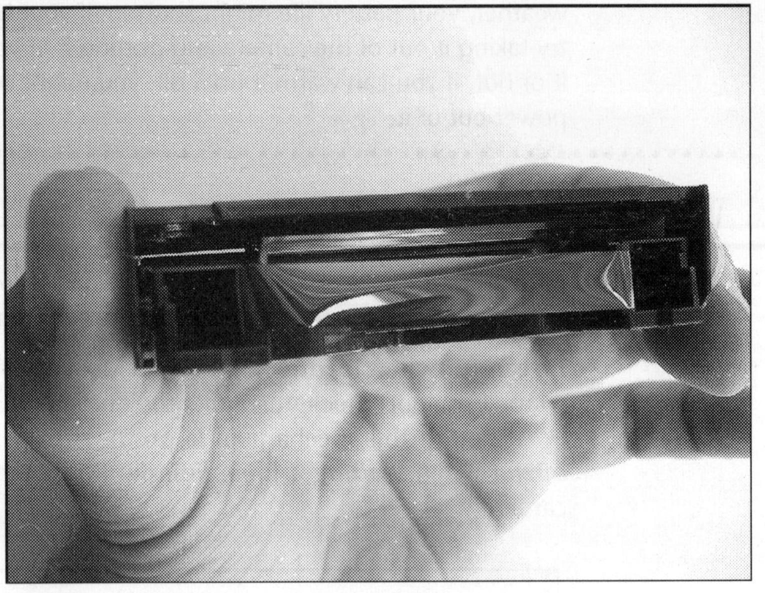

FIGURE 5.4 Don't ever touch the tape inside a videocassete that you're using. If you're curious about how a videocassette works, then get an old tape—or a tape that you don't intend to use—and take that apart. Messing with a good tape can render it useless.

- **Don't worry too much about the brand of tape you use.** In most cases, if you're buying a name-brand tape, it will be fine. You probably won't be able to see a difference in image quality from one brand of tape to another.

WATCHOUT!

Sony sells some very expensive videotape that has an extra memory chip built into it. If you're not using a Sony camera, you don't need this extra chip. If you *are* using a Sony camera, you only need it if you plan on shooting lots of stills and want quick access to those stills. In other words, save your money and buy cheaper tape.

Viewfinder

Your camera's viewfinder probably displays all sorts of setting and readouts while you're shooting. It's important that you understand what these different readouts mean.

Check your camera's manual and be certain that you know what all of its display icons mean. Also, find out if there's a way to turn off these readouts. There will be times when you want them out of the way so that you can see what's behind them in the frame.

Controls

Your camera is most likely covered with all sorts of buttons and controls. Although it's best to know what all of them are, you'll really only regularly use a few, essential ones. To shoot good video, you *must* know how these controls work!

ZOOM

Your camera's zoom control lets you "zoom in" on an image to make it appear larger and closer, or "zoom out" to make your subject look smaller and farther away (Figure 5.5).

Your camera's zoom control probably looks something like the one shown in Figure 5.6. Push it one way and the camera zooms in; push it the other and the camera zooms out. Play around some with your zoom control to get a feel for how quickly it can zoom. In addition, see if it zooms at different speeds depending on how far you press the zoom control. A variable speed zoom will allow you to speed up or slow down the speed of the zoom by pressing harder or softer on the zoom control. This can be essential for creating certain types of effects.

HINT

Turn Off Digital Zoom

Some cameras have a *digital zoom* feature, which creates a "fake" zoom effect by digitally enlarging the image that your camera sees. Digital zoom is usually used to achieve a ridiculously high zoom amount like 40x or 200x. However, digital zoom always looks terrible—grainy and noisy, with bleeding colors—so turn it off. If you don't know how, check your camera's manual.

FIGURE 5.5 For these two images, our camera stayed in the same position (relative to our subject), but in the lower image, we zoomed in closer.

Start and Stop

In addition to the zoom, the other control that you absolutely *have* to be able to find by feel is the start/stop control—the control that starts and stops recording. Usually located under your thumb, some cameras actually have more than one start/stop control (Figure 5.7).

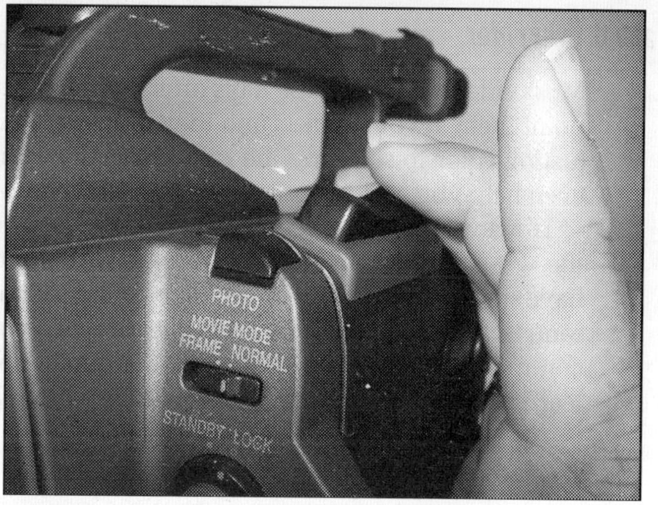

FIGURE 5.6 A good zoom control rests comfortably beneath your fingers and is easy to access at all times.

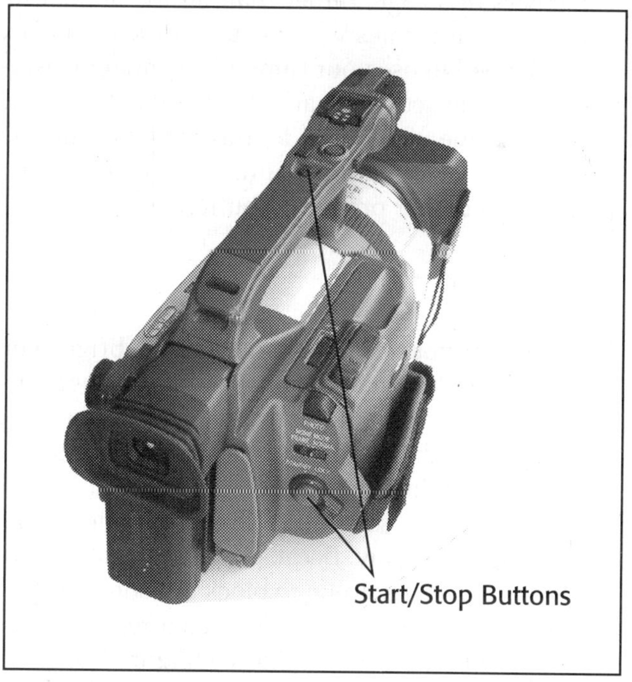

FIGURE 5.7 You need to be able to find your camera's Start/Stop button by feel. Some cameras actually have more than one so that you can hold the camera in different positions.

Manual Overrides

Most video cameras these days offer complete automatic operation—just point them at your subject and they'll do everything from focusing to adjusting color to selecting the right exposure settings. Some cameras will even help you steady your shot if you don't have a tripod!

However, even the best camera isn't perfect, and will sometimes make the wrong choice about focus or exposure. Fortunately, many cameras have special manual options that give you control over your shooting parameters. Later in the book, you'll learn when you might use some of the controls. For now, you should take a quick look at what they do, and learn how to access the controls on your particular camera.

MANUAL FOCUS

Although your camera's autofocus might be very good, there will be times when it will be "fooled" into focusing on the wrong thing. If you're shooting an animal at the zoo, for example, your camera might focus on the bars of a cage, rather than on the animal inside the cage. For these times—or for times when you want to create a very unusual framing—you'll need to use your camera's manual focus.

After you activate manual focus, most video cameras will place a small gauge in the viewfinder to indicate what distance the camera is focused on (see your camera's manual for details). You can adjust the focus by turning a dial or pressing a button.

MANUAL IRIS

The iris in your camera controls how bright your image is. If the iris is open wider, the image is brighter; if it's closed down, the image is darker. Your camera will automatically measure the light in a scene and select an iris opening that is appropriate. However, its iris choice might not always be the best thing for a scene.

For example, say you're shooting a shot of someone standing in front of a bright window. Because of the bright window, the camera will most likely turn its iris down to block out some of the light. This will make the window look okay in the final picture, but the person in the foreground will become dark and shadowy (Figure 5.8).

With a manual iris control, you can open up the camera's iris so as to better expose your subject. The window will end up *blown out*—that is, it will be overexposed, too bright, and washed out—but your subject will

FIGURE 5.8 In the top image, the bright light is causing our camera to underexpose the image, leaving our subject's face hidden in shadows. With a manual iris control (sometimes called Manual Exposure, or Manual Aperture), we can force the camera to overexpose. Therefore, although the background blows out to white, we can now see our subject's face.

be visible. Manual iris controls usually work the same way as a manual focus control does. Check your camera's documentation for details.

SHUTTER SPEED

Your video camera contains a shutter that opens and closes just like the shutter in a film camera. Shutter speed is another way that the camera controls how bright the camera's image is—a faster speed lets in less light, while a slower speed lets in more. Shutter speed also affects how sharp or blurry an individual frame is.

In an image with a fast shutter speed, every frame will be sharp and in focus. At slower shutter speeds, each frame will appear blurrier. A faster shutter speed can make the motion in an image appear stuttery, since the individual frames don't blur into each other (Figure 5.9).

If you're shooting sports, you might want to set your camera to a faster shutter speed to shoot clearer action. Similarly, if you want to grab still images from your video, a higher shutter speed will improve your chances of getting clear stills.

For most shooting, though, a slower shutter speed—around 1/60th of a second—will produce the best-looking motion.

White Balance

There are many different kinds of light in the world—sunlight, fluorescent light, candlelight, and on and on. Each type of light has a different color. Fluorescent light, for example, is much more blue than the yellowish light that comes from the incandescent light bulbs that you use in a table lamp. The color of sunlight, meanwhile, can actually vary slightly from place to place and from one time of day to the next.

You probably take all of this for granted because your eye adjusts on-the-fly as you move from one type of light to another. Because it can do this, colors usually look the same as you move from indoors to outdoors or from one type of artificial lighting to another.

Your camera is not so lucky; it can't do nearly as good a job as your eyeballs do of knowing what a particular color is supposed to look like. In fact, to accurately reproduce color, it has to be told exactly what type of light is currently available. You tell a camera about the available light through a process called *white balancing*.

The idea is pretty simple. As you probably already know, light is made up of bunches of different colors. When you see a rainbow, what you're

FIGURE 5.9 When shooting with a slower shutter speed (as in the upper image), each frame is rendered pretty blurry, resulting in smoother motion when the video is played. When shooting with a higher shutter speed (lower image), each frame is perfectly sharp, resulting in stuttery, jerky motion that contains lots of detail.

actually seeing is normal sunlight being split into all of its separate colors by drops of rain. The idea behind white balancing is that if the camera knows what white looks like under the current light, then it will know what every other color is supposed to look like, since white light is composed of every other color.

Most cameras have an automatic white balance feature that tries to locate a white object in the current scene and adjust itself so that that white object actually looks white. If it looks white, then the other colors will probably look right.

As with all automatic features, though, automatic white balance can become confused under certain situations. For example, if you shoot an Irish marching band marching on a golf course on St. Patrick's Day, pretty much everything in the scene will be green. The camera will most likely assume that the brightest object in the scene is white, when it will actually be green, which will throw off the color balance of the entire scene.

White balance troubles also crop up when you're shooting in a situation with mixed lighting. Say you're shooting in a room with fluorescent lighting, but there's sunlight coming in through a window. Because the sunlight is one color, and the fluorescent lights are a different color, your camera might have a very difficult time figuring out what color things are supposed to be.

White balance problems show up in your final video in the form of color "casts." If an image looks too blue or green overall, it is said to have a blue or green "cast." These types of color issues are really troublesome, because they can make your video look awful, and because they're *very* hard to correct.

Fortunately, if you pay attention to the lighting in your scene, and learn how to use your camera's white balance controls, you can avoid these troubles. Read your camera manual to learn how to change your camera's white balance.

AUTO WHITE BALANCE

In general, auto white balance will work fine. If you're shooting outdoors in direct sunlight, or indoors with a single type of light, you can probably get by with leaving your camera on auto.

However, if you're shooting in either situation and there is a dominant color in the frame—a big red fire truck or a bright blue building, for example—then your camera's auto white balance could get screwed up. At this point, you'll want to switch to manual. As you spend more time with your camera, you'll get a better idea of when you can rely on its auto white balance, and when you need to take the controls yourself.

WHITE BALANCE PRESETS

Most video cameras include a number of predefined white balance settings. For example, your camera probably provides special white balance settings for daylight, tungsten (which are the types of light bulbs you usually find in your house), fluorescent, and cloudy days. These settings are usually a little more reliable than auto white balance if you're shooting in these situations. They're also handy for times when your scene might be corrupted by a dominant color of some kind.

If you're really concerned about color, or if you've discovered that your camera can't auto white balance in certain situations, these presets might be just the answer.

MANUAL WHITE BALANCE

For *really* reliable color and white balance control, you'll want to use your camera's manual white balance. To manually white balance a camera, put someone in an area that's lit by your lighting and have them hold up a piece of white paper. Point your camera at the paper and zoom in all the way until the paper fills the whole frame. Press the manual white balance button. The camera will take a reading and then white balance itself accordingly.

Manual white balance is ideal for mixed lighting situations or any other time when your camera's auto white balance feature isn't working. This is really the white balance mode you should be using all the time. Unfortunately, it's often not practical to take the time to manually white balance.

Widescreen

You know that notice you see at the beginning of some movies that says, "This movie has been modified to fit your set"? That notice is there to let you know that a whole bunch of the image has been cropped off to fit onto your TV screen.

HINT

Aspect Ratio—A Fancy Term for *Shape*

The ratio of an image's width to its height is called its *aspect ratio*. This term comes up a lot among filmmakers as they discuss different film and tape formats. Video has an aspect of 4:3, while HDTV and many film formats have an aspect ratio of 16:9. Most computer screens have an aspect ratio of 4:3, although some wider screens have a 16:9 or 3:2 aspect ratio. For the most part, you can always assume that you'll be working in 4:3, unless you use your camera's wide-screen mode or switch to a fancy video or film camera with a different ratio.

Movies are typically shot using formats that are very wide—much wider than they are tall. Television, on the other hand, is almost square. Figure 5.10 shows the difference between a number of different movie frames sizes alongside a television frame size.

When it comes time to transfer a movie to make it fit onto a TV, a studio has two options: they can either "letterbox" the movie—put black bands across the top and bottom of the screen to effectively change the

FIGURE 5.10 Regular video has a very different shape, or aspect ratio, than does HDTV or the typical movie. The inner square shows the aspect ratio of regular video—the kind your camera shoots—while the larger square shows the aspect ratio of HDTV and some movie formats (there are other movie formats that are even wider).

shape of your TV screen into something more rectangular—or they can crop the edges off to make the movie fit your TV.

Obviously, you can't chop off the edges without chopping off some image, which is why you often see scenes in videotape movies where someone's head is hanging half off the frame. Or someone might be talking to someone else who's not even in the frame. Needless to say, if you're a director who's carefully created a shot, having it chopped up in this manner can be very frustrating.

Most filmmakers find wide formats to be much more appealing than the square TV format. With a wide format, you can capture wide landscapes and create an epic, sprawling landscape on the screen.

Many video cameras include special widescreen modes. It's important to note that these modes don't actually shoot a wider image. Rather, they chop off the top and bottom to make the image into a wider shape (Figure 5.11).

FIGURE 5.11 Although many cameras feature a "widescreen" option, it doesn't actually shoot a wider image. Instead, it just crops the top and bottom of the frame so that the image looks rectangular instead of square.

If you want to use one of these modes, be aware that they won't necessarily look wider in your viewfinder. What's more, you'll need editing software that supports widescreen mode—if yours doesn't, don't shoot with the widescreen feature turned on. You'll learn more about this in Chapter 8, "Editing."

Other Effects

Most cameras include loads of other special effect features that let you make your image all funky and weird looking. Although these effects can be fun to play around with, they're not really practical for anything. What's more, you can make *much* cooler effects on your computer. In general, it's best to always shoot the cleanest, most normal footage you can, and then use your computer to add any special effects and weirdness later.

Timecode and Record Search (Sometimes Called "Edit Search")

Your video camera captures 29.97 frames per second. (The odd number has to do with some technological changes that were made when color television was invented—in the days of black-and-white TV, video was 30 frames per second.) Each frame of video is numbered using a special *timecode* (Figure 5.12).

FIGURE 5.12 Each consecutive frame of video on a piece of videotape has its own unique timecode that marks its location on the tape in hours, minutes, seconds, and frames.

As you shoot, the camera lays down a continuous track of timecode. If you pause and start shooting again, the camera picks up the timecode where it left off. However, if you roll the tape at all between shoots (perhaps when reviewing your footage), there will be a break in your timecode.

Your computer uses timecode for any number of different things, from capturing and logging clips when editing, to synchronizing audio and video from different sources. Although you can most often get by with bad timecode, many things are easier with good timecode.

To help ensure that you have healthy, continuous timecode, many cameras include a *record search* or *edit search* feature that looks for the last piece of good timecode and cues the tape to that point. When you start shooting, the camera can pick up the timecode exactly where it left off, and avoid a timecode break. Check your camera's manual for details.

FIVE THINGS YOU SHOULD ABSOLUTELY DO BEFORE SHOOTING

There are a number of things that you should always do before shooting. If you start practicing them now, they'll quickly become habit. The items in the following list will help ensure that there aren't too many unpleasant surprises when you get back to the editing room. Note that this is a partial list; we'll be adding some more things to it later.

- **Check your battery level.** Make sure your battery isn't going to die in the middle of a take.
- **Make sure your tape is properly cued.** If you've been reviewing a scene, make sure you've wound the tape forward so that you don't accidentally erase it! Use your camera's Record Search or Edit Search feature to find the ending.
- **White balance!!** It doesn't matter what method you need to use—auto, preset, or manual—just make sure you do it!
- **Check your manual settings.** If you're using manual focus, iris, or shutter speed, check them now to make sure they're properly set.
- **Check your settings.** Make sure you don't have any extra, undesirable settings turned on (special effects, widescreen, etc.).

DEALING WITH MICROPHONES

This book is going to teach you a lot about how to shoot a really good image. However, in any scene involving dialog, sound will often be more important to your final product than picture.

In recent years, it has become very hip to shoot beat-up, grungy-looking video. You've probably seen lots of music videos (and maybe even some movies such as *Three Kings*) that were shot using grainy film with *lots* of texture and weird color. What you've probably never seen are music videos or movies where the *audio* has been beaten up and made grungy. No matter how bad the picture, filmmakers always go to great pains to make certain that their audio tracks are crystal clear.

You should do the same, and the easiest way to do that is with the clever use of some external microphones.

WATCHOUT!

Remember, no matter what type of camera you have, the microphone that's built into it is pretty inferior! Unless you're shooting very close to your subject (and are standing in a very quiet room), your on-camera mic will produce boomy, echo-y, terrible sound. Take the time to learn how to use an external mic.

In Chapter 2, "What You Need," you learned a lot about microphones and how to pick one that's right for you. In Chapter 6, "Shooting," you're going to learn more about using your microphone. For now, it's important to just learn the basics:

- **How do you change the mic's battery?** If your microphone uses a battery (usually either a AA, AAA, or a watch battery of some kind), make sure you know how to change it when it dies.
- **How do you turn the mic on?** If your mic uses a battery of its own, it will need to be turned on.

WATCHOUT!

Always remember to turn your microphone off when you're not using it. Leaving the microphone turned on will drain its battery, even if the mic's not being used. Since you never know when a mic battery might die, be sure to keep an extra in your camera bag.

- **Where do you plug the mic into your camera?** Be certain you know where your camera's external mic jack is. It should be clearly labeled, but if you can't find it, check your manual.

ALL THAT OTHER GEAR

For certain types of shoots you're going to need some other types of gear. We'll discuss microphones and lighting in more detail in Chapter 6.

In Chapter 2, "What You Need," you read about tripods, the handiest piece of equipment you can buy! There should be a tripod mount located somewhere on the bottom of your camera (Figure 5.13).

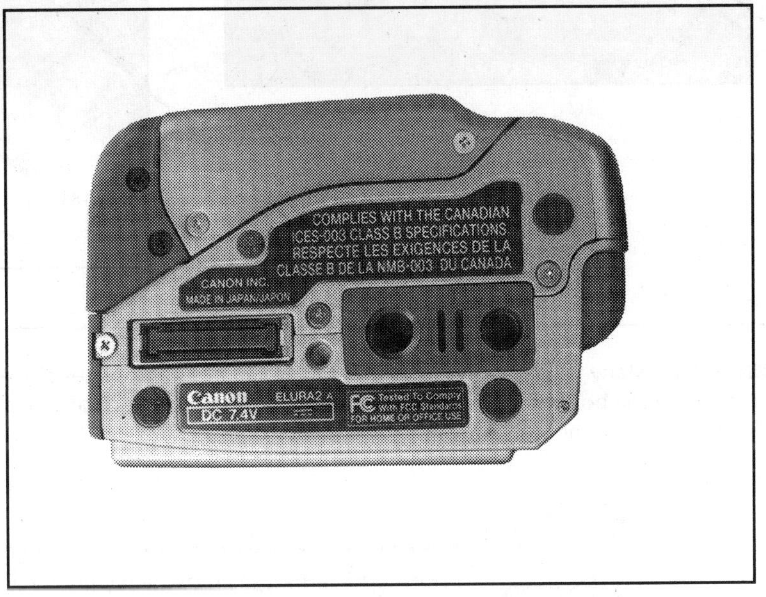

FIGURE 5.13 Somewhere on the bottom of your camera, there should be a tripod mount, ideally a metal one (as opposed to a flimsier, plastic mount).

The mount is really just a simple hole with screw threads. Some cameras also have an extra unthreaded hole next to the tripod mount to add extra stability. To mount the camera on the tripod, simply screw the tripod's mounting screw into the bottom of the camera.

Some tripods have a removable mounting plate that you can screw on to the camera. You can then fit the camera with mounting plate onto the tripod (Figure 5.14).

This type of tripod is usually easier to work with since you don't have to try to hold both the tripod and camera at the same time.

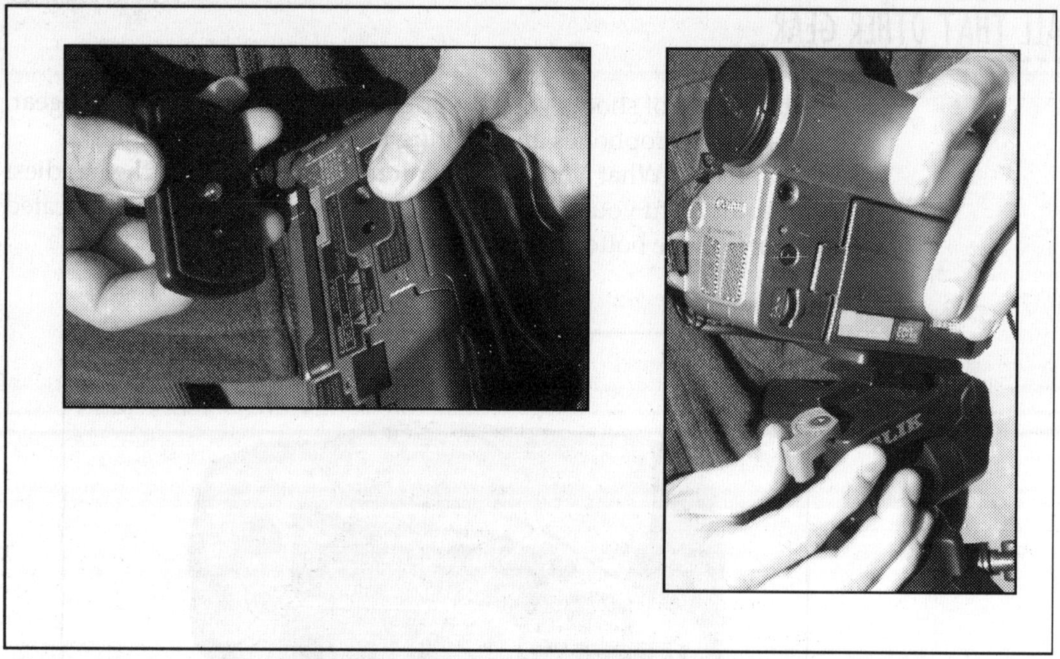

FIGURE 5.14 Many tripods are equipped with special mounting plates that attach to the standard tripod screw on the bottom of your camera. With the plate mounted to your camera, you can then quickly mount and unmount your camera from your tripod.

WATCHOUT!

Tripods and cameras can be heavy and awkward. Be very careful when mounting the camera on the tripod, as it's very easy to drop either. Although your tripod will probably be okay if you drop it, your camera probably won't. Take your time! In addition, on some cameras, you can't remove the tape or battery without first removing the camera from the tripod, so you might find yourself having to mount and unmount the camera a lot. Practice at home before you go out in the field.

External Monitors

The LCD screen on your camera is great for most types of shooting, but if you're working in dark situations, it just won't cut it. Moreover, the color on an LCD screen is not very accurate, which can create troubles if you're shooting scenes where lighting or color is very important.

If you're shooting in either of these situations, it will be worth lugging along an external monitor such as a small TV set (obviously, carrying around a TV isn't practical all the time). You can connect the camera to the monitor and use the monitor as a viewfinder, or you can simply use the set when you want to review your footage.

Obviously, to view your footage on your TV, you need to connect the TV to your camera. Most cameras provide a composite connection, an S-video connection, or both. Composite connections usually come in the form of a mini jack and require a special cable, usually included with the camera (Figure 5.15).

S-video connectors require a special S-video cable. However, even if your camera has an S-connection, your TV might not, so don't worry too much about S-video until you've determined that your TV set supports it (Figure 5.16).

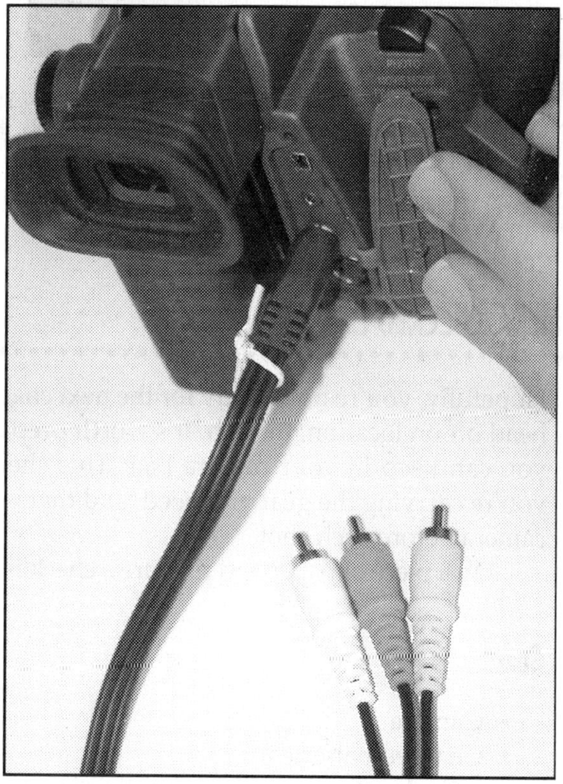

FIGURE 5.15 Most cameras include a special AV cable for taking video and two channels of audio out of your camera. The yellow connector plugs into the Video In jack on your TV, VCR, or Analog capture card, while the red and white connectors plug into the audio jacks.

FIGURE 5.16 If your camera has an S-video jack, you can use it to get slightly higher video quality when plugging into TVs, VCRs, and analog digitizing cards (provided those devices also have S-video ports).

ACTIVITY: CAMERA CHECKLIST

Hopefully, you're now ready for the next chapter on shooting. Before you head off on location, though, it's worth preparing a simple checklist that you can keep in your camera bag. This checklist will help ensure that you're carrying the gear you need, and that you adequately prepare your camera before each shot.

Grab a piece of paper and prepare a checklist that includes the following:

Gear:

- Camera
- Charged batteries
- AC adapter (if you'll be shooting in a location that has power)
- Tape (always take more than you think you'll need)
- Microphone, mic cable, and extra microphone battery
- Headphones

Grab a piece of paper and prepare a checklist that includes the following:

Gear:

- Camera
- Charged batteries
- AC adapter (if you'll be shooting in a location that has power)
- Tape (always take more than you think you'll need)
- Microphone, mic cable, and extra microphone battery
- Headphones

Now, on the back of the paper, write a checklist of all of the things to check before you start shooting. If need be, you can also note the exact buttons to push on your camera.

Camera settings:

- Check the battery level.
- Make sure your tape is cued (use Record Search or Edit Search).
- Set the white balance.
- Set any manual settings (focus, iris, shutter).
- Turn off any extra, undesirable settings (special effects, widescreen, etc.).

Print out these lists on a small piece of paper and stick them in your camera bag. Most important, though, *remember to use them!*

You're now ready to start shooting!

CHAPTER

6

Shooting

IN THIS CHAPTER

- Preparing
- Composition and Framing
- Camera Movement
- Shooting to Edit
- Lighting
- Microphones
- Troubleshooting

In many ways, shooting is the best part of the entire movie-making process: you get to go out to fun locations, you get to boss people around, and you get to use cool gear. It's also the first time that you can start to see the ideas in your head turn into something real.

Unfortunately, shooting can also be really hard. Many things can go wrong, there are lots of things to keep track of, and you're usually working against the clock.

In this chapter, you'll learn how to deal with all of those concerns, as well as learn how to get the best-looking, most usable footage that you can manage.

There are really two types of shooting: on-the-go shooting (you could also think of this as "vacation" or "home-movie" style shooting), where you simply document an event or activity; and planned, scripted shooting, where you set out to shoot a story or script that you've written and prepared ahead of time. No matter what type of shooting you're doing, you need to understand the skills and techniques presented in this chapter.

ROLL 'EM

If you read the last chapter then you should have a better idea of exactly how your camera works, as well as what all of those controls and buttons do. However, what should you do when you're actually ready to start shooting?

Shooting a Script

Who doesn't want the chance to shout "Lights! Camera! Action!" at some point in their life? Well, when you're shooting a scripted movie, you just might find yourself yelling these words. First, though, there are a few things you need to prepare.

When you first get to your location or set, spend some time making sure everything's ready:

- Check your set or location to ensure it looks the way you want it to.
- Make certain all the necessary crewmembers and actors have arrived with their gear or costumes.
- Check that you have all of the power, cables, lights, and other necessary pieces of hardware.
- Make sure that nothing unexpected has come up that might adversely impact your shoot—bad weather, noisy construction workers, and so forth.
- Finally, talk to your actors to find out if they have any questions about what they'll be doing in the scenes that you'll be shooting.

Once you've double-checked all of these details, you're ready to start setting up your camera. If you storyboarded your script, you should have a pretty clear idea of what shots you need. Now it's time to actually place the camera, lights, and microphones. We'll cover that process in the rest of this chapter.

With your scene lit and miked, and your shot composed, you're ready to roll. Review the camera checklist that you made in the last chapter, just to ensure that your camera is prepared. Next, make sure your crewmembers and actors are in place and ready. Make certain that they understand that they are not supposed to do anything until you yell "action."

If you're shooting on location, listen for any loud noises—airplanes, traffic, etc.—and wait for them to finish before you start shooting.

Now you can start your camera rolling. After pressing the Start button, let the tape roll for a few seconds. This extra few seconds of footage is called a "handle," and it can be essential when editing.

At last, after all this preparation, it's finally time to yell "action!"

When the scene has played out, let the camera roll for a few more seconds to create another handle; yell "cut," and stop your tape. Your actors should know to stay in character until you yell "cut." Similarly, your crew should know to stay quiet until the shot is complete.

With that shot "in the can" you can now start the process all over again to get another take, or you can set up the camera again for a different angle, or move on to another shot.

Shooting "On the Go"

If you simply want to shoot footage of your friends "on the go"—perhaps they're skateboarding, or just hanging around, for example, or maybe you're shooting while on vacation—there are still some guidelines you should follow to ensure you get good, usable footage.

- **Follow your checklist.** Get in the habit of working through the checklist you made in the last chapter. This will ensure that your camera is properly white balanced and that you have no unwanted settings activated.
- **Compose your shots.** You can't just point your camera at your subject and get nice-looking, usable footage. To get a good shot, you have to take the time to compose and frame your image. We'll cover composition and camera movements later in this chapter.
- **Shoot with handles.** Always let the camera roll for a few seconds before and after your shot, to provide handles. These handles will make things much easier when you start editing.
- **Shoot steady.** When shooting on the go you won't always have the luxury of shooting from a tripod, but this doesn't mean that you have to shoot shaky footage. If your camera has a stabilization feature, make certain it's turned on. To get even steadier footage, find something you can lean against, or that you can prop your arm and/or camera on. Anything you can do to steady the camera will improve your chances of getting good footage.
- **Be careful with that zoom control!** There is absolutely nothing more annoying than a video with too much zooming! Zooming

video is really frustrating to the viewer. It's usually ugly, and it makes editing very difficult since it's nearly impossible to make a smooth cut into or out of a shot that is in mid-zoom. If you need to zoom in or out of a shot, either pause the tape to do your zoom, or do the zoom quickly and then steady the camera for your shot. You can always edit out the reframing later.

WATCHOUT!

Zooming Is Dangerous for the Health of Your Movie

Although we're trying to avoid any hard-and-fast rules in this book, this is one rule that it's best to follow: don't zoom in a shot. You can zoom in or out to set up a shot, but using a zoom well is very difficult. Rules are made to be broken, of course, and there are times when zooming is very effective. In general, though, try to avoid them.

Once you start editing, you'll have a much better idea of what makes good and bad "on-the-go" footage. And, once you read the rest of this chapter, you'll hopefully have a much better idea of how to shoot pretty, effective footage.

Shooting a Music Video

Music videos pose their own unique challenges, both technically and creatively. If you read Chapter 2, "What You Need," then you've probably spent some time trying to come up with a concept, and possibly even a rough script, for your music video, and by now you've probably done all of the preproduction you need to do to get started shooting.

As discussed in Chapter 2, music videos are really kind of like silent films in that the stories they tell are conveyed without dialog. However, there is sound in a music video, of course, and shooting that sound is your main technical challenge.

Here's the main problem you'll face: In most music videos, you'll want to shoot footage of your musicians (or actors) lip-syncing to the music video's song. However, as with any type of shoot, you'll most likely need to shoot multiple takes when shooting a music video, and you'll also probably want to shoot different angles of the same scene in your video. In addition, while shooting all of these takes, you'll want to be sure that the lip-syncing is consistent so that your various shots will edit together well.

To ensure that your actors are always lip-syncing the same way, you'll need to have a recording of the song available for playback on your set while shooting. In other words, you'll play this song during the shoot, the actors will lip-sync to it, and then you'll edit all of your footage using that same recording for your audio track. This will ensure that your actors are always performing at the exact same tempo.

Depending on the editing software you're using, you'll most likely end up having to sync your video and audio by eye. That is, you'll need to try to match the performer's mouth to a particular moment in the song. This is not as hard as it sounds, but there are things you can do to make it easier:

- In shots where the actor's face will be visible, be certain that there's at least one or two moments where you can clearly see the movement of their mouth. Ask them to enunciate very clearly in those moments, as you'll be using that as your reference for syncing.
- If the actor's mouth is not visible in the frame, then sync doesn't matter so much for that shot. However, if the actor is dancing, you want to make sure that they're dancing to the beat, so you'll still need to play audio for them on-set.

COMPOSITION AND FRAMING

Composition is simply the way an image is put together; that is, which visual elements are included in the image, and how they're arranged. While shooting, you'll *frame* your scene in your camera's viewfinder to build a composition.

Composition and framing are essential to creating video images that are attractive, and that serve to tell your story (Figure 6.1).

The upper image is not very well composed and is poorly framed. The lower image is a much better framing of the same subject matter. Notice that in the lower image, our attention is more focused on our subject. As a viewer, it's easier to tell what the image on the right is about.

Notice, too, that the lower image is simply prettier. In addition to having a more focused center of attention, the image is has a more interesting sense of scale – the trees and bandshell tower over the woman. What's more, the image is "balanced." Although our attention might be focused on the woman—lending a lot of weight to the right side of the image—the trees and sky balance her presence with their own weight on the left side of the image. Later in this chapter, you'll learn some basic skills that you can use to create good compositions.

FIGURE 6.1 Learning to create better compositions will improve the look of your movie as well as make your story easier to follow.

Using Composition to Tell a Story

Good composition skills let you do far more than simply create pretty images. By carefully crafting your compositions, you can convey important information to your audience. For example, look at the images in Figure 6.2.

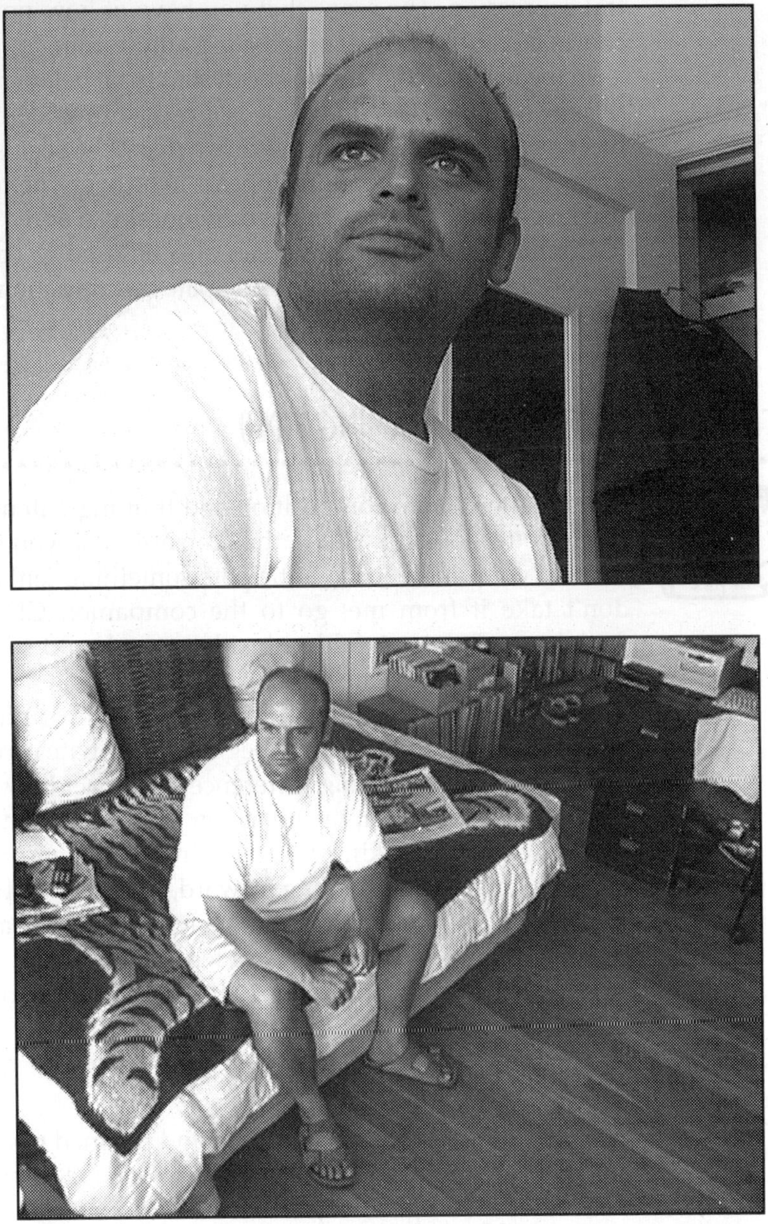

FIGURE 6.2 The different compositions of these two images present two very different impressions of this man.

In the upper image, the man looks confident and powerful, while in the lower image, the same man looks lonely and possibly afraid. In both of these images, the man is striking a similar pose and a somewhat neutral expression. The sense that you have of how powerful or weak he is comes mostly from the composition and framing of the shot.

In the upper image, he has been shot from below and framed so that he fills the frame. In this image, he is a very strong-looking, imposing figure. By contrast, the lower image shows a man who seems small. He is literally lower than us, and therefore appears to be overwhelmed and weak. When used well, these compositional differences can add a lot to your story.

Composition and framing can also be used to create tension in your audience by helping them to anticipate certain actions, as you'll see in the following activity.

ACTIVITY: COMPOSITION AND FRAMING VIDEO

Careful attention to composition and framing will not only allow you to create better-looking videos, they can also help you to build suspense, or to force your audience to anticipate something (either good or bad). But don't take it from me; go to the companion CD-ROM and find the Activities>Chapter 6 folder. Inside, you should see a document called *compandframe.mov*. Watch it now.

As you saw in the compandframe movie, if you frame a shot in a particular way, the audience will begin to anticipate certain actions.

To recap: There's a big difference in impact between the two images shown in Figure 6.3. In the image on the left, we simply see a woman—a scared woman—looking forward. In the image on the right, she is a scared woman who's looking forward, but there's a big space behind her. As an audience, we know that that big space is probably there to be filled by something, and so our level of tension increases. This is a tension created almost solely by the composition and framing of the shot.

Basic Composition Rules

Whether you're shooting a scripted and planned movie, or you're simply out shooting footage of your friends, you need to pay attention to some basic rules of composition, both to make your video more interesting and comprehensible, and to make your images more attractive.

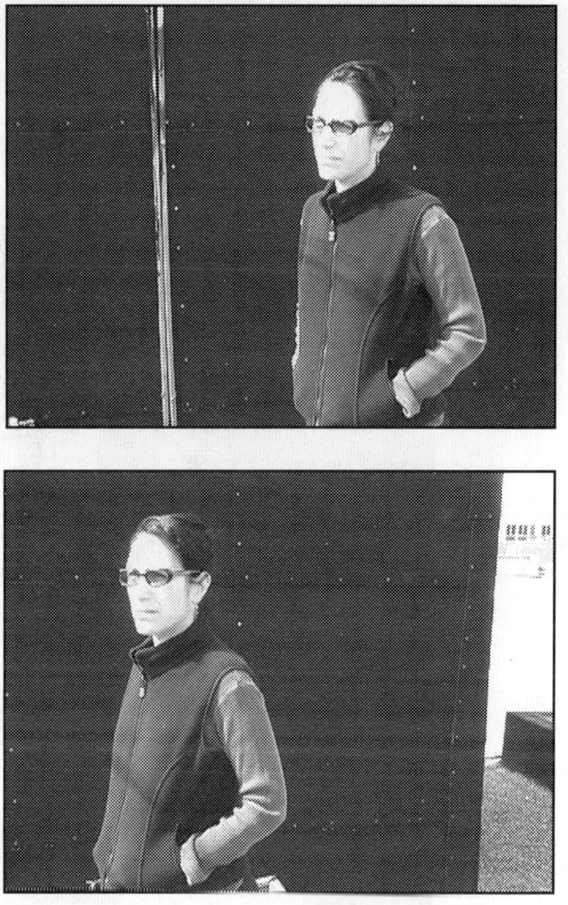

FIGURE 6.3 As you saw in the Composition and Framing movie, different compositions can make your audience anticipate different things.

If you're shooting from a script, you have the luxury of setting up your shots ahead of time. If you're shooting "on the go," then you'll need to create your framings and compositions as you shoot. Fortunately, you can follow the same compositional rules for both types of shooting. As you gain more experience, you'll get a better eye for composition and develop some compositional habits. Soon, you'll be quickly framing and composing without even thinking about it. To get started, though, try to learn these basic ideas.

USE THE WHOLE FRAME

This one's pretty easy. Look at the two images in Figure 6.4.

Which one looks better? The lower one, right? The upper image is really kind of silly. There's all that extra space that serves no purpose and

FIGURE 6.4 Let's say your goal in this shot was to get some footage of that guy who's standing there. Which image works better?

tends to distract the viewer from the subject. What's more, the subject is so small that even when you do notice him, you can't see a tremendous amount of detail.

Although this problem is easy to spot when you're back home looking at your footage, it can take some concerted effort to recognize it when you're actually shooting. Here's the problem: your brain is very good at focusing on a faraway subject and filtering out or ignoring all the extra stuff that your eyes can see. Unfortunately, even when you're looking through a camera, your brain continues to do this. Therefore, when you're shooting a shot like the one shown in Figure 6.4a, your brain is focused on that tiny little figure and fails to notice that what you're really capturing is a frame filled with extra, unnecessary scenery.

HINT

The first step in achieving better compositions is to get in the habit of looking at the image in the viewfinder, rather than looking through the viewfinder at your scene!

You probably had no trouble looking at Figure 6.4 and seeing that it was poorly composed. If you look at the image in your viewfinder as if it was a finished image (like a picture in a book), then you'll have a better idea of what your viewers will be seeing when they watch your movie later on.

Another way to avoid an image like Figure 6.4a is to get in the habit of checking the edges of your frame when composing. Before you decide that the image is well framed, take a minute to move your eyes around the entire perimeter of the frame. You might be surprised to see that you left a lot of space around your subject, or that you've framed your subject in such a way that the foreground interferes with the background, as in Figure 6.5.

WATCH THAT HEADROOM!

This is really just a variation of the last tip, but it comes in particularly handy for shooting on-the-go, documentary-style footage. Beginning shooters have a tendency to place their subjects—either their entire body or just their head—at the very center of the frame. Unfortunately, this

FIGURE 6.5 If you're not paying attention when framing your shot, you might accidentally end up with your background interfering with your foreground, as in this image where it looks like the windmill's arms are sticking out of the woman's head.

doesn't always produce the best-looking image. Look at the difference between the two images in Figure 6.6.

See all the space above the person's head in Figure 6.6a? That's called *headroom*, and that image has too much of it! Think about newscasters you see on TV; they're usually framed with little headroom, and cut off just a little below the shoulders. This is a very comfortable distance for the average interview shot.

If you want to convey more intimacy—say, for a more serious subject—then zoom in closer. The only time you zoom way out on an interview subject is if you need to see the person's entire body, or something that person is referring to in the background. Even then, watch the headroom and make sure the image is well balanced. Figure 6.7 shows two different "interview" shots, composed with different framings.

LEAD YOUR SUBJECT

This tip is handy for on-the-go interview footage or prescripted dialog scenes. When you have a single shot of someone speaking, "lead" that person by putting some empty screen space in front of him.

FIGURE 6.6 The upper image has too much headroom—that is, there's so much space around the man that it's difficult to tell what the subject of the image is. Because the lower image is framed tighter, the audience's attention is drawn to the actor.

FIGURE 6.7 Although we needed a wide shot to get all four subjects of this interview, for a more personal touch, we shot close-ups and two-shots of individual speakers.

For example, Figure 6.8 shows someone talking to another person who is off-frame. If we put the blank space in front of her, we get a much more comfortable sense than if we put the space behind her.

FIGURE 6.8 Leading. When shooting someone who is looking or talking in a particular direction, it's usually best to "lead" them with extra space in the direction in which they are facing.

Obviously, if you have a special need to create tension—as in the composition and framing example you saw earlier—then you can break this rule. In general, though, leading the front of a person is the best way to go. Obviously, in a dialog scene, if you lead the first person in one direction, you should lead the second person in the opposite direction, as shown in Figure 6.9.

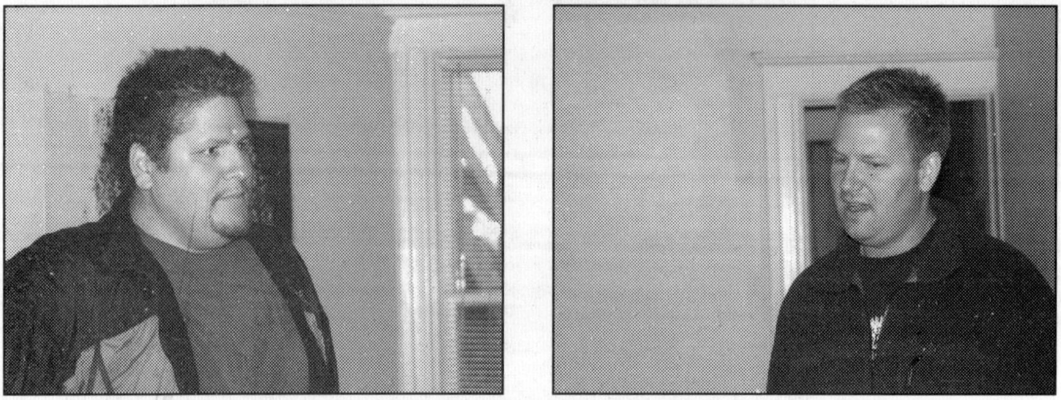

FIGURE 6.9 Dialog leading. When shooting dialog scenes, be sure to lead and frame your subjects so that when you cut from one shot to another, it will be obvious how the people are positioned relative to one another.

ACTIVITY: LEADING LEARNING

To learn more about leading, look at the leading.mov movie, located in the Activities>Chapter 6 folder on the companion CD-ROM. In it, you'll see examples of good and bad leading and why it's important to carefully consider how you frame people who are speaking to each other.

THINK IN THIRDS

One of the most basic composition concepts is to imagine your image divided into thirds, both horizontally and vertically. Instead of placing your subject in the dead center of the frame, place them (or it) at the intersection of these imaginary dividing lines (Figure 6.10).

Similarly, there are times when you'll get a more interesting composition by violating the symmetry in your frame, as shown in Figure 6.11.

It's important to notice that in all of these examples, even though we're moving the location of the subject, the images are still balanced. In Figure

FIGURE 6.10 Composing in thirds.

FIGURE 6.11 Although the man could have been framed in the middle of the shot, the composition is a little more interesting if we break the symmetry of the shot and frame him off to the side.

6.11, the presence of the man on the right side of the screen is balanced by the door on the left.

DON'T BE AFRAID TO GET TOO CLOSE

Although it's important to have the proper headroom and leading in a shot, there are times when a shot calls for something more dramatic. Don't be afraid to get in close to your actors, and to crop their heads and bodies out of the frame, as shown in Figure 6.12.

FIGURE 6.12 You can increase the drama and suspense of a scene by getting in really close to your subject. Although this "tight" framing cuts off some of our actor's head, it's still a well-composed, effective image.

This is a very "dramatic" type of framing; in this case, it's being used to heighten suspense. In a more dramatic moment, it could be used to give the audience time to see an actor's mood change or develop.

GO FOR THE INTERESTING ANGLE

It's important to not overdo this one, but there are times when you can make a somewhat boring scene more interesting by finding a different angle. Remember that your camera can move up and down as well as from side to side, so consider shooting from the ground, or from up in a tree, as in Figure 6.13.

FIGURE 6.13 It's important not to be too "clever" in your framing, but sometimes going for the interesting angle can spice up an otherwise boring scene. Remember, though, don't draw so much attention to yourself that the viewer is distracted from the story.

Be careful, though; too many "interesting" angles can leave your audience confused. You don't want them spending so much time asking "what is that?" that they lose track of your story.

Choosing a Focal Length (or, "Where Do I Stand and How Far Do I Zoom?")

Focal length is the distance from the front of the lens to the camera's imaging chip. The longer the focal length, the more magnifying power a lens has (or, the more "telephoto" it is). Therefore, when you zoom in on a subject, you're effectively increasing the focal length of your lens (Figure 6.14).

FIGURE 6.14 If you zoom in more, your camera has a longer focal length, and your subject appears closer.

Note that, when you zoom, your camera's lens won't necessarily get any longer or shorter. Instead, its internal parts will move and rearrange to create a longer or shorter focal length.

Focal length is usually measured in millimeters, so a 100mm lens is more telephoto than a 50mm lens. Unfortunately, most video cameras offer no markings on the lens to indicate the current focal length. You usually don't need to even think about focal length or millimeters, but it's still good to know the terminology.

NOT ALL FOCAL LENGTHS ARE CREATED EQUAL

If you're like most people, when you want to frame a shot a particular way, you simply zoom in or out to position your subject in the frame. For example, let's say you want to shoot an image that's framed like the storyboard shown in Figure 6.15.

Depending on where you're standing, you'll have to zoom different amounts, as shown in Figure 6.16.

Obviously, having a zoom lens is very convenient because it means you often don't even have to move to get the shot that you want. How-

FIGURE 6.15 Suppose your storyboard calls for a shot that looks like this.

FIGURE 6.16 There are many different ways to shoot the image shown in the storyboard on page 127. In the first shot, we stood close to our subject and zoomed out, while in the second shot, we stood far away and zoomed in. Although one approach might be more convenient at the time, the different tactics result in very different images. Notice how the tree seems farther away in the first image, and how the man's face is a little distorted. It's important to choose your camera position and focal length carefully!

ever, this laziness comes at a price, because your zoom lens will produce *very* different pictures depending on how far in or out it is zoomed.

Here's the deal: a lens magnifies the area it's looking at. However, at wider angles (shorter focal lengths), it will magnify close objects *more* than it will magnify faraway objects. In other words, if you shoot someone's face with a wide-angle lens (that is, with your lens zoomed out all the way), your subject's nose will be magnified much more than their ears. The result can be seen in Figure 6.17 (a and b).

Quite a difference, huh? Notice how it looks like there's a much greater distance between his nose and ears in the second picture than there is in the first. Have you ever had your picture taken and then thought, "that doesn't look like me"? If so, it's probably because the photographer was using a wide-angle lens, which distorted your features.

So, as you can see, when setting up and framing a shot, it's *very* important to think about where you position the camera and how much you're

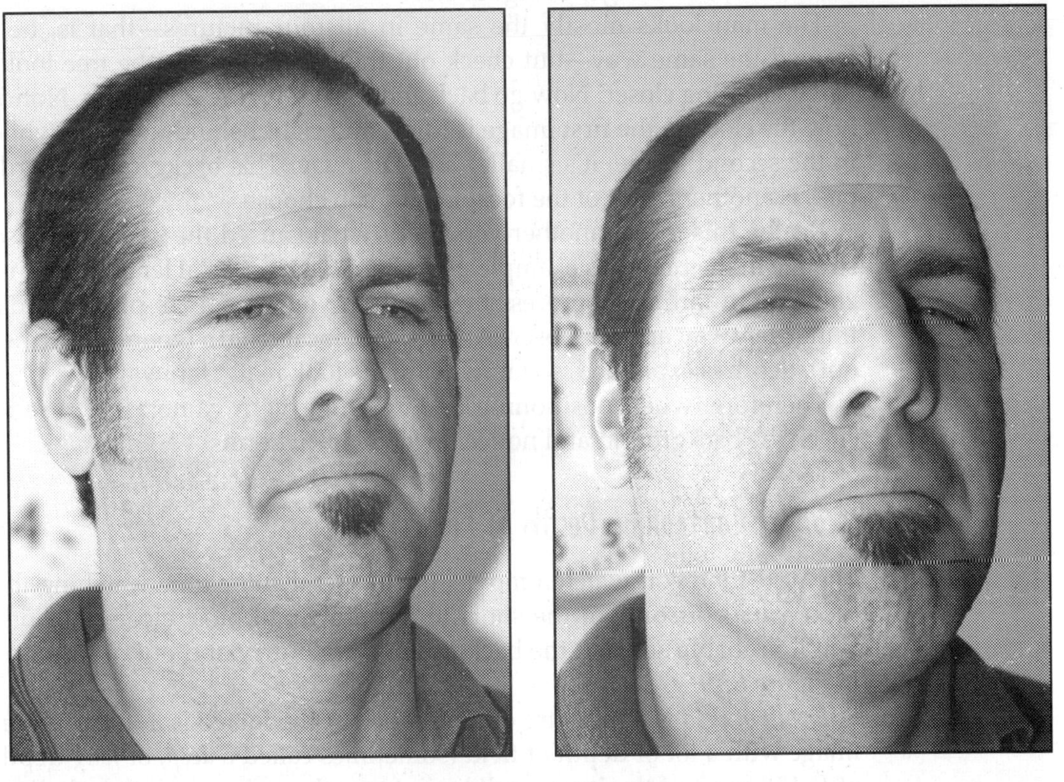

FIGURE 6.17 (a) An image shot with a long focal length looks very different from (b) an image shot with a short focal length.

zooming. Most people look best when shot with a slightly telephoto lens; that is, a lens that magnifies just a little more than your eyes do. This means that if you don't want your actors to look weird, you should place the camera farther away and zoom in slightly to a focal length that is more flattering.

There are times, though, when you'll *want* to make your actors look weird. Almost all comedies are shot with very wide-angle lenses, since they tend to make the actors look just a little funnier and a good deal more clownish. Next time you're watching a really out-there comedy, try to pay attention to how wide the lens is. You'll be able to tell that a wide-angle lens is being used because people will look something like the guy in Figure 6.17b, and because you'll often see a very wide expanse of background behind the actors.

MORE FOCAL LENGTH WEIRDNESS

Look at the two images in Figure 6.18.

The man looks mostly the same in all four pictures—that is, he's framed the same way—but check out the backgrounds—the tree looks like it's getting closer! Now go back and look at Figure 6.17 again. Notice how the clock in the first image is huge, and right behind the man, while in the second image, it's smaller and far away. This background weirdness is another result of the focal length you choose.

Really, this is just another version of what caused the guy to look so strange in the previous example. Simply put: longer focal lengths (that is, zooming in farther) compress the depth in your image. In other words, things faraway appear closer. At a shorter focal length (zooming farther out), depth is expanded, so faraway things look really faraway.

Therefore, when positioning and zooming your camera, be sure to check the background and notice how "deep" it seems.

Losing Focus, or Controlling Depth of Field

The next time you watch a movie, try to spend some time watching the *backgrounds* of some of the shots in the movie. In most close-up shots, you'll probably see that the backgrounds are blurry and out of focus, as in Figure 6.19.

Depth of field is a measure of how much of the image is in focus. In an image with a lot of depth of field (sometimes called a *deep*, or *long* depth of field), most of the image will be in focus. In an image with a shallow depth of field, very little of the image will be in focus.

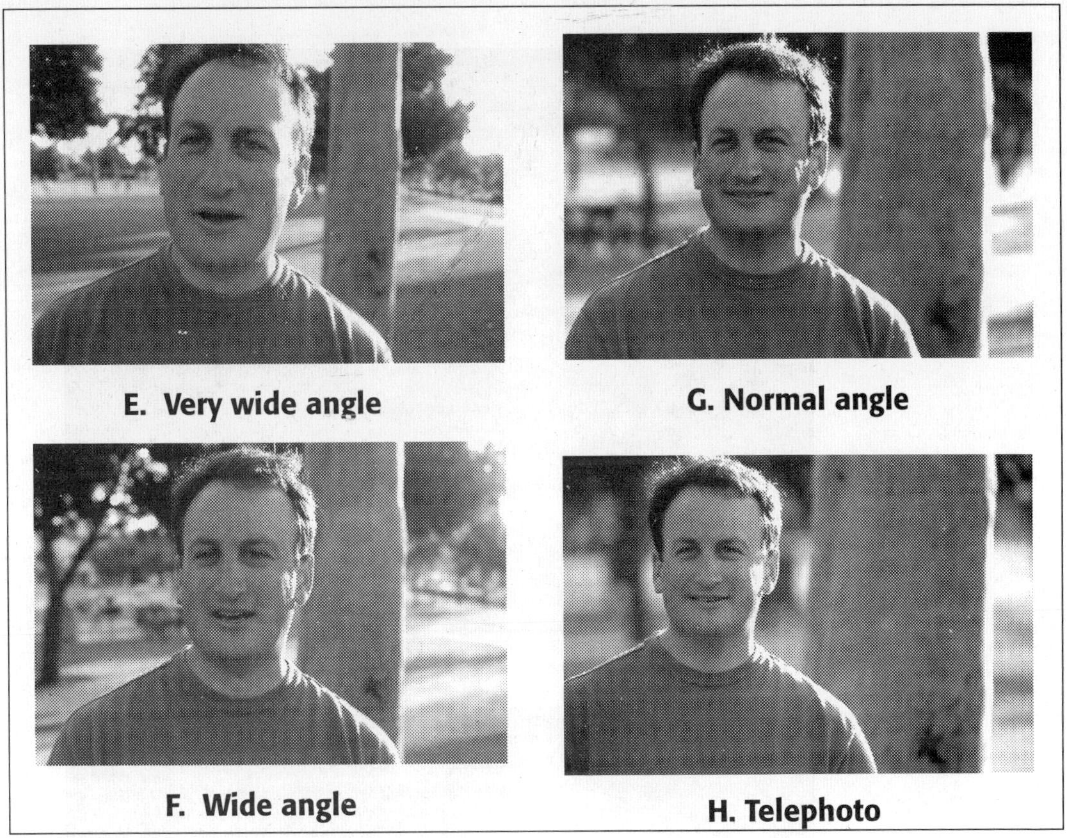

FIGURE 6.18 Are those trees moving around? No, they simply look like they're in different positions because of the focal length that we choose to use.

Shallow depth of field is one of the things that makes film look so different from video. It's very hard to shoot video with shallow depth of field, which is unfortunate, since choosing a shorter depth of field is a great way to focus attention onto the subject in your image.

The amount of depth of field in an image is controlled by two things: how wide the camera's iris is, and how far in the camera's lens is zoomed.

APERTURE AND IRIS

Inside every video camera is an aperture, or iris that controls how much light passes through the lens. This aperture also has a lot to do with how much depth of field an image will have. *When the aperture is opened wider, the image will have less depth of field.*

FIGURE 6.19 The lower image shown here is said to have much less depth of field, which is why the background is out of focus. Controlling depth of field lets you bring focus to particular areas of your image.

Therefore, if you want to try to shoot a shot with a shallow depth of field, you'll first need to open the camera's iris. To do this, you'll have to have a camera with a manual iris control. Check your manual for details.

FOCAL LENGTH

You can also shorten the depth of field in your image by *lengthening* your focal length. In other words, if you're trying to shoot an image with a shallow depth of field, position yourself away from your image and zoom in as far as possible. This will, of course, compress the depth in your image (as explained in the last section), but if the background is blurry, this won't really matter. To increase the shallow depth of field effect, open your camera's iris, as explained previously.

CAMERA MOVEMENT

Now that you've mastered composition and framing, let's complicate things a little further and talk some about camera movement. There are *many* different ways to move a camera and, just as different framings and compositions convey different information to the audience, different types of camera movements can have different meanings to the audience.

The main purpose of camera movement, though, is simply to keep your image in frame and to follow the action in your scene. The easiest way to understand camera movements is to see them in action.

ACTIVITY: CAMERA MOVEMENT MOVIE

Go now, and watch the cameramovement.mov movie, located in the Activities>Chapter 6 folder of the companion CD-ROM. This movie will show you all of the different types of camera movements. When you're finished, come back here.

You usually only need to be concerned with camera movement when you're shooting a scripted movie. If you're simply shooting on the go, you'll most likely just shoot everything handheld and attempt to follow the action as it develops.

Like good composition and good editing, good camera movement is something that you don't even notice when you're watching a movie. When planning your shots, your goal is simply to create movements that will allow you to cover the action in your scene in an elegant, attractive manner.

To recap what you saw in the camera movement video in the last activity, take a look at the camera angles and movements shown in Figure 6.20. Once you start thinking about moving your camera, you might want to go back and rework your storyboards to include more camera motion.

SHOOTING TO EDIT

Shooting nice-looking video is one thing; shooting video that can be edited into finished scenes is another. In other words, you often need to shoot your shots in a very particular way to get them to edit together into effective scenes. In this section, we're going to look at what you need to do to ensure that you're getting good coverage of your scene. Many of the concepts discussed here will make more sense once you have some editing experience.

Establishing Shots

Most scenes begin with an *establishing shot*. An establishing shot is simply whatever shot is necessary to establish the location and setting of the scene. Remember, your audience doesn't necessarily know where a scene is taking place; therefore, with a quick establishing shot, you can quickly orient your audience (Figure 6.21).

Even if you hadn't planned or storyboarded an establishing shot, shoot one anyway. Once you start editing, you might find that you need it. Remember, it's better to have too much footage than not enough.

Masters and Cut-aways

Let's say you need to shoot a fairly typical scene: two people, at a location, talking. Whether the location is a local café or the backside of the moon, you'll most likely shoot the scene the same way: by shooting a *master shot* and a sequence of *cut-aways*. This is a very common way of putting a scene together because it's easy to shoot, gives you a lot of leeway when editing, and makes for a well-covered scene. Unfortunately, it means you'll usually need to shoot your scene at least three times!

Let's go back to our previous example and say that we're shooting a scene of two people having a conversation on the front steps of their

FIGURE 6.20 There are lots of different ways of moving your camera, and each one has a name. You'll want to learn these names both for storyboarding and for describing shots to your crew and actors.

FIGURE 6.21 Establishing shots are used to quickly give the viewer a sense of where the scene is taking place.

apartment building. First, we would start, of course, with an establishing shot of the locale.

As explained previously, the actors would actually have to perform the scene several times. First, we would shoot a *master shot* of the scene, framed to show both of our actors. This will serve as the base shot into which we will edit the rest of our coverage (Figure 6.22).

The actors would play out the entire scene, and we would keep shooting takes of that one master shot until we were pleased with the way the actors performed.

Next, we would reposition and reframe the scene to get a single *over-the-shoulder* shot of one of the actors, as shown in Figure 6.23.

Now the actors would play the scene again. At this point, we have a two-person master shot of the entire scene, and a shot of just one of the actors performing the entire scene. This second piece of footage can be used as *cut-away* footage when we edit. Finally, we would reposition the camera and reframe to shoot the other actor and, again, the actors would play out the scene. This gives us yet another reel of cut-away footage.

There might be other cut-aways that we'd like to shoot as well. Perhaps what they're reading in the newspaper is important. If so, we might

FIGURE 6.22 This two-shot, or *master shot* shows both of the people involved in the conversation we're shooting.

need to get an over-the-woman's-shoulder shot of what she's seeing in the paper.

Once in the editing room, these cut-aways would be edited into the master shot to create a sequence like the one shown in Figure 6.24.

The master shot alone is enough for the audience to see and hear everything in the scene, but the cut-aways allow us to move in close to get personal with the actors. You'll learn more about master shots and cutaways when you start editing in chapter 8.

Reaction Shots

Reaction shots are simply a particular type of cut-away. It's very important to think about reaction shots when planning your shoot, as they're an essential part of your storytelling arsenal.

A reaction shot is simply a shot of an actor reacting to something. That something is usually a thing, action, or event that the audience has just seen in another shot. For example, let's say we have a script that reads as follows:

FIGURE 6.23 After shooting your scene the first time using the master shot framing, you'll be ready to set up and shoot it a second time. This time, move your camera and frame a 1-shot of one of the actors. Then, shoot it a third time, and get the other actor.

FIGURE 6.24 With all of this *coverage*, you can now start editing your scene. In addition to having angles that cut together sensibly, you also have three different performances, meaning that—with some clever editing—you can choose the best parts of each.

> Bob lives in an attractive Victorian house in San Francisco. One day, after a hard day of working in his law office, he returns home and opens his front door, only to find a very healthy-looking Tyranosaurus Rex standing in his living room.

To shoot this scene, we would start with an establishing shot of an attractive Victorian house in San Francisco. Next, we would show Bob—dressed in his work attire and carrying a briefcase—ascending the stairs and opening his front door. We would see that he looks tired and ready to relax.

After seeing him open the door, we would cut to a shot of his living room, now mostly filled with a large dinosaur.

Stop for a moment and think about what you know so far about this scene—not much. You know that there's a guy coming home from work, and you know that there's a dinosaur in his living room. However, you don't know if that dinosaur is supposed to be there, or if this is as much of a surprise to Bob as it is to us.

In a movie, the audience has to be told what to feel, and it's the characters in the story that will tell the audience what's going on. Most often, they will do this by *reacting* to what's going on around them. (This is all related to the "show it, don't say it" concepts discussed in Chapter 3, "Writing.")

So, now that we've seen the dinosaur, we need to see Bob's reaction. If he screams, then we know that the dinosaur was uninvited. If he walks in, sees the dinosaur, and tiredly says "Hi Rex" as he walks on into the apartment, then we know that the dinosaur is a pet—two entirely different stories all told by a simple reaction shot.

POV Shots

A POV shot is a variation on a reaction shot. P.O.V. simply stands for *point-of-view*. To go back to our previous example: if after Bob enters the apartment, we move our camera to his position to show the dinosaur, then we are shooting a "Bob's POV" shot.

Most of the time, the camera is an impartial observer that comes along for the ride through the character's story. When you use a POV shot, you're letting the audience see the scene just as the character does.

FILM SCHOOL: REAR WINDOW

Hitchcock relied heavily on reaction shots and POV shots in his masterpiece, *Rear Window. Rear Window's* story is very simple: Jimmy Stewart plays a man with a broken leg who is stuck at home, confined to a wheelchair. After spending a few days watching his neighbors out his window, he begins to suspect that one of them has committed a murder. Go rent this movie and notice how the shooting of the story is very simple: Hitchcock shows us what Jimmy Steward has seen, and then shows us his reaction. Over and over, the movie alternates between scene and reaction. Hitchcock knew exactly how to get the actor to guide the audience through the emotional landscape of his story.

Continuity

Continuity is simply the process of making sure that your images are consistent from frame to frame. Say you're going to shoot a person standing in one position in one shot, and then stop shooting, change camera positions, and reshoot from another angle. To preserve continuity, you'll need to make sure the actor is standing in the same position (as well as wearing the same clothes, holding the same props, and so on) in both shots. Continuity can get very complicated when you figure that it might take 20 minutes or longer to move the camera. Moreover, if you're shooting in one location over several days, things get even harder.

Big Hollywood movies have whole mobs of "continuity" people who watch scenes—and even go so far as to take Polaroid pictures of scenes—to try to find continuity problems. And even *they* don't always get it right! Try to keep an eye on the following:

- Obviously, make sure that costumes, props, hairstyles, and other "actorly" things are consistent from shot to shot.
- Check for actor position, posture, gesture, and expression from shot to shot.
- Check for lighting continuity from shot to shot. If you're shooting at a location during late afternoon, and if you come back the next day to shoot some more, be sure to shoot at roughly the same time.
- Don't hesitate to review your footage—a huge advantage of video over film—as you set up new shots.

Continuity is another thing that you'll develop an eye for as you keep making movies.

Don't Make Small Changes in Camera Position

If you're shooting two different angles of a scene, and intend to edit those two shots together, be aware that the second shot needs to be quite a ways from the first shot. If your two angles are too close together, the edit will look strange.

I know, that doesn't make too much sense. Fortunately, you'll see an example of this problem in the following exercise.

Control the Pacing of a Scene

In movies, less is almost *always* more. Less movie usually means a tighter, more efficient movie that stands less chance of boring its audience. As the director, you are in complete control of the pacing of a scene. Yes, an actor can speak faster or slower, but it is mostly the shooting and cutting of a movie that determines its pace.

For example, let's say you're going to shoot a scene of someone leaving their house and getting in their car to drive to work. You could frame the shot so that the audience gets to watch them walk out the door of the house, go to their car, unlock it, and get inside (Figure 6.25a). This might take 15 to 20 seconds of screen time (half a script page!).

Alternatively, you could shoot a shot of them leaving their house and then cut to a shot of a car. The audience would see them walk up to the car, unlock it, and get inside. Now we're down to 5 to 10 seconds

FIGURE 6.25 As a director, it's your job to control the pacing of a scene. Consider these two approaches to the same scene. In the first sequence, we show each step of the man's progress from his house to his car. In the second sequence, we show far fewer steps. Even though both sequences convey the same information, they have very different pacings.

(Figure 6.25b). (Of course, you could economize even further by showing them leaving home, and then showing them at work. Things can go *too* quick, though. Finding the balance is part of the skill of being a movie maker.)

DON'T TRY THIS AT HOME!

ON THE CD

Sure you can learn a lot by watching how a master filmmaker does something, but you can often learn more by watching how a novice filmmaker messes things up. Fortunately for you, I'm as big a hack as the next guy, and so have compiled some examples of the Top 10 Worst Shooting Problems into a movie that you should go watch right now. In the Activities>Chapter 6 folder, check out shootingproblems.mov for examples of:

- Bad lighting—Take the time to do the minimal lighting (avoid backlight, use a reflector). Show the difference.
- Not moving the camera far enough between angles.
- Not using a tripod.
- Composing so that weird things stick out of people's heads.
- Crossing the axis of action.
- Continuity problems (include the Token Soap driving scene).
- Zooming and panning too much.
- Bad framing (headroom).
- Keeping the camera at eye level, in one position.
- Not using close-ups.
- Not controlling the pacing of a scene. (Show a scene that's too long, a scene that's shorter, and an example of the fast-zoom technique of accelerating a shot. In addition, show the difference between telephoto and wide angle for making distance look shorter.)

This movie, in fact, covers some important problems not described here in the book, so it's worth watching. Come back here when you're done.

LIGHTING

Alright, I've gone six chapters without laying any guilt on you, but now it's time. Why? Because I know that, in addition to not using a tripod when you should, you're usually not going to do even minimal lighting. Yes, it's true. You're going to be so impatient and in such a hurry that you're going to shoot poorly lit, dark video even though I'm going to take such pains to explain how you can use some simple lighting techniques to make your video look a *hundred* times better. It just breaks my heart…

Reflectors

They say a picture is worth a thousand words, so let's give it a try. Check out the two images in Figure 6.26.

FIGURE 6.26 These two images show what a difference a simple reflector can make when shooting. In the lower image, notice the extra light on the woman's face.

The one on the bottom looks a lot better, doesn't it? That's because I had someone hold a white reflector below the subject. The reflector bounced a very small amount of light into the woman's face, eliminating the weird shadows under her eyes and nose, and generally making the image look better. Figure 6.27 shows a photo of the actual shoot.

FIGURE 6.27 This was how the reflector was configured to take the bottom picture in Figure 6.26.

As you can see, it's a pretty simple setup that yields a *dramatic* improvement in image quality. You can use any type of white cardboard or stretched fabric as a reflector. If you do nothing else in the way of lighting, at least use a reflector of some kind when shooting people—Please, make me proud.

3-Point Lighting

If you're lucky enough to have some lighting equipment (either because you managed to swing enough money to rent some, or were otherwise able to beg or borrow some), then you're sitting pretty. With even a small lighting kit, you can usually greatly improve the look of your video.

Lighting is, of course, an art, and there are many different ways to light a scene. You're going to learn one method here, a standard 3-point lighting scheme that can be used in most any situation, indoors or out.

It's important to realize that good lighting is much more than simply illuminating your subject so that it can be seen. Your goal when lighting is to add depth and shape to your scene, as well as to eliminate shadows and contours that would otherwise make your subject less attractive.

As you'd expect, 3-point lighting uses three different lights to illuminate your subject. Figure 6.28 shows how the three different lights work.

If your set is very large, you might need to use additional lights, but you can often double up the roles of some lights. For example, your scene might only need a single backlight to cover the entire set, while each actor might need their own key light, and possibly more than one fill light. Finally, some additional reflectors and bounce cards might be needed to get rid of extra shadows.

When setting lights in any situation, remember the following:

- The light bulbs in a professional lighting kit are very fragile. In fact, the oil from your fingers can cause the bulbs to explode! Handle them with extreme care, and remember that they get *hot* very quickly!
- Because lights can get so hot so quickly, be sure that you don't accidentally let anything brush or hang up against them; you might start a fire!
- Tape down the power cords! You don't want anyone tripping and knocking over your fragile lights.
- Some lights can use a lot of power. If you're shooting on location, you might want to talk to an experienced lighting person or electrician to determine how many lights you can plug in at once at your location.
- Look at your subject when lighting. This may sound obvious, but sometimes you won't notice a weird shadow or contour until your back in the editing room. When setting lights, try to notice all of the shadows on your subject's face and take whatever action is necessary to remove (or, in some cases, increase) them.

WATCHOUT!

Stay Away from Open Windows

Probably the single biggest lighting problem is also the easiest to shoot. When you shoot into a window or other strong backlight source, your subject will end up underexposed and dark, as shown in Figure 5.8. What should you do? Don't shoot in front of a window!! If you absolutely have to, then use your manual iris feature to overexpose the shot so that you can see your subject's face.

Here's how 3-point lighting works:

First, set a key light. This is a fairly tightly-focused light that is simply pointed at your subject so that they can be seen.

A. Diffuse key light

Next, set a backlight. A backlight should be positioned behind and above your subject, and pointed at the back of their head. Notice how the backlight creates a "halo" around the man's head. This halo serves to separte him from the background.

B. Key light and back light

Finally, set the fill light. Like the backlight, this is a more diffuse, spread-focused light that is intended to cover a wide area. As you can see, the fill light serves to fill in dark shadows and to simply throw more light onto the subject.

C. Key light, back light and fill light

FIGURE 6.28 In this example of three-point lighting, the actor is first lit with a diffuse key light (a), then a hard back light is added (b). Finally, a soft, subtle fill light is used to bring out the left side of his face without losing the high-contrast look (c).

MICROPHONES

As stated earlier, the microphone on your camera probably doesn't produce very high-quality audio. Because they're very *omnidirectional* (that is, they pick up sound from all directions), they tend to produce sound that is very echo-y or "boomy." Because of this, it's best to use an external microphone.

In this section, you'll learn some quick tips and tricks to get better sound no matter what type of mic you're using.

On-Camera Mics

There's not much you can do to improve the audio quality of an on-board mic, but there are some simple things to be aware of to keep the audio from getting worse:

- **Pay attention to where the mic is.** Most cameras keep their onboard mics somewhere inside the camera body. Get familiar with its location so that you can avoid bumping or hitting it with your fingers when you handle the camera.
- **Remember that the mic can hear *you*.** Because on-camera mics pick up sound from all directions, they sometimes pick up sounds from *behind* the camera, which means you need to stay *quiet* so that you aren't recorded.
- **Learn the range of your mic.** Different mics have different ranges, and there's a distance at which your on-camera microphone will produce significantly poorer sound. Check your camera manual to find out the effective range, and do some experimentation with your camera to find out how far away you can be from your subject and still get good audio. You may want to rethink your camera positioning for a shot once you know how far the microphone can "listen."

Handheld Mics

A good handheld mic is the most versatile microphone option you can choose. Your main concern with handheld mics is where and how to position them. Obviously, if you're shooting an interview, your subject can simply hold the mic. If you're don't want the mic to be visible, though, you'll need to hide it, or put it on a *boom*.

HIDING MICROPHONES

You can often simply hide a handheld microphone on your set, in a plant, under a prop, or taped to a piece of furniture. If you're hiding a mic, though, you need to think very carefully about the following:

- **Where should you point the mic?** Whether your mic is omnidirectional or unidirectional, it should always be pointed toward subject(s) you want to record. If your subject is moving, then you might need to do multiple takes with different microphone setups.
- **Is your subject within range of the microphone?** Just as with an on-camera mic, a handheld mic will have a range. Make sure that your subject is staying within the range of your mic.
- **Will the mic get bumped or moved?** Make sure that you choose a microphone location that won't be disturbed during recording. You don't want your actors to bump into the microphone or set props down on top of it.

MICROPHONE BOOMS

The ideal way to use a handheld microphone is to stick it on the end of a boom, a long pole with a microphone mount on the end. Although you can buy specially made booms, it's not to hard to fashion your own. Simply get a lightweight microphone stand or pole, and rig up an attachment for your microphone.

When shooting, you'll need a boom operator to hold the microphone above the head of whomever is speaking. Obviously, they need to hold it high enough so it's not in the shot.

The main advantage to a boom microphone is that it can be pointed at different people on-the-fly. What's more, because it's pointed down at the ground, it won't pick up any other noises that are coming from behind the actor.

Your boom operator will need to remember the following:

- **Handle the boom gently.** Unfortunately, the sound of the operator's hands on the boom pole can be transmitted up to the mic. It's best to hold a boom pole with the fingertips, and to try not to move your hands too much while shooting.
- **Put a brightly colored sticker on the microphone.** This will make it easier for the camera operator to notice if the microphone has dropped into frame.

- **Read the script!** To follow the dialog, the boom operator should be familiar with the script so that he can anticipate who might speak next.

Lavalier (Clip-On) Mics

The advantage of lavalier mics is that they are positioned so close to the speaker's mouth that they usually record very good audio. The downside is that if you want to record more than one person, you'll need more than one mic, and a mixer to mix the audio from those mics into a single signal that can be plugged into your camera. For this reason, you'll probably only want to use a lavalier mic when recording interviews or other shots that only have a single speaker.

To use a lavalier mic you simply turn it on, clip it to your subject's clothing, plug the other end into your camera, and start shooting. Figure 6.29 shows an example of good lavalier mic placement. As you can see, you don't want the mic too close to your subject's head, or too far away. In addition, it's best to loop the microphone's cord as shown in Figure 6.29. This will help keep your subject from ripping the mic off or moving it around.

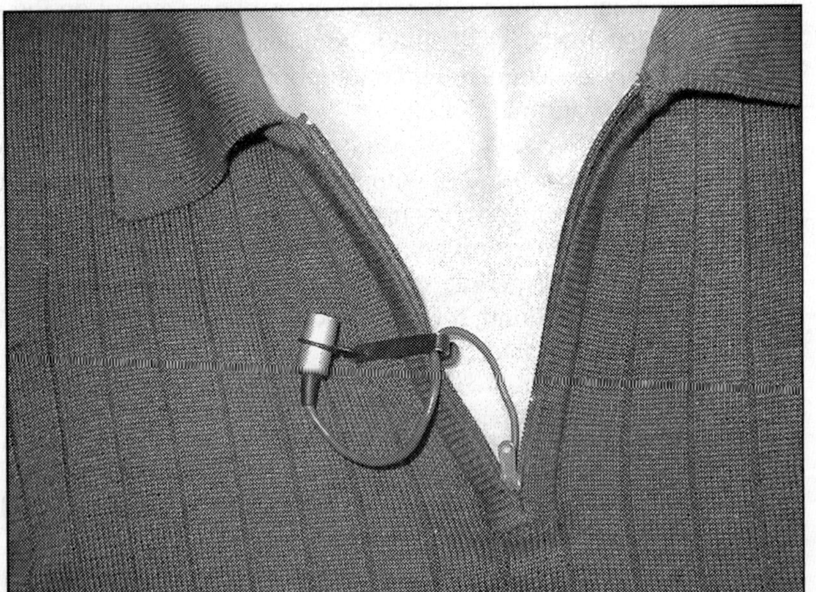

FIGURE 6.29 When using a lavalier (clip-on) microphone, position it roughly as it's positioned in this picture.

Finally, if your subject's head will be turned a particular direction—say, to talk to an interviewer—then try to position the mic more on that side of the subject's body.

WATCHOUT!

Use Those Headphones!

As you can see, a lot can go wrong with microphone placement and recording. To be safe, you *have* to use your headphones to monitor and test your audio while you're at your location! You often only get one chance for certain shots, so you don't want to waste them!

TROUBLESHOOTING

A lot can go wrong when you're shooting. Although this book can't help you with actors who don't show up, uncooperative rain clouds, or locations that are too noisy, it can offer you some advice for dealing with your technical concerns. If you're having a problem, you might find the answer in this section. If you don't, then go to www.dvhandbook.com and try posting your problem in the Production forum. Perhaps someone online can offer you a solution.

The Color in My Video Is All Weird!

This is almost always a white balance problem. If you're still at your location, double-check your white balance settings—perhaps you have the wrong setting. If you've been manually white balancing, perhaps you should re-white balance. *Remember, if you've changed to a location with a different type of lighting, or changed the lighting in your location, you might need to change your white balance settings!*

If you're done shooting and are only now noticing the color problem, you're in trouble. To fix video with bad white balance, you'll need some editing software with color balance controls—and you'll need a lot of time.

My Video Looks Squished!

If your video looks stretched or squished horizontally, you've probably got your camera's wide-screen (sometimes called "16:9") feature turned on. Deactivate it, and everything should go back to normal. If you've already shot some footage this way, go back and shoot it again (or commit to shooting your entire movie in wide-screen format).

My Camera Won't Start!

First, be certain that your camera is in shooting mode, rather than playback mode. Make sure your batteries are charged, or that you're plugged into a wall and that the outlet you're using works. If your camera has a standby mode, make sure it's turned off.

There's a Weird Block in My Video!

If you see a weird block of pixels appearing on your video, then you have a dropout on your tape. About the only way to fix this is to rotoscope it out by hand. See Chapter 9 for details on rotoscoping. Some weird image artifacts can be the result of dirty heads in your camera or deck. Get a head-cleaning tape and follow its cleaning instructions carefully.

There's No Audio!

If you're using an external mic and there's no audio, make sure your microphone is securely plugged into the correct socket on your camera, and make certain that the microphone is turned on. If all that checks out, but there's still no audio, try replacing the microphone's battery.

The Image Is Completely Black!

Make sure you removed the camera's lens cap. This might sound silly, but there've been one or two times when, exhausted from too much shooting, I've looked through the viewfinder to see a black image. Of course, my immediate thought is "oh no, what's wrong? There's no way I could've left the lens cap on; it must be something else." Don't be shy! Check that lens cap!

My Shot Won't Stay in Focus!

The autofocus mechanism in most cameras tries to identify the subject of your shot, and focus on that. Unfortunately, most autofocus mechanisms simply look at the very center of the image. Therefore, if your subject is moving around, your camera might keep refocusing on what's *behind* your subject. This is the time to resort to your manual focus control. Before the shot, have your actor stand where you want him, and use your manual focus control to get him in focus. Now you can shoot your scene.

Be aware, though, that if he moves closer or farther from the camera, he'll go out of focus. If you want him to stay in focus, you have to limit his movements to only moving horizontally across the frame.

Pulling focus (sometimes called *racking focus*) is the process of changing focus *while you're shooting*. It's typically used to shift attention from something faraway to something close up. Unfortunately, it's pretty much impossible to do this on most video cameras.

I Can't Focus on What I Want to Focus On!

This is kind of related to the last problem. If you want to frame a shot like the one in Figure 6.30, you might have to resort to manual focus.

FIGURE 6.30 If your subject is on one side of the frame, your camera might end up focusing on something behind them, because cameras typically analyze the center of the frame to calculate focus. You might need to switch your camera to manual focus to frame this type of shot.

Because your autofocus mechanism tries to focus on the middle of the image, it will end up focusing on the background. Your subject will be left blurry. Switch to manual mode and bring your subject into focus.

My Shot Gets Brighter and Darker!

Your camera's iris opens and closes automatically to let in more or less light. If something comes into frame that changes the overall illumination of the scene, your camera's iris will open or close to compensate, sometimes lightening or darkening the scene. Unfortunately, it sometimes does this too much. You can get around this by switching to manual mode and setting the iris (sometimes called *aperture*) yourself.

My Actors Keep Walking Out of Frame!

Sometimes, you'll go to lots of trouble to set up a perfectly composed shot, only to see it all go to pieces when you start rolling and your actors walk to the wrong place. The easiest way around this is to get some masking tape and make marks on the floor. The actors can then simply learn which mark they're supposed to walk to for different parts of the shot. This is what people mean when they say an actor is "hitting his marks."

I'm Having Trouble Controlling My Tripod!

A good tripod can move in many different directions—it can pan and tilt and swivel and pedestal. However, if you *only* want it to pan, it can be a real drag if it starts tilting and swiveling also. Fortunately, most tripods provide locks and restraints that let you limit the camera's motion to a single axis on the tripod. Check your tripod's manual for details. If you have a "pistol grip" tripod, you're probably out of luck; they simply don't let you constrain motion to a particular axis.

There's a Hum in My Audio!

Hums can be caused by many different things, ranging from air conditioners to refrigerators. It's *imperative* to listen closely before you start shooting to ensure that there are no humming machines running near your shoot. It's easy for your ears to tune these sounds out, so you have to actively listen for them.

If the hum sounds more like an "electronic" hum—say, an up-close, buzzing sound—then you might have a bad microphone cable, or your microphone battery might be dying. Try swapping out the cable or battery. (You might also be getting hum from an ungrounded DC plug.)

My Actor's Clothes Have Weird Lines Moving All Over Them!

Video cameras don't like clothes with really small checked or lined patterns. These patterns create waves of interference in your final image, and there's nothing you can do about it. Your only option is to make sure that your actors don't wear any clothes with fine textures. If you're unsure about an actor's clothing, shoot some test footage and look at it on a monitor (don't trust the LCD screen on your camera).

I'm Trying to Shoot through a Window, but All I See Are Reflections!

If you need to shoot through a window—say, a car window or storefront—then you might have a problem with reflections in the window obscuring the action taking place on the other side. Buy a *circular polarizing filter*, and attach it to your camera. A circular polarizer will let you filter out the reflections to see what's on the other side (Figure 6.31).

When People Watch My Footage, They Say They Can't Understand My Actors!

If you wrote your own script, you already know what your actors are saying. Consequently, you can probably understand the actors even when they're mumbling. When you're shooting, make sure you can really hear your performers. Make sure they're speaking clearly and, most importantly, *slowly*! Nervous actors tend to speak quickly and mumble. Be harsh on this one and demand as many takes as you need to get good, clear dialog. Don't rely on what you *know* they're saying; try instead to *hear* what they're saying.

My Friends Keep Getting Bored When We're Shooting!

One of your hardest jobs as a director is keeping everyone motivated and excited about the job at hand. With good preparation, your actors won't have to stand around as long, but there will always be some waiting. Try

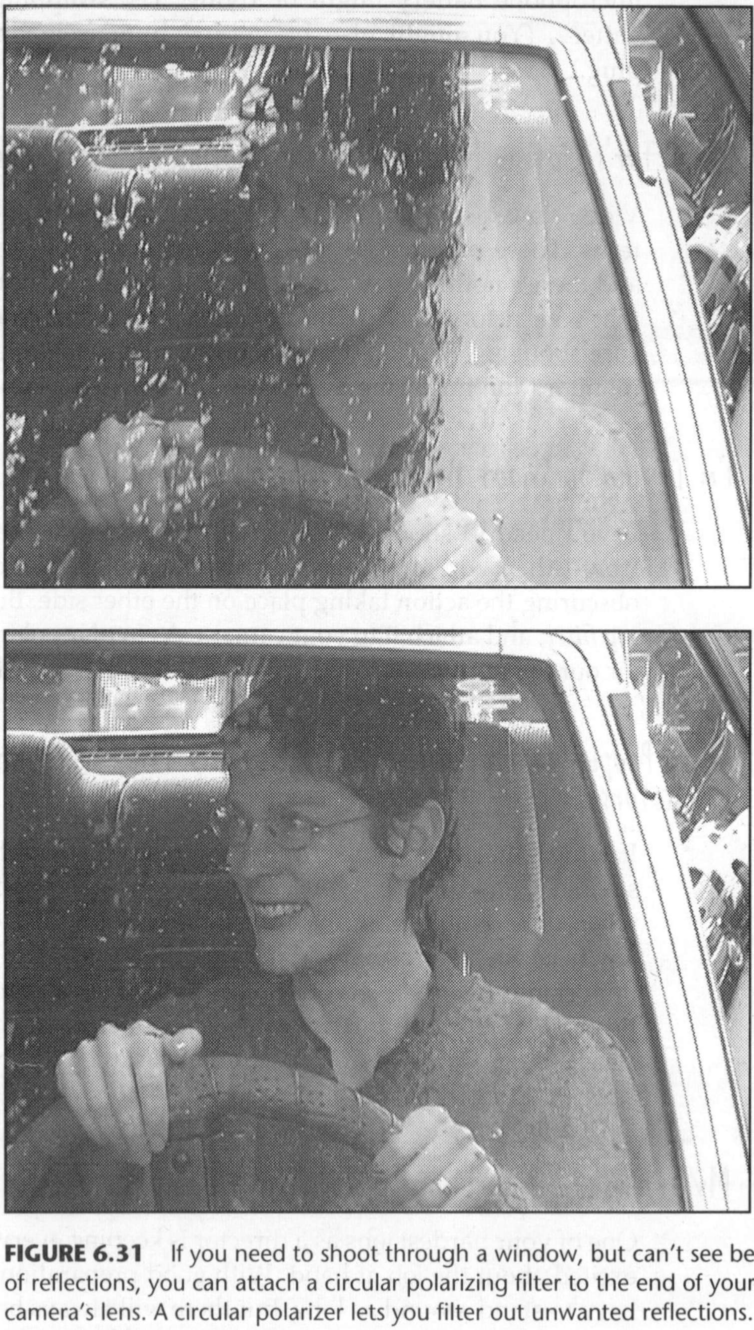

FIGURE 6.31 If you need to shoot through a window, but can't see because of reflections, you can attach a circular polarizing filter to the end of your camera's lens. A circular polarizer lets you filter out unwanted reflections.

Note that you can only use iMovie to edit video shot with a DV camera. If you're shooting with an analog camera (see Chapters 1 and 2 if you're confused about the difference), then you'll need some special hardware to capture video into your Mac.

For analog editing, check out www.dazzle.com. This company makes inexpensive analog digitizers that let you connect your analog camera to your Mac's USB port. You won't be able to edit full-screen video, but for creating movies for Web, e-mail, or CD delivery, Dazzle's the cheapest way to go (see Figure 2.10 on page 29).

Finally, there are more powerful, more expensive editing programs such as Adobe Premiere and Apple's Final Cut Pro. In addition to hefty price tags, these programs are much more complex to learn; however, they offer editing tools that go far beyond the simple cutting tools provided by iMovie. If you have a choice, start out with iMovie, and work your way up to these more serious programs if you find that you want more power.

Once you've chosen an editing program, follow its installation instructions, and then skip ahead to the sections *Connecting Your DV Camera* and *Connecting Your Analog Camera* to learn how to connect your camera.

Editing on Windows

Unless you bought a Windows system specifically tailored for video editing, your computer probably didn't ship with a preinstalled video editing program, so odds are that you're going to have to find some software. If you shot your movie with a FireWire-equipped DV camera, then you'll also need to make sure that your computer has a FireWire port.

Fortunately, you can usually kill two birds with one stone by buying a FireWire card that includes an editing package. Pinnacle Systems' StudioDV package is a great choice for Windows users (www.pinnaclessys.com) who need both a FireWire card and an editing program.

ON THE CD-ROM

If you already have a FireWire card and are looking for editing software, you might want to consider Adobe Premiere. A demo of Premiere is included on the companion CD-ROM. There are also many good shareware applications available on the Web. The best way to find one is to go to www.download.com and do a search for "video editors."

You'll need to make sure your computer has everything it needs to run a particular editing program. If you're not sure how much RAM and what type of processor your computer has, then choose Start> Settings>Control Panels, and click on System (Figure 7.2).

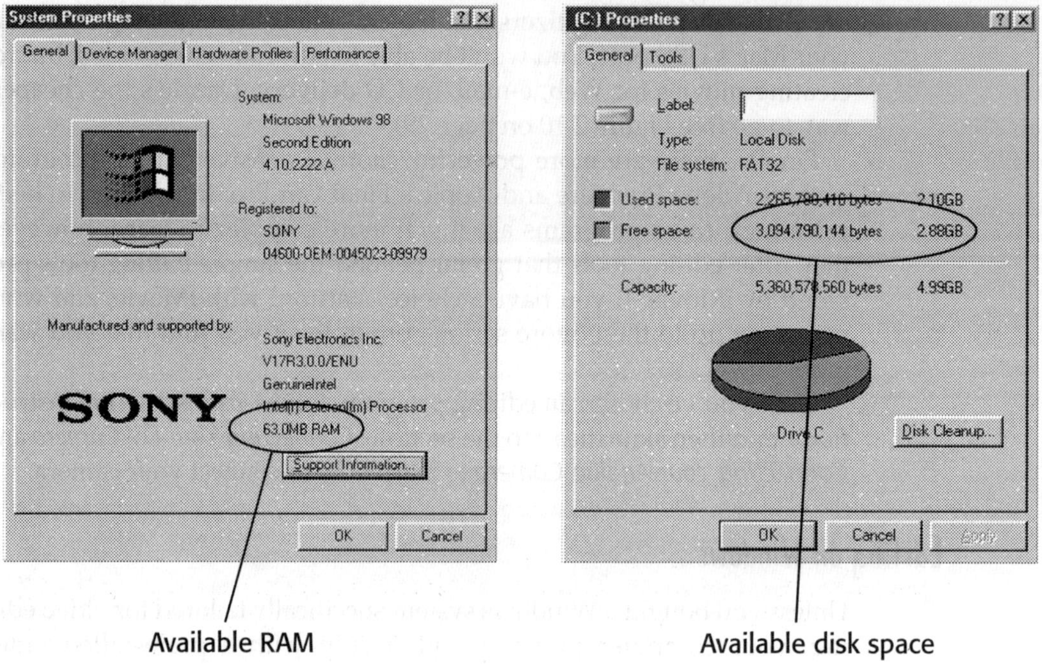

FIGURE 7.2 If you're unsure of how much RAM and disk space you have, or what type of processor, you can check Windows' Properties dialogs.

To determine how much disk space your computer has, click on its icon and choose File>Properties.

Once you've selected a package, follow its installation instructions and install the software on your computer. If you need to install a FireWire card, you might have to take your computer apart. Follow the card's instructions closely.

When you're finished, you'll be ready to connect your camera.

CONNECTING YOUR DV CAMERA

Obviously, before you can do any editing, you have to get your video from your camera to your computer. If you have a DV camera, you can transfer the video through a FireWire cable. A FireWire cable not only lets you copy video into your computer, it also provides a way for the computer to control your camera, allowing you to search, rewind, play, and pause your camera, all from your computer. Moreover, when transferring through FireWire, you'll experience no loss of quality as you pour video into your computer. (When using an analog digitizer, your video quality will degrade a bit.)

There are two types of FireWire connectors: 6-pin and 4-pin (Figure 7.3).

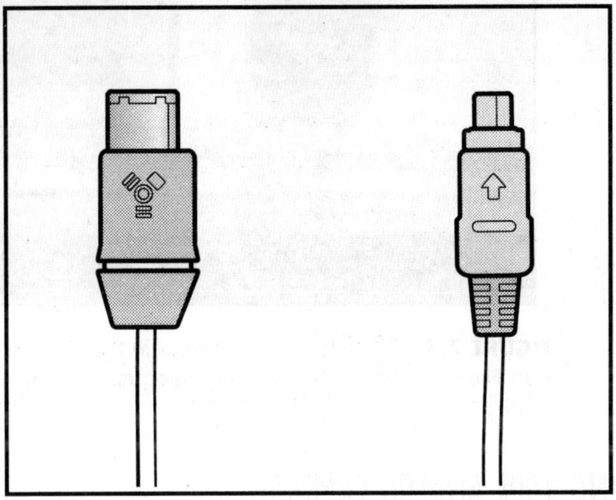

FIGURE 7.3 There are two types of FireWire connectors, and you might need cables that go from one type to another.

Your DV camera most likely has a 4-pin connector on it, while your computer probably has a 6-pin connector (Figure 7.4). Therefore, you'll need to get a 4-pin to 6-pin FireWire cable. There's a good chance your computer shipped with one of these. If not, you'll need to buy one at a computer store. You should be able to find one for around $20. Some computers have 4-pin FireWire connectors. If yours does, then you'll need a 4-pin to 4-pin FireWire connector.

FireWire connectors can only be plugged in the right way, so hooking up the cable is straightforward. Be sure to position your camera where it can also be plugged in to a wall outlet for power. It's best to save your battery power for shooting, and to use DC power when editing.

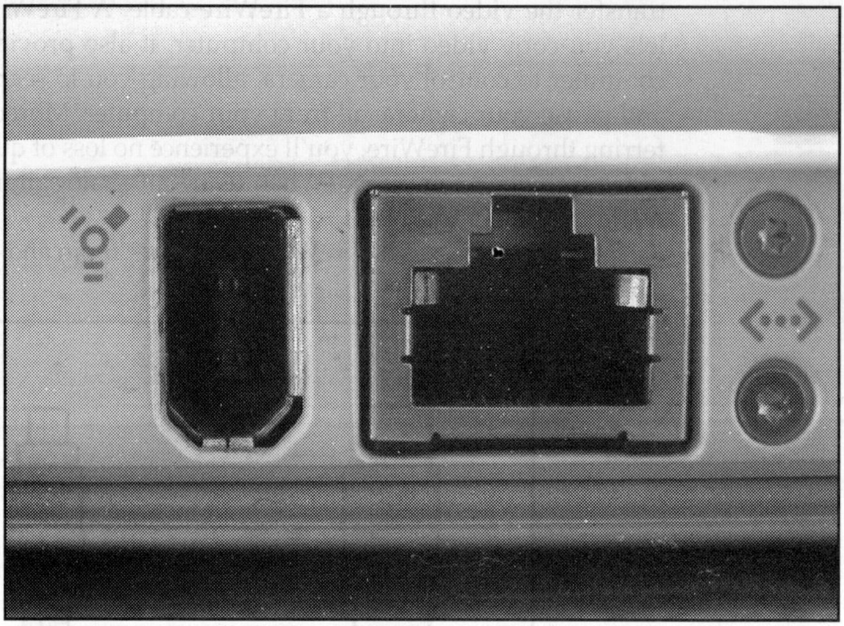

FIGURE 7.4 The leftmost connector in this picture is a standard 6-pin FireWire port like you'll find on most FireWire-equipped computers.

CONNECTING YOUR ANALOG CAMERA

If you'll be capturing video using an analog capture device, (such as the Dazzle devices discussed earlier), you'll need an appropriate video cable to patch your camera's video and audio out to your analog capture ports.

There are a few different kinds of video connectors; which one to use depends on your camera. If both your camera and capture device have S-video connectors, then you should use an S-cable to patch video from your camera to your computer.

S-video cables do not carry any audio, so you'll need to patch audio from your camera separately. Most video cameras use a single mini jack for audio output. Your analog capture device probably uses either a single mini jack, a single RCA jack, or a pair of RCA jacks.

If your camera doesn't have an S-video port, then it probably sends video and stereo audio out through a single mini jack. These camera usually include a cable with a mini plug at one end and three RCA plugs at the other (See Figure 5.15 on page 103).

Note that the RCA jacks on most camera cables are color-coded. Red and white cables carry left and right audio channels, while yellow cables carry video. Make sure you plug each cable into the appropriate jack on your analog capture box. You won't hurt anything if you connect them incorrectly; you just won't be wired right for audio and video capture.

As with a DV camera, you'll want to plug an analog camera into a wall socket for power. No need to waste your battery when you're editing.

CONNECTING A TELEVISION TO YOUR DV CAMERA

If you're using a DV camera, you might want to connect your camera to your television, in addition to connecting it to your computer's FireWire port. Connecting to a TV will let you see a higher-quality image than what will display on your computer screen while you're editing.

You connect a monitor to your camera using the same types of cables that you use to connect an analog camera to an analog capture device. However, instead of plugging into a capture box, you plug the video and audio connectors into your television. Refer to the previous section *Connecting Your Analog Camera* for a detailed description of the different types of connections that you'll need to patch the analog video and audio outs of your camera into a television.

ACTIVITY: LEARN YOUR SOFTWARE

Unfortunately, there's not enough space in this book to teach every detail of every software editing package. However, most programs include good instructions of their own. Before you move on to the next chapter, you need to learn some of the basics of your chosen editing program. Many programs include online documentation and tutorials that you can read on-screen.

Take some time now to work through any tutorials that were included with your editing program. If your program didn't include any hands-on tutorials, then read through the documentation and learn how to do the following:

- Capture video from your camera into your editing program.
- Organize your video into "bins" or trays.
- Trim individual clips.

- Place clips together to create a finished product.
- Add titles and graphics.

Once you're comfortable with these activities, you'll be ready to start learning some of the rules of good editing. We'll cover these in Chapter 8, "Editing."

SUMMARY

That's it. If you've followed these instructions, you should be ready to start editing. Double-check to make sure that you have:

- Selected and installed some video editing software on your computer.
- Connected your camera to your computer using the appropriate cables.

CHAPTER

8

Editing

IN THIS CHAPTER

- The Language of Film
- Where to Start
- Editing Basics
- Creating a Rough Cut
- Titles

By this point, you've hopefully managed to get your actors and crew together and you've shot your script. Or, maybe you've just taken your camera with you on an outing with your friends and shot a bunch of footage. Either way, you now have a bunch of video. Some of it's probably interesting, some of it probably isn't—it's time to start editing.

Hitchcock once said that drama was "life with all the boring parts removed." A large part of good editing involves removing the boring parts from your footage. Editing is also where you'll create a lot of the drama (or suspense, or comedy, or terror, or any number of other emotions) in your finished movie. It is during editing that your scenes and shots will begin to turn into a story. What type of story depends largely on your editing skills.

Editing can be a somewhat tricky thing to get a handle on because when editing is done well, you don't even notice it's happening. Consider the James Bond scene discussed on page 73. I included this scene as an example of how many camera setups and shots you might need to shoot a single minute of finished movie, but this scene is also a good example of excellent editing. If you're like me, when you first watched the scene, you were not even aware of how many different shots there were. When the cuts and edits came, you didn't see them, you simply saw the unfolding story.

This is your goal in the editing room: to lead your audience to the story and emotion that you want them to feel, without letting them know that they're being led in a particular direction.

In this chapter, you're going to learn about the aesthetics and vocabulary of editing. If you read the last chapter and worked through the last activity, we'll assume that you are already familiar with your editing program, and that you know how to import video and perform basic editing tasks using your editing program of choice. If you haven't done this, go back now and do the activity on page 165.

THE LANGUAGE OF FILM (OR TAPE)

Editing has a language all its own. Imagine the following scene:

> A man and a woman walk into an antique shop. As they browse around the store, the woman suddenly freezes, her eyes locked on a small statue that sits on a table. The man notices her sudden change in demeanor and asks her what's wrong. She stares at the statue as the camera slowly zooms in on her face. We hear a swell of music as the image slowly dissolves to a shot of a small girl holding the same statue.

So, who is the small girl in that story? If you said it's the woman as a young girl—that the woman was having a flashback to an earlier time—then you're exactly right. But how did you know that? Because you understand the language—the vocabulary—of film editing. So, when you see a camera slowly push in on someone's face, when you hear a particular type of swelling music, when you see a long dissolve, you know that a story is going into flashback. When you see these techniques being used, you understand that you are now seeing events that took place a long time ago—events that are out of sequence with the main flow of the story.

You might be thinking, "well, of course, everyone knows that." But everyone *doesn't* know that. The language of film is something you've learned from watching TV and movies. The techniques of flashbacks, intercutting scenes, reaction shots, establishing shots—all of the vocabulary that we take for granted—had to be discovered. Over the years it has been refined, reinvented, and changed.

The good news is that your exposure to TV and movies means you're probably already well versed in the language of movie editing. Now you just have to learn how to apply this vocabulary to your own project.

ON THE CD-ROM

Activity: History of Cinema Revisited

In Chapter 1, "Introduction," you were pointed toward the *History of Cinema* essay on the companion CD-ROM. If you didn't read it then, take a look at it now to learn more about the development of editing.

Montage

One of the most interesting things about editing is that, very often, the emotional impact of a scene comes not from the content of the individual shots, but from the way they are edited together. In the early 20th century, a Russian filmmaker named Sergei Eisenstein performed a very interesting experiment. He took a shot of an actor making a dramatic expression and cut it next to a shot of a beautiful woman. Then he took the *exact same* footage of the actor and cut it next to a shot of something less savory.

When the audience was shown these two clips they were stunned at the versatility and skill of the actor. They couldn't believe that the actor could so completely convey both desire and revulsion. They had no idea that what they were seeing was the exact same shot of the actor in both scenes. They "read" his performance differently when it was placed in different contexts—this is the power of editing (Figure 8.1).

Eisenstein called this type of editing *montage,* from the French word *monter*, meaning "to assemble." One of the best modern examples of montage is the shower scene in Alfred Hitchcock's *Psycho*. This scene is famous for its horror and for the huge number of quick edits. Most curious of all, though, is that you never see the knife touch the woman's body. The violence in the scene is completely implied by the way the different shots are combined.

FIGURE 8.1 If we first show a clip of the *San Joaquin Valley Swiss Club* and then show a clip of our actor, he looks confused. However, if we first show a clip of a knife-wielding maniac, and then show *the exact same clip* of our actor, the actor will look terrified. This is the power of *montage*.

ACTIVITY: SHOTS AND CUTS

It's impossible to talk about editing without talking about shooting, since you often plan your shots based on how you expect to edit them. In other words, you might plan to shoot a scene by having an establishing shot and a cut-away. When you set up and shoot these shots, you'll probably have some idea of where you will cut between them.

Take a moment to review the shot descriptions on page 134, and pay attention to how certain shots ("over the shoulder" to "reverse," for example) require a particular type of edit.

WHERE TO START

Editing can be a big job, particularly if you have a lot of footage. To keep from getting overwhelmed, it's best to have a plan of attack when you start your editing process. Although all projects are different, in general you can expect to proceed something like this.

Log Your Footage

You cannot edit without being familiar with all of your footage. This means that before you start any cutting, you need to watch everything that you've shot. As you watch, you should *log* all of your shots; in other words, make a list of every shot you have, including a description of the shot, which tape it's on, its location on the tape (its timecode listing), and how long it is. If you've shot multiple takes of the same scene, then you should note which take is the good take, the one you want to use. When you go to capture your footage, you can just capture the good takes, and not waste disk space on the bad ones.

You can also log your footage as you import it into your editing program. Higher-end programs such as Final Cut Pro and Adobe Premiere have their own logging facilities that let you create a log as you import (Figure 8.2).

Don't just skim through your tapes to create a log. Watch your footage closely while you log, and try to become as familiar with it as you can. You will have a much easier time editing if you have a clear idea of the footage at your disposal.

Find Your Base

The best way to get started editing is to identify if there's some type of "foundation" for your project. For example, if you're editing a music video, then you know you'll want to edit and lay down the music first and then cut your video to fit it. With other types of projects, you'll probably opt for different starting points. Moreover, as discussed in Chapter 2, "What You Need," you'll want to find the beginning/middle/end

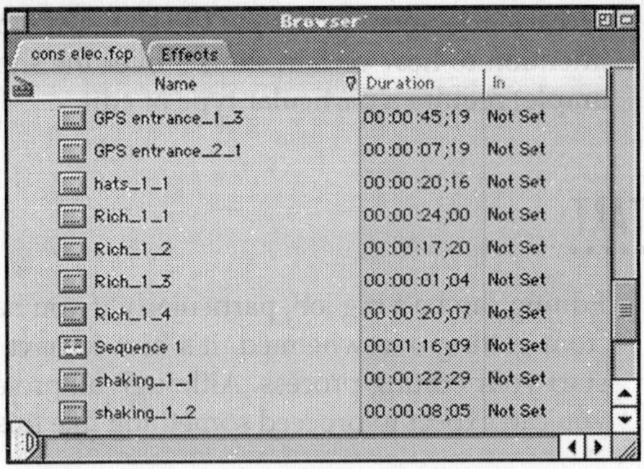

FIGURE 8.2 In many editing programs, you create a log when you import clips. This log lets you create a description of each clip, in addition to storing the start time and duration of each clip.

structure of your story. As you watch your footage, this structure will hopefully become clear.

Documentary. If you've shot a documentary, your biggest chore will be to sort through all of your footage. After that, you might find that you want to build your piece around a particular interview or group of interviews. Those interviews will be your starting point. Cut them first, and then begin laying in your supporting footage and other scenes. Or, perhaps your documentary will center on a particular event or a specific person. Find footage that serves as a good introduction to that event or person, and use that as your beginning. The rest of your structure should follow from there.

Music video. Starting a music video is pretty easy: just get your audio track in order. If it needs any editing, do that right away. Once you've "locked sound," you can start editing video to fit the music.

Stories. If you've shot a narrative story of some kind, you already have a starting point: your script. If you've completely finished shooting, you might as well start at the beginning of your movie and start cutting from there. If you've only shot a little footage, there's no reason you can't start editing it while you wait to shoot more scenes. If your project has a deadline and requires any special effects, you might want to start working on the effects scenes first, as they tend to take the longest to produce. If you put them off until the end, you might not get them finished in time.

Casual video. If you've simply gone out and shot footage of you and your friends, then there are a number of ways to get started. If there's a particularly enjoyable moment, you might want to cut it first, and then start adding new scenes around it. Or, maybe you want to start with a music track and proceed as if you were cutting a music video. Most importantly, though, no matter how you choose to start, try to find a beginning/middle/end structure as soon as possible.

Once you have a rough idea of structure, you're ready to start on a rough cut. Before you do, though, you'll want to think about some editing basics.

EDITING BASICS

As an editor, you have a number of techniques at your disposal that you can use to tell your story. Your job is to figure out how to present your footage in a way that tells your story clearly, while delivering the emotional impact you want. As an editor, you control what the audience sees—and in what order they see it—and thus are in complete control of what the audience knows. And, as you saw earlier in the Montage discussion, the order in which the audience sees something has a great effect on what they understand.

In addition to controlling what the audience sees, you also want to control the way they see it. By presenting shots in a particular manner, you can make the audience feel tense, relaxed, suspenseful, frightened—any number of different emotions. To achieve all this, you'll use some basic editing concepts.

Pacing and Rhythm

In Chapter 6, you learned about the idea of controlling the pacing of a movie. In the shootingproblems movie, you saw how the same footage can be edited two different ways to make a faster or slower scene. Fast is not necessarily better than slow (and vice versa), as each scene has its own pacing needs.

Concepts such as pacing and rhythm might sound rather abstract at first—after all, they're usually used to describe music, not movies—but you can quickly understand the concept of cinematic pacing by simply watching some music videos. Music videos are tied very closely to a particular piece of music; in fact, they're often cut directly to the beat of the music. If it's an upbeat song with a fast beat, you'll see lots of quick cuts between short shots. The video for a lyrical ballad, on the other hand, will usually be made up of longer shots with slow dissolves. Because these two types of music have very different emotions and pacings, the video is cut in very different ways, using particular pacing and rhythm.

Pacing and rhythm in a movie are controlled by the length of the shots you choose and the type of edits you choose to use between those shots. However, the effect of pacing has a lot to do with the type of story you're telling. Say you have a scene of a character wandering through a big empty house, thinking about whether he's made the right decision about something. Deliberately slow pacing during this scene will make it more introspective and dramatic.

If, on the other hand, you're editing a scene from a horror movie where a frightened girl walks through a big empty house, terrified that a knife-wielding killer lurks in the corners somewhere, then a deliberately slow pace will make the scene more tension-filled and scary. As you can see, a slow pace doesn't mean a particular thing, and increasing the pace of either of these scenes will convey completely different moods and emotions. Those moods and emotions are neither right nor wrong, but some may be more appropriate to your story than others are.

When you're editing you need to constantly ask yourself, "what information does this shot convey?" If it's something the audience already knows, then there's a good chance you can get rid of it. However, the shot might serve a purpose beyond presenting information if it helps lengthen a scene to improve the pace of your movie.

Pacing is largely controlled by the length of the shots you choose to use. Choosing lots of short shots will create a final scene that feels frantic and fast-paced, while choosing lots of long shots will create a more somber, meditative scene (see Figure 6.25).

Finding the right number of shots can be tricky. Too many long shots can seem dull; too many short shots can seem *cutty*—conspicuously edited—or disjointed. The most effective use of pacing involves a variety of fast and slow cuts as in the famous shower scene in Hitchcock's *Psycho,* which starts out with a long, slow shot and ends with a series of very short, fast cuts.

As an editor, you'll often cut and recut scenes, experimenting with longer or shorter shots and different kinds of cuts, to get a feel for different pacings. So, how do you find the right one? "Right" and "wrong" are really just a matter of how the scene feels when you watch it. In general, though, it's safe to say that if you're aware of the editing when you're watching—that is, if you find yourself thinking "that was a long shot" or "boy, there sure are a lot of cuts in this scene"—then the scene is probably not very well edited.

Every time the audience becomes aware of some aspect of the *making* of your movie, they also become distracted from the *story* you are telling.

This is true of the shooting, the editing, the audio quality—everything. The best way to tell if something is right or wrong in your movie is to ask yourself if it serves the story. That is, does it make the story better (the right choice), or does it distract the audience (the wrong choice).

Hard and Soft Cuts

Cutting between two shots that are visually and narratively similar is called a *soft cut*. Soft cuts (sometimes called *seamless* cuts) are ones that your audience probably won't even notice because they are so unobtrusive and natural.

Conversely, a hard cut is one that occurs between shots that are very different. Your audience won't necessarily notice a hard cut either, if it's done well, but it will have a very different effect on them (Figure 8.3).

FIGURE 8.3 Cutting between these two images is a hard cut. In addition to the content of the shot changing, the audience's focus and eye movement is dramatically shifted from the upper-left corner of the frame to the lower right.

Hard cuts typically make your audience's eyes move around, and when their eyes are moving, they feel more action or tension. Holding your audience's eyes in the same place, even across cuts, will keep them calmer and more relaxed (Figure 8.4).

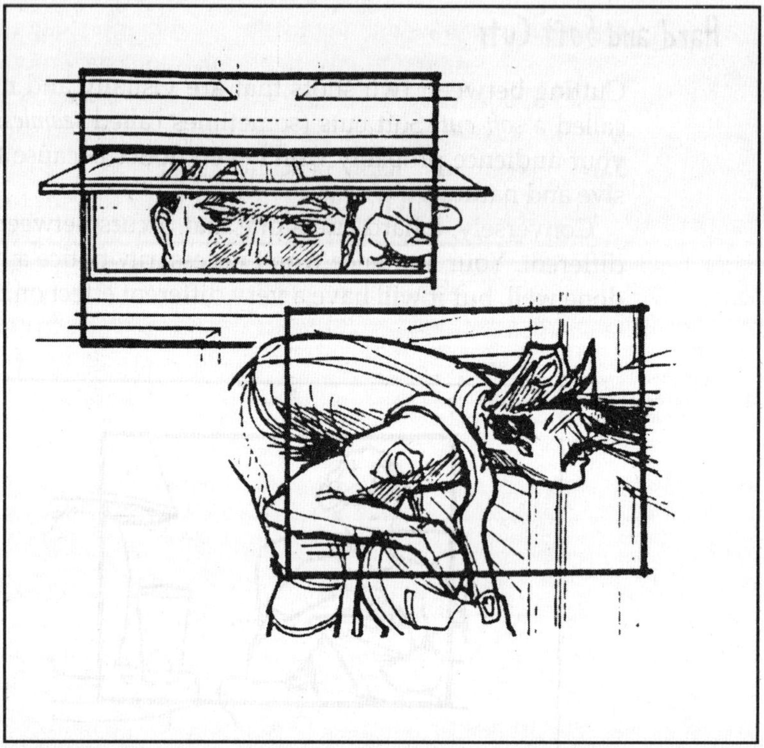

FIGURE 8.4 Although the content of these two shots is very different, notice that the main focus of each shot is in roughly the same place on the screen. This means that your audience will barely move their eyes as you make the cut. This softens the cut, and keeps them calm during what is a slow-moving, quiet sequence.

Hard cuts typically occur when any of the following change dramatically between shots:

- **Camera angle.** Wide, tight, and so forth.
- **Screen position of the subject.** Where is the subject positioned in the frame?
- **Color.** Is there a strong change in color; for example, shifting from night to day?

- **Movement and action.** Are you cutting between a static shot and a moving shot?
- **Story.** Are you cutting between two shots in the same scene, or cutting to an entirely new scene?

The softest cut of all is to *dissolve* between two shots. You'll learn more about dissolves when we talk about transitions later in this chapter.

When shooting and editing, think about the emotional content of your scene. If you want to create a tense, fast-paced scene, you'll probably want to plan on lots of hard cuts, and will need to shoot accordingly. Similarly, if you want a slower scene, you'll need to plan on softer cuts.

Your choice of hard or soft cuts will have a lot to do with creating an overall "style" or feel in your movie. Learning to create style that adds to the story, rather than distract from it, is an important skill for every editor.

Structure

In Chapter 2, you learned about three-act structure, the basic organizational structure of most movies. As you learned, three-act structure is simply a fancier, more organized way of saying that your story has a beginning, middle, and end. Whether you're shooting a scripted project or simply shooting footage of you and your friends, you'll probably shoot much more footage than you need for your finished project. When editing, you'll want to think about your story's beginning, middle, and end. You want to make sure that each section is proceeding at the proper pace and is the right length. If you're unsure about the details of three-act structure, check out pages 45–47.

Another way to think of three-act structure is as a setup, an action, and a payoff. The setup occurs in Act 1, the action occurs in Act 2, and the payoff occurs in Act 3. Thinking of structure in these terms is particularly appropriate to very short projects, such as commercials and sketches. For example, in a commercial, the setup (Act 1) might be a woman cleaning a kitchen. The action (Act 2) occurs when a mouse runs across the floor, causing the woman to scream and leap onto a chair. The payoff (Act 3) is the tag line "Johnson's multipurpose chairs. Sturdy. Taller than a mouse."

When you think of three-act structure this way, you begin to understand that it can, and should, be applied to every scene in your movie. In other words, the individual scenes in your movie—or sequences of shots within a scene—should also have definite beginnings, middles, and ends.

For example, although it's a simple scene without much action, the Controlling Pacing section of the shootingproblems movie that you saw in Chapter 6 has a well-defined structure: the man leaves his house, the man walks to his car, the man drives away. It might not leave you on the edge of your seat, but it does progress in a rather sturdy fashion (Figure 8.5).

FIGURE 8.5 Beginning, middle, and end of the Controlling Pacing section of the Shooting Problems movie.

Although you can vary widely from three-act structure, it's a very good starting point. No matter how you structure your movie, it's important to introduce a problem or situation in the beginning, so that the viewer is intrigued enough to keep watching, to expand upon the problem so as to provide content and new information for the viewer, and to reach a conclusion to provide a sense of closure. Projects that fail to achieve these things are often perceived as boring (bad first act), lacking in substance (bad second act), or pointless (bad third act).

OTHER STRUCTURES

Three-act structure may be the most common form of movie structure, but there are other approaches. Some people prefer to look at a feature film as 12 10-minute sequences (or roughly 10 minutes). Each sequence ends with some sort of revelation that leads the viewer onto the next sequence, eventually building to a conclusion. Ernest Lehman says he used this concept of structure when he wrote Hitchcock's *North by Northwest*. Another type of structure is the narrative build, or intensity build, where the story gains in intensity as it progresses, much like a musical crescendo (this structure is often accompanied by a musical crescendo on the soundtrack). This type of structure is usually not sturdy enough to sustain a feature-length project, but can be quite successful for a short format piece such as a music video. One-hour dramatic television shows use a variation of three-act structure, but they are broken into five acts to accommodate commercial breaks.

NO STRUCTURE

Whether you're cutting a documentary with hundreds of hours of material, a feature film shot with improvised acting, or simply a montage sequence of you and your friends, you're going to find yourself faced with editing some unstructured material. Earlier in this chapter, you learned about some ways to find structure in documentaries, music videos, and scripted material. Here are some more tips for working with unstructured material.

Use *chronology* to create structure. For example, if you're editing a birthday party, you can simply manipulate the real chronology of events to create a setup (everyone arrives, people greet each other, presents are stacked on a table), the action (the cake is brought in, candles are blown out, the presents are opened), and the payoff, (everyone's happy and having a good time; finally, everyone leaves).

Use three-act structure to help you figure out each scene. Say you need to edit a scene that shows a mugging victim going to take her first karate lesson (she wants to learn how to defend herself). You have a ton of footage of the lesson, but what do you show? You need to serve the story, which is about how the woman is timid at first, but then gains confidence. To do that, you need to pick the moments that show this arc in the victim's character. Perhaps a hesitant moment at the door (setup), some week attempts at a karate kick, then stronger (action), and then a good solid kick and a smile of confidence (payoff). In addition to creating a solid scene, you've also reinforced the content of your overall story by mirroring it within this one scene.

Paper edits are a good way to work toward the first rough cut if there is no script. You can use transcripts of your footage, or your own notes to outline a structure, and basically create a script before you start to edit the material itself.

CREATING A ROUGH CUT

The first cut of a film is called the *rough cut,* and the goal of a rough cut is to figure out exactly how you'll create the film's structure with the footage at hand. Just as you might actually write several drafts to arrive at your "first draft," you'll probably make several passes at your initial rough cut.

Once you've chosen a starting point for your story, you'll be ready to start on your rough cut. Hopefully, you've already reviewed and logged your footage, so you have a good idea of what takes are good and what footage is useful. Start trimming your scenes to roughly the right length, and then quickly put them in order. When you make a rough cut, you're simply trying to get an idea as to which takes work and which don't. You also want to get a feel for your story, how things are paced, which areas need to be faster or slower, and so on. Don't worry about making every cut perfect; you can do that later.

Once you have a preliminary rough cut, go back and start cutting your dialog. Getting good timing and pacing for the dialog in your project is one of your most critical editing tasks.

Finally, when you're comfortable with the dialog scenes, you'll take a series of passes to refine the cut. In these passes, you'll focus on the picture—covering jump cuts with reactions or cutaways, establishing each scene, making sure each edit works, making good transitions, and aiming for a rhythm and pace that's on track with the content of the project.

The result of all this work is the first rough cut. It might not sound all that rough after all that work, and it probably isn't—it's supposed to be a watchable version of the film and it should be ready to be screened and reviewed.

Creating a rough cut can be a big job, particularly if you're working on a feature-length project that might have 15 hours of footage. Most important of all, though, is that your individual edits "work." No matter what the subject matter or style of your movie is, there will also be some edits that work and some that don't. To create better edits, think about the following.

Motivating Your Edits

Many beginning editors get nervous if they don't make a lot of cuts. After all, are you really doing any editing if all your shots are long? Bear in mind, though, that knowing when *not* to cut is as important as knowing *when* to cut. So, how do you know when to cut and when not to cut?

Sometimes it's very simple. If you shot an establishing shot and a cutaway, with the intent of cutting between them, then you'll pretty much know where to cut. Say, however, that you have a dialog scene between two people, Dick and Jane. When shooting, you asked the performers to do the scene twice, and you shot a close-up of each actor doing the whole scene. You now have footage of each actor delivering every line. So, how do you choose which actor to show and when?

You could, of course, cut between every line, but this might result in too many cuts, and create a scene that's much faster-paced than you wanted. Rather than cutting simply to show all the footage you have, watch the scene and ask yourself what you *want* to see at any particular time. In other words, look for a motivation for cutting from one scene to another.

If Jane tells Dick that she just burned his house down, we're probably far more interested in seeing Dick—so that we can see his reaction—than we are in seeing Jane.

Cuts can also be motivated by action. If we see a man throw a tuba out of a window in an office building, we'll really want to know where that tuba lands. Cutting from the office to a shot of the tuba crashing through the window of a car is a well-motivated cut.

Finally, sometimes a cut will be motivated by the need to solve a technical problem. Perhaps you need to cut away from a shot that is out of focus or shaky—hopefully, you won't have to do this too often.

Continuity

If you've spent much time watching movies, you've probably spotted a simple continuity mistake at one time or another. For example, a guy has his arms folded in one shot, but not in another, or something like that. These types of mistakes happen when editors choose clips from different takes—sometimes takes shot on different days. It's rare to see a huge continuity mistake—an actor's clothes or props changing—but it can happen. Obviously, you need to keep an eye on continuity while shooting (feature films employ people with Polaroid or digital cameras to constantly monitor continuity concerns while shooting), but there are also some continuity issues to be aware of when editing.

MATCHING ACTION

Matching action means that movement within a scene flows naturally from one shot to the next. For example, say you have two shots—a wide shot of an actor opening a door, and a close-up of his hand on the doorknob—and you want to cut from the wide shot to the close-up to show the actor opening the door. What's difficult about this type of edit is making the action appear continuous and properly timed.

Often, if you're cutting from a wide shot to a tight shot, you'll need to skip part of the motion to make the flow seem natural. In other words, don't worry about showing all of the wide shot and the close-up. Experiment with cutting the wide shot early, or cutting into the close-up late. Your audience has a good sense of how long it should take, in real time, to open a door, and your edit needs to match that sense (Figure 8.6).

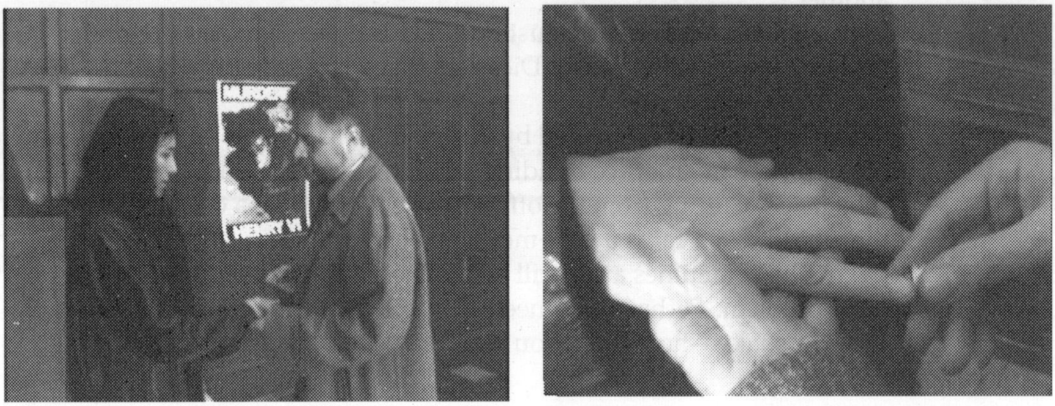

FIGURE 8.6 Sometimes, when you're cutting from a wide shot to a close-up, you'll need to edit out a little bit of action to get timing that feels right. For example, in this sequence of a man putting a ring on a woman's finger, you'll need to cut away from the wide shot a little before he gets the ring on her finger. Although some action will, technically, be missing, the cut will feel more realistic and properly timed.

MATCHING EYELINES

Eyelines are a rather abstract concept, but they make sense once you pay attention to them. If you have two characters holding a conversation and you want to cut between them, you need to make certain that the characters appear to be looking at each other (Figure 8.7).

If you can draw an imaginary line from one actor's eyes to the other's, then you have matching eyelines. Unfortunately, if your eyelines don't match, there's not really anything you can do other than flip the incorrect frame.

JUMP CUTS

A jump cut is a radical break in continuity and occurs any time you cut between two different clips shot from the same angle (Figure 8.8).

FIGURE 8.7 When cutting dialog, you want to make certain that your *eyelines* match. That is, that the characters actually appear to be looking at each other when you cut between them.

You usually want to avoid jump cuts, because most people are not used to seeing them in normal scenes. However, you can use them for certain stylistic effects. For example, locking your camera in one place and jump cutting between lots of different actions taking place in the same room can be a way to show the passage of time.

Jean-Luc Goddard very famously used jump cuts to create tension in his movie *Breathless*.

Action and Reaction

As explained on page X, most of your editing centers on establishing a scene or moment and then showing your characters' reactions to that scene or moment. As discussed previously, which reactions you choose to show, and in what order, is largely how you control what the audience feels and believes (see "Montage" on page 169).

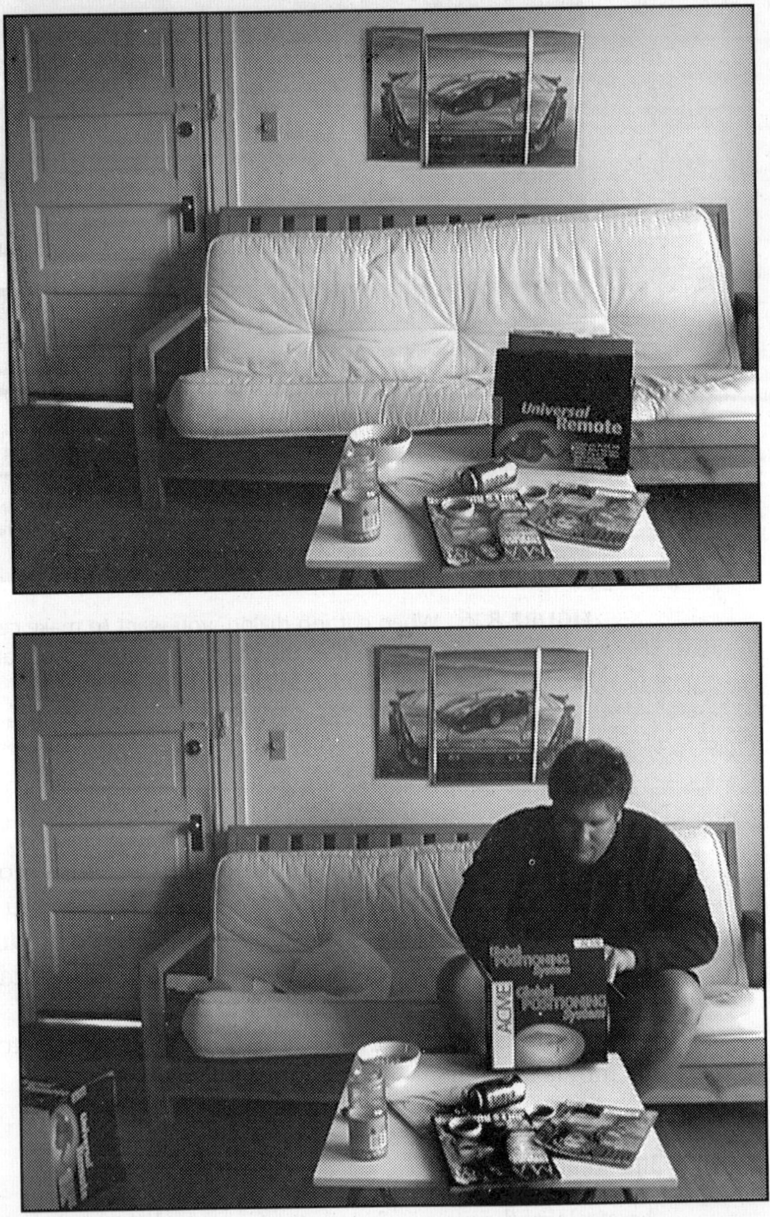

FIGURE 8.8 Cutting from the first shot to the second shot would be a *jump cut*. The guy would seem to suddenly appear in the frame and many of the props would jump around. Jump cuts are usually something you want to avoid, as they don't make visual sense to your audience.

Editing Dialog

You might think that editing dialog is very simple: just show the person who's speaking when they're saying something. However, good dialog editing is much more complex. As discussed previously, the audience is often more interested in seeing the person who's *listening* so as to see their reaction. Moreover, if you cut to a new shot every time someone different speaks, your scene will suddenly have a *lot* of edits in it. No matter what type of project you're working on, editing dialog will be a big part of your editing job. Consider the following:

Conveying information. At its most basic level, dialogue conveys information about a story or a subject. The first priority in editing dialogue is to make sure that all the necessary information gets in the scene.

Tightening the dialog. Getting rid of the ums, breaths, and other hesitations can be very important to the successful pacing of a scene. Obviously, if the speakers are on camera, you're going to be stuck with whatever they said. However, if they are covered by a cutaway, you can tighten any unnecessary pauses and get rid of partial sentences and stutters so that the actors speak concisely.

Overlapping dialog. You can make a conversation between two people sound more natural by overlapping the dialogue, especially during more intense moments. In real life, people don't always wait for the other person to finish talking—they interrupt, talk over them, and so forth. Conversely, if a scene was shot with overlapping dialogue in it, you might have less freedom to edit the scene as you wish. You'll be locked into the pacing of the overlapping dialog as it was recorded.

Expanding a moment. Adding pauses, or *beats*, in a conversation is an important tool for intensifying a moment. In a scene where a man asks a woman to marry him and she says "Yes," a carefully placed pause can change the meaning entirely. With no pauses, it plays as a happy agreement. A pause before he speaks plays up his nervousness. A pause before she answers builds suspense if the shot stays on him, and implies hesitation if the shot is on her.

Starting late and getting out early. Sometimes, dialogue scenes, as scripted and shot, are much longer than they need to be. The characters enter the scene, greet each other, have a conversation, make plans, and exit. It might help the overall pace to start the scene in the middle, or get out of it early, and hard cut to a new scene.

Sometimes long stretches of dialogue can seem boring or present too much information. With dialog, less is usually more.

Fixing and cheating dialog. Sometimes dialogue problems—a messed-up line, for example—can be bad enough to wreck an entire scene. Sometimes you can cheat a word or phrase from another take. Or, you might be able to save the scene by starting the dialogue under an establishing shot, or by editing around it. These types of issues are unique to each project, but if you keep an open mind and think on your feet, you just might be able to pull off a miracle save. Just remember, if you do your job right, no one will notice!

Transitions

Almost all editing programs these days allow you to create all sorts of crazy transitions between scenes. In addition to the usual dissolves, you can also create pushes, wipes, spins, 3D movements, and all the other slick transitions that you see on sports programs and some commercials.

Every program provides a different way of applying these transitions, and you shouldn't have any trouble learning how to add transitions to your edits. *However, you should be very careful about when you choose to use fancy transitions!*

For any type of narrative story, it's safe to say that the only type of transition you should ever use is a dissolve (sometimes called a *cross-fade* or *lap dissolve*). In general, though, no matter what type of project you're editing, dissolves will distract your audience and generally appear as excessively flashy. Use them with caution.

TITLES

Your editing program most likely includes a titling facility of some kind, which you can use for everything from adding subtitles to beginning and ending credit sequences. If you want to create a really fancy, animated title sequence of some kind, then you'll need to learn how to use an animation or motion graphics program such as Adobe After Effects or Pinnacle Commotion. For simple graphics and title rolls, though, your editor's titling facility should be all you need.

When you create titles, there are a few things to keep in mind. First, legibility is your primary goal. If people can't read your titles, why have them? You'll need to carefully consider color, typeface choice, and font size when creating your graphics.

Creating Titles for Video

If you plan on outputting your final movie to videotape, you'll need to make some careful considerations when creating your titles. First, you'll want to be cautious when choosing colors. Bright reds and blues will often bleed and smear when shown on TV. Pick more muted colors and be sure to output some quick tests before you print your final movie to tape.

In addition, any single-pixel horizontal lines will most likely flash when transferred to video. This can be really annoying, so be careful when creating graphics or choosing typefaces with very thin lines.

Finally, not all TV sets show the same amount of image; some show a lot, while others crop the edges of the image. To be certain that your titles are always visible, be sure to stay in the *title safe* area of the screen (Figure 8.9).

FIGURE 8.9 When creating titles for video, you want to be sure to keep them within the *title safe* area of the screen. If your editing program doesn't include title safe guides, then try to make sure that your titles don't cross into the outer 5% of the screen.

Some editing programs have a title safe display that can be superimposed on the screen while creating titles. As with color choice, you might want to test your titles to make sure they fit on the screen before you print your final video.

Creating Titles for the Web or CD-ROM

If you plan to e-mail your final movie, post it to a Web site, or burn it to a CD-ROM, then you'll ultimately be shrinking your movie down to a rather small frame size (you'll learn about this in Chapter 10).

Because movies viewed "online" are usually small (320 × 240 pixels), you need to be extra concerned about legibility. Be sure to use a typeface that's easy to read, and choose a large type size. It's also best not to superimpose your titles over an image, as this will make them less legible.

EDITING A MUSIC VIDEO

ON THE CD

Becoming a good editor takes practice, and because there's no time like the present to start learning, why not dive in right now and start editing a music video. Although I'm sure that Chapter 6's discussion of how to shoot a music video has left you more than ready to start shooting, you might not yet have had a chance to get something "in the can." Not to worry. In the Tutorials>Chapter 8>MusicVideo folder is all of the raw footage from a video by singer/songwriter Kim Petrowski. You'll also find an audio file of the song itself, *Sweet Sound.* In this tutorial, you'll get started on editing the footage together into a finished rough cut. Although a finished, final cut is also included in the Music Video folder, try not to watch it until you've taken your own pass at editing.

What You Need to Know

This tutorial assumes that you have already set up your computer hardware and installed your editing software. In addition, it also assumes that you've already learned how to do the following things with your editing program:

- Import files that have already been captured
- Place clips into a project
- Setting in and out points for a clip

- Trimming and rearranging clips
- Inserting an audio track

If you're unclear about any of these, you'll need to go to your software's documentation or tutorials and brush up.

For this example, we'll be using Apple's iMovie, but just about any editing program will do. The point of this tutorial is not to learn how to use specific parts of a particular program, but to learn how one goes about organizing and approaching a music video editing job.

Step 1: Get Your Media

ON THE CD

First, you need to copy the appropriate media from the companion CD-ROM to your hard drive. The footage for this video was actually shot on 16mm film, then transferred to Digital Betacam videotape, and then finally dubbed down to MiniDV tape and dumped into the computer. Copy the Tutorials>Chapter 8>MusicVideo folder to your computer's hard drive. In the music video are two different folders: "Sync video" and "Non-Sync video." You'll learn more about these in a minute.

Special Step for iMovie Users

If you're using iMovie, you need to take an extra step to convert the music video clips into footage you can use with iMovie. To save space on the companion CD-ROM, these clips were compressed with the Sorenson compressor. Unfortunately, iMovie can't work with Sorenson-compressed video, so you need to use the Apple QuickTime Player to convert the clips into something that iMovie can use.

The QuickTime is installed on any Mac that has QuickTime. If you don't know where it is, use Sherlock to find it. Once you've opened the QuickTime player, open the first clip in the Sync video folder that you just copied to your hard drive. Go to the File menu and choose Export (or just press command-F). In the Export dialog, choose "Movie to DV Stream" from the Export pop-up menu, and "NTSC 48 kHz" from the Use pop-up menu. The QuickTime player should automatically add a .dv extension to the filename.

Save the file, and then convert all of the other clips using the same process.

Step 2: Start Your Software

Next, open your editing program, create a new project, and import all of the footage from the music video folder. When you're finished, your editing program should show you some type of catalog of your media (Figure 8.10).

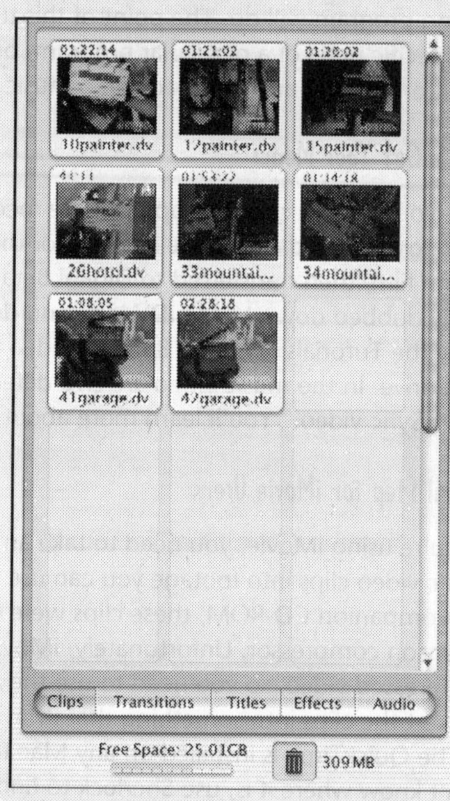

FIGURE 8.10 Once you've imported your media, you should see a list of clip names or, as in the case of iMovie, a display of thumbnails.

Step 3: Import the Audio Track

ON THE CD

The song for this video is called *Sweet Sound* and it's located in the Tutorials>Chapter 8>MusicVideo folder. The file, sweetsound.aiff, should have been copied to your hard drive along with the video. Import it into your editing program. Now, listen to the track, as you're going to need to be a little familiar with it to cut the video.

Step 4: Review the Footage

Now, take a look at all of the footage you imported. If you had started this job from scratch, you would have already reviewed your footage when logging, and you probably would have watched it again when you were importing. Because you didn't have to do those steps, you should watch it all now to see what footage you have at your disposal.

As you watch, you'll see some things that obviously need to be edited out—slates, crewmembers, bad camera movements—but you should also keep an eye out for shots that you like (Figure 8.11). Some of the shots overlap each other (that is, they cover the same part of the song), so you're going to have to choose which of the shots you prefer for each bit of song.

FIGURE 8.11 As you review the footage you've imported, keep an eye out for shots that you like.

All of the footage included in the Sync folder is footage of the woman singing, with accompanying audio. All of the footage in the Non-Sync folder is footage without any lip-syncing so it can be used anywhere.

Step 5: Make a Plan

Your biggest concern when editing a music video is to maintain *sync*; that is, to make sure that the video always stays in sync with the audio. As explained in Chapter 6, the best way to shoot a music video is to have your actors lip-sync to an audio recording that you play on set. This ensures that during multiple takes and camera angles, your actors will always be synced to the same music source.

This video was originally shot with no audio at all; instead, a CD of the song was played on-set. The CD player was able to generate timecode that was sent to a *timecode slate*. That's the slate with numbers that you see at the start of some of the shots, and it makes it easier to synchronize the video with the appropriate part of the song. When you're shooting with a DV camera, you'll almost always be capturing sound, so you'll have footage that includes the audio that was playing back on-set. You can use that audio to figure out where in the song each particular clip goes.

For this footage, I've gone ahead and synced the video to the appropriate part of the CD track, so your editing experience will be exactly the same as if you'd shot using the method described in Chapter 6.

Knowing this, you're ready to start making an editing plan. Obviously, any music video needs to be edited to the music, so your first course of action should be to lay down your music track. Because the Sync footage clips contain video of the woman lip-syncing, those clips must go in particular places. Other pieces of footage are not tied to particular parts of the song, so they can go anywhere. With this in mind, let's start editing.

Step 6: Lay Down Your Music Track

If you followed step 3, you should have already imported the *sweetsound.aiff* into your project. If you're using iMovie, that sound file will already appear in one of the audio tracks in your project's timeline (Figure 8.12). If you're using another editing application, you might have to put the file into an audio track.

Step 7: Pick Some Footage with Vocals

Now that you have an audio bed, you can prepare to lay in the shots that have footage of the vocalist. You don't have to use all of these shots, but you'll probably use most of them to get the coverage you need.

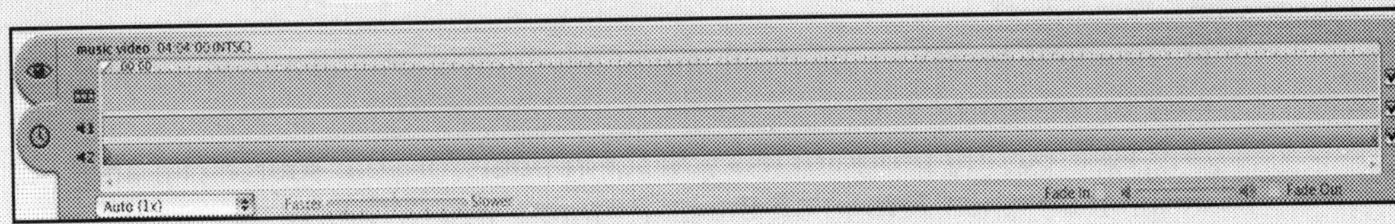

FIGURE 8.12 iMovie's timeline with audio in the audio track.

Before you can begin editing, you need to figure out roughly where each shot fits into the song. A couple of hints: the "painter" shots cover the first verse and chorus of the song; the "garage" shots cover the second verse and chorus; and the "mountain" shots cover the last two choruses. Watch all of these shots and pick the performances you like best. These shots will comprise the "spine" of your rough cut—that is, when you have nothing else to show, you'll show these shots. When picking a shot, pay attention to how well the singer's performance matches the music, and zero in on any camerawork that you particularly like. Sometimes you won't have too many choices, and you'll probably have some rough spots that you'll need to cover later. In addition, remember that this is a "rough" cut; you don't have to get it perfect as you'll have plenty of time to fine-tune it later. In particular, don't obsess too much about hitting the beat of the music; you'll fix those things later.

Another hint: for the "painter" shots, try the start of 11painter, even though it's not a complete take, and use 10painter for the rest of the scene.

Step 8: Insert the First Shot

Now that you've picked some shots, it's time to get them into your project. First, you need to trim any unwanted material off of the head or tail of your shot—the timecode slate, and so on. Do this using your program's trim features.

The rest of your task is mostly trial and error. You've got to get the woman's mouth synced to the appropriate part of the audio track. Your task is a little easier since you have audio on each of your clips, but mostly this will be a visual chore.

Let's start with the *12painter* clip. After you've trimmed the ends of the clip, look for a hard, distinct sound to use as a sync point. The start of the word *breath* in the third line of the song works well, and *b's* are easy to recognize.

If your editing program lets you set in point for your source clip and destination, then zero in on the exact frame where the "b" occurs in both the video clip, and in the timeline where your audio is, set an in-point, and then insert your footage. After inserting, you'll need to expand backwards from your in point to get the earlier part of your footage back into your project, but your clip should be in sync.

If your program doesn't let you set in-points, then you'll simply have to insert the clip into your timeline and drag it back and forth until the "B" in the video clip matches the "B" in the audio track. Once those points are aligned, the entire track will be in sync.

Step 9: Insert the Rest of the Sync Footage

Using the same technique used in step 8, insert the rest of the footage of the woman singing.

Step 10: Insert the Nonsync Footage

Now you're ready to start cutting in the footage included in the nonsync folder. Because there's no lip-syncing in these clips, you can insert them anywhere. These clips can be used to cover areas of the song where there's no lip-syncing, or places where you couldn't find lip-sync footage that you liked.

For these clips, you should try using hard cuts, rather than dissolves. This will make a nice contrast with the tone of the other footage. In addition, if you place your hard cuts on the beat of the music, or edit so that the camera movement or other action occurs on the beat, then you'll be able to reinforce the rhythm of the soundtrack.

(By the way, the shots *02woods, 04woods,* and *05woods* were designed to cover the intro to the song.)

Step 11: Finishing Touches

Once you have your first rough cut, try experimenting with some dissolves of varying lengths. The beginning and ending are obvious places for dissolves, but you might find some other places within the video itself where you can add some moody transitions.

Finally, when you have everything cut, you can think about adding appropriate titles.

That's it! Remember, there's no right or wrong way to edit, but if you'd like to see someone else's take on how to edit this video, check out the *sweet.mov* document located in the Tutorials>Chapter 8>Music Video> Final Movie folder. This was cut by editor Sonja Schenk and includes a list of credits at the end. If you'd like to make a credit sequence that includes your names, you can copy down the credits listed in the movie—just substitute your name where it says *editor*!

SUMMARY

There's a good chance that you'll spend more time editing than shooting, so don't be surprised if your editing phase goes on longer than you were expecting. Hopefully, by now, you're comfortable with the following concepts:

- Logging your footage
- Finding a starting point
- Knowing some basic editing pitfalls to avoid
- Knowing what makes a good edit, and what makes a bad one
- Basic titling

If there's one single rule to remember when editing, it's this: if the audience notices your edit, it's probably not a good one. *Don't be flashy!* The most satisfying edits, the ones you'll be especially proud of and want everyone to know about are the ones that people won't ever mention or give you credit for. In the end, though, you'll have a better movie if you set your ego aside, don't show off, and choose the edits that best serve your story.

CHAPTER

9

Special Effects

IN THIS CHAPTER

- Practical Effects
- Filters
- Compositing
- Rotoscoping

Personally, I think special effects work is one of the most enjoyable parts of post-production. The tools are fun, the problems are weird, and you get to make cool-looking stuff. Special effects work is also the most time-consuming part of the post-production process, so you need to plan and choose your special effects very carefully.

Although heavy-hitting effects professionals might use rooms full of computers to create stomping dinosaurs and liquid-metal robots, you'll be glad to hear that even with your desktop computer, you can create realistic-looking, impressive special effects. In this chapter, you're going to learn some basic effects processes. Most of these effects can be achieved using software you probably already have. Some techniques, though, might require you to buy some new tools.

Special effects work is a complex subject, and detailed descriptions and explanations are way beyond this book. In this chapter, you're going to learn the fundamental concepts and practices of several basic special effects techniques. These techniques form the foundation of all effects work, and with some experimentation and play, you can build these techniques into many other effects. By the end of this chapter, you should have a good idea of the types of questions you need to consider when you set out to make a special effects shot. Once you understand the questions, you should have an easier time tracking down the answers on your own.

PRACTICAL EFFECTS

Although most special effects these days are done using computer-generated imagery (CGI), there are still many effects that are created using "old-fashioned" methods: props, sets, trick photography, and so on. These "practical" effects are often much easier to pull off than digital effects, and you should consider all practical options before turning to your computer to create an effect.

For example, a friend was recently shooting a commercial wherein a character in a business suit needed to slip on something and slide along a sidewalk. Although there were lots of digitally enhanced options for creating the effect—towing the actor on a wire and removing the wire later, digitally animating the actor along a shot of the sidewalk—it was finally decided that the best choice was simply to get a roller skate shoe and modify it to look like a dress shoe.

Once you start post-production, you're going to have enough to do without worrying about creating one more special effect. Therefore, the more you can do in-camera, the better.

Here are some tips for creating practical effects.

Props and Costumes

Although it is possible to create digital props that can be inserted into a scene, it's almost *always* easier to create actual props for your actors to use. In addition to eliminating a lot of post-production hassle, your actors will have an easier time working with real objects instead of imaginary ones.

A simple prop choice can make all the difference in the believability of a scene. For example, in the *Consumer Electronics* video, simply sticking a framed Mona Lisa on the wall immediately changed the mood of the shot. To create that prop, I went to a prop store and rented a frame ($15 for a week). Then I downloaded a JPEG image of the Mona Lisa from the Web, resized it to fit the frame, and printed it out on a friend's large format inkjet printer.

Finding props. Ideally, of course, you already have all of the props you need. If you don't, ask your friends if they have what you're looking for—perhaps you can borrow the props you need.

Renting props. If you don't have, or can't borrow, the props you need for a particular shot, you might be able to rent them from a prop shop. Check your local telephone book to see if there are any prop rental houses in your area. You might also be able to rent or borrow props from university theatre departments or community theatres.

Building props. If you can't find or rent a prop, or if you need a very special, unusual prop, then your best choice might be to build it yourself. Props can be built out of anything, of course. Your main concern when creating a prop, though, is to build something that will look believable on-camera. Be careful not to over-build. That is, if a detail on a prop is not going to be visible on-camera, then don't bother to create it.

Fortunately, with DV, it's very easy to set up your camera and grab some quick shots of your prop while you're building it. Then you can easily see what it needs or doesn't need (Figure 9.1).

Trick Photography

In the *very* old days of moviemaking, all special effects were done "in-camera" using trick photography. Many of these effects are still practical and are still used. For example, for some of the shots in the recent *Lord of the Rings* movie, actors playing Hobbits were made to look short by simply sticking them on an oversized set. In other shots, actors playing hobbits were placed farther from the camera than actors playing humans. When framed properly, the shot looked like a tall actor talking to a really short actor.

With some clever framing, angles, and set creation, there are all sorts of effects you can achieve without any digital manipulation. In most cases, these effects require very careful control of the camera's depth of field. Check out pages 125 through 132 for more information on controlling depth of field in your image.

Some Strings Attached—Mostly Practical Effects

Many effects are partly practical and partly digital. For example, if you have a prop that you need to make hover or levitate, you can easily use a string to dangle it into your shot, and then erase the string digitally. Similarly, you can push or pull props with rods, cables, wires—anything thin that can be easily painted out. Painting on your image in this fashion is called *rotoscoping* and we'll cover it in more detail, later.

You can, of course, use wires and cables to make actors levitate and perform seemingly impossible physical feats. These types of effects,

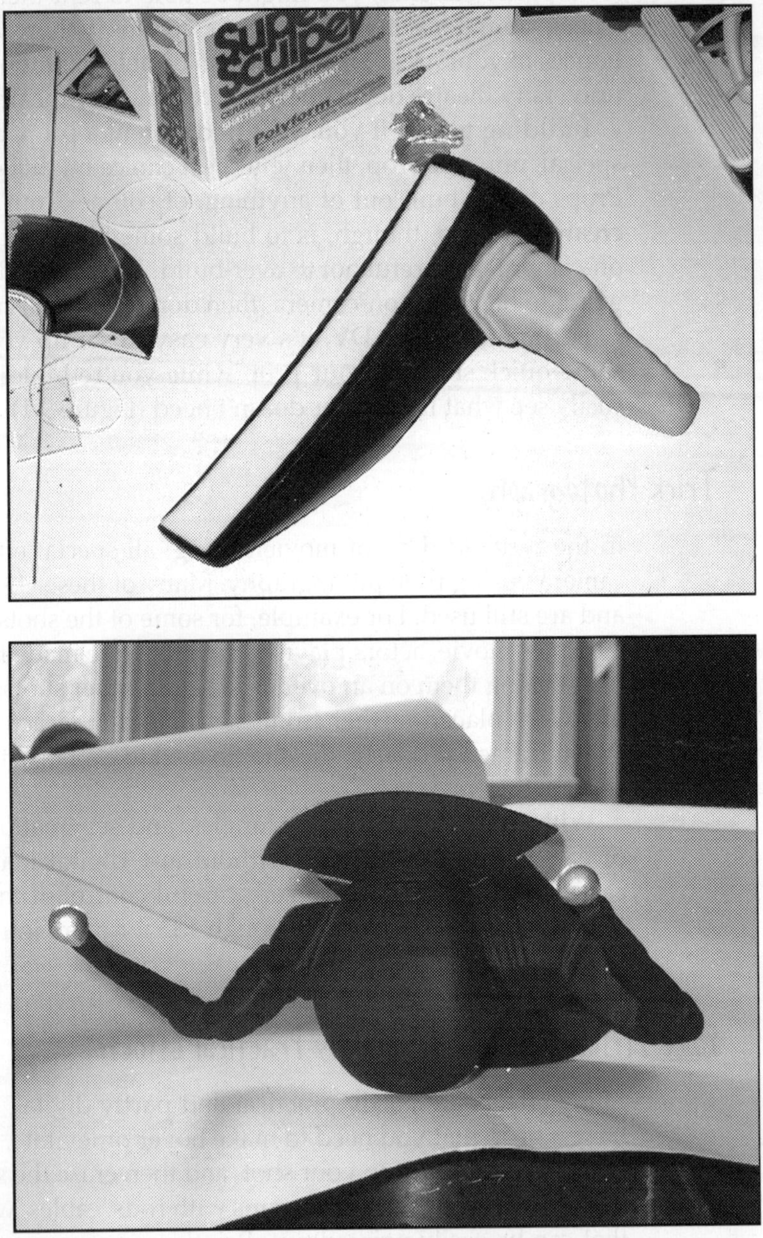

FIGURE 9.1 If you can't find the prop you need, you can always build it yourself. I built the Universal Remote prop for my *Consumer Electronics* short using a telephone handset, a cut-up CD, some super glue, and a *lot* of Sculpey modeling clay.

though, require special rigs and trained performers—definitely not something you want to try at home.

FILTERS

If you've spent much time playing with your editing software, you've probably already discovered that it can produce some cool effects on its own. Even simple editing programs such as iMovie are capable of creating cool transition effects. Most basic video editing programs also provide some special filters that you can use to change the color or look of your video.

For example, iMovie includes filters that can adjust colors and contrast, sharpen, or convert your video to black and white (Figure 9.2).

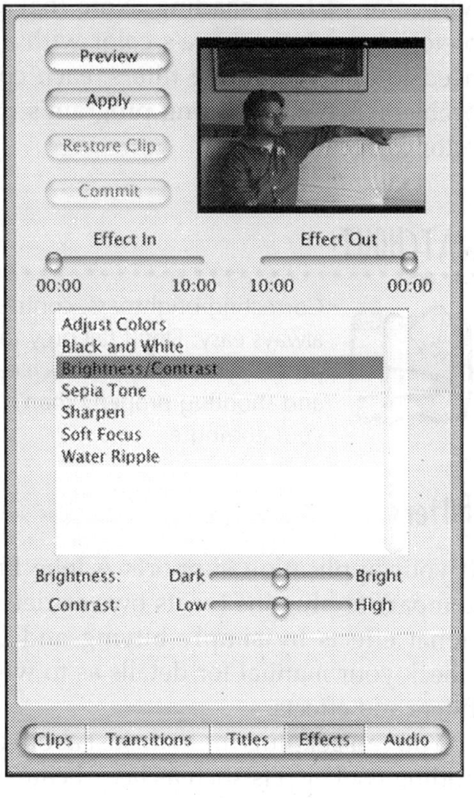

FIGURE 9.2 Many editing movies include special effects filters like the filters built into iMovie. You can use these filters to automatically create all sorts of special effects.

In most editing programs, you use filters in roughly the same way: select a piece of video, and then choose the filter that you want to apply to it. Many filters have settings and controls that you can use to fine-tune the filter's effect.

You can use filters such as these to make your movie look weird or surreal, but you can also use them to correct poorly shot video. For example, if your editing program has a Brightness and Contrast, or Levels filter, you can use it to brighten up video that might have been underexposed (Figure 9.3).

If your editing program, has a Color Balance, or color adjustment filter, then you can change or correct the color in your image. Note that these kinds of filters won't let you do radical color correction—like quickly changing an orange basketball into a blue one—rather, they let you perform general corrections to an entire image. Sometimes, you can use these filters to correct images with bad white balance, or that have an odd color *cast*, or shading. Note that it's very rare that you can completely correct an image's color with a single color filter. Usually, you need to apply multiple filters, each configured to correct a particular problem. See your editing program's manual for more details on using color correction filters.

WATCHOUT!

Correcting brightness, contrast, and color in an image is not always easy. Don't fall prey to the "oh, I can fix it in the computer" syndrome. It's *much* easier to spend the time lighting and shooting properly than it is to fix poorly shot video in your computer.

Effects Filters

If your application supports Adobe Premiere or Adobe After Effects-compatible plug-ins (or its own variety of plug-ins), you can add additional effects by simply buying and installing special plug-in filters. Check your manual for details as to whether your app supports plug-in filters and effects.

You can get plug-ins to do just about anything, from correcting color to adding cool effects such as laser beams, lightning bolts, snowflakes, and on and on (Figure 9.4).

Plug-ins can be expensive, but for many types of effects, they're the simplest, most cost-effective way of getting the results you want.

FIGURE 9.3 You can use a Brightness and Contrast or Levels filter to make dark, underexposed video brighter and more legible.

COMPOSITING

Compositing is the process of layering different pieces of video—stacking one on top of the other to create a finished image. You'll use compositing effects any time you want to take video of one thing and include it in video of another thing. For example, if you want to create a shot of a

FIGURE 9.4 Special plug-in filters allow you to automatically create all kinds of special effects such as this Snowstorm filter from DigiEffects.

person walking across the Sahara, you could shoot footage of the person walking and then composite them into footage of the Sahara to create a finished shot.

You can also use compositing programs to create video collages with lots of different layers of video, and you can even make the layers move around. You see collages on TV all the time, from commercials to the opening of news and sports programs.

Although there are many different methods for creating composites, the fundamental process is always the same: shoot one piece of video, create a mask (sometimes called a *matte*) to mask to control which areas of each piece of video are visible, and then layer another piece of video on top of it (Figure 9.5).

It's that "creating a matte" part that can be tricky. Fortunately, there are a number of tools that make the process easier, and there a few things you can do to generate masks automatically.

Keying

Perhaps you've seen documentaries or pictures of actors performing in front of a blue screen or green screen. If you've ever wondered why, it's

FIGURE 9.5 All compositing operations follow the same basic idea: different layers of video are stacked on top of each other. Special masks are used to control which parts of a layer remain visible.

really pretty simple. Blue and green are not colors that appear in skin or hair tones (at least, not in healthy people). Therefore, in post-production, it's very easy to filter out the blue or green background and replace it with something else.

You can do the same thing digitally through a process called *keying*. If you shoot actors in front of a blue screen, you can tell the computer to *key out* the blue and replace it with a different piece of video (or a still image, if you've photographed or painted a background) (Figure 9.6).

Keying is a great way to make your actors look like they're on location—say, the moon—or on a really expensive set, perhaps mission control at NASA.

FIGURE 9.6 To put images of billowing smoke behind this actor, he was shot in front of a blue screen. In our editing program, the blue was *keyed* out and replaced with footage of billowing smoke.

You can also use keying for adding or changing foreground elements. For example, when preparing the remote control prop for the *Consumer Electronics* video, I couldn't figure out how to build a realistic-looking control panel, let alone one with lots of cool animated stuff on it. So, instead, I painted the front of the face blue and then used an illustration program to create an image of what the face should look like. Then, I keyed out the blue of the remote control face, and replaced it with my computer-generated face image (Figure 9.7).

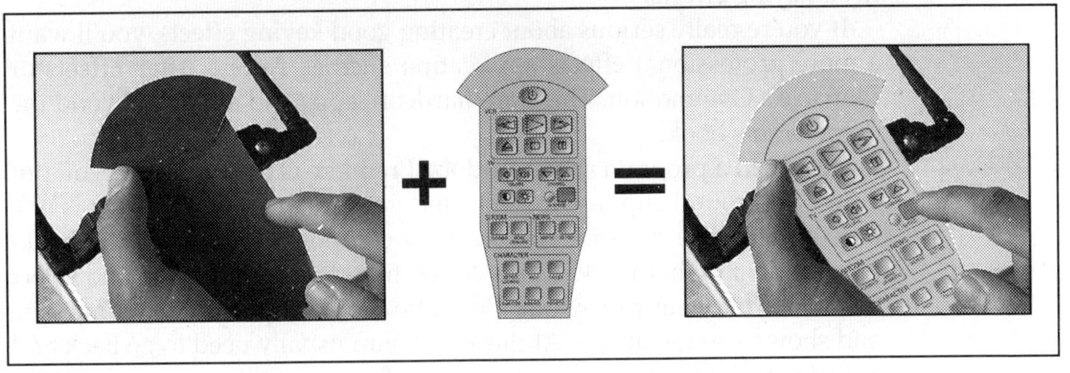

FIGURE 9.7 We painted the face of this prop blue so that we could chroma key a computer-generated surface onto it.

Getting keying to work can be complicated. First, you have to shoot "clean" blue-screen footage, and then you have to tweak settings in your editing program to create a good composite. Finally, you need to think about ways to make your actors interact naturally with the missing environment. Here are some of the things you need to think about when creating keying effects.

HINT

Be Wary of Keying with Older Formats

Don't expect to get good keying results with older analog cameras that use VHS or Hi-8 tapes. You really need to be using a digital format such as MiniDV if you want to do any type of keying.

FINDING A PROGRAM THAT CAN KEY

First, you need to make sure that your editing program knows how to perform chroma key operations. Simple programs such as iMovie don't provide such features, so you might have to move up to a more sophisticated application. Pinnacle Studio (available for Windows) and Adobe Premiere (available for Mac and Windows) provide good keying controls, as does Final Cut Pro (for Mac). Premiere and Final Cut are expensive, though, so you might want to think carefully about how much you need keying effects.

If you're really serious about creating good keying effects, you'll want a more professional effects application such as Adobe After Effects or Pinnacle's Commotion. These are hardcore apps and are *way* beyond the scope of this book.

Keying in a program such as Adobe Premiere is pretty simple: you put your background clip in one track, and your foreground clip (that is, the blue-screen clip, the one you want to composite on top of the background) in a higher track. Apply a Key filter to the upper clip and select the color you want to key out. Premiere then computes your composite and shows you the image. At this point, you usually need to go back and adjust your key settings to make a smoother composite.

If you're using a program other than Premiere, you'll need to read your manual for more on how to create a key. Look in the manual's table of contents or Index for such terms as "keying," "chroma key," "blue-screen," and "compositing."

CREATE A BLUE-SCREEN KEY IN PREMIERE

Once you've shot your blue-screen footage and your background image, you're ready to use your editing program to create your chroma key composite. Although the procedure varies somewhat from application to application, most programs use a somewhat similar technique to create a key effect.

In this tutorial, you're going to see how to create a chroma key effect using Adobe Premiere. If you don't already have a copy of Premiere, a demo version is included on the companion CD-ROM. If you haven't done so already, install the software and move on to the

ON THE CD

first step in the tutorial. When you first launch Premiere after installation, it will give you a choice of two different editing styles. Select "Single Track Editing."

Step 1: Launch Premiere

Go ahead and launch your copy of Premiere. If you installed the demo version that's included on the CD-ROM, be aware that this version will not let you render a finished movie. Don't worry, though, you'll still be able to see how keying works.

Step 2: Create a New Project

When Premiere launches, it asks you to create a new project. In the Load Project Settings dialog that appears at launch, choose the *NTSC 640 x 480 QuickTime* setting, and click OK.

Step 3: Import Your Media

You'll use two movies to create this composite, and both are included in Tutorials>Chapter 9>Keying folder on the CD-ROM. Jay.mov is a short clip of a man sleeping in front of a blue-screen background. LA140.mov is a clip of a surreal watery background. This clip is part of the Liquid Ambience Collection from the ArtBeats Digital Film Library (www.artbeats.com).

Import both of these clips into your project by choosing File>Import> File. You'll need to do this twice, once for each clip.

Step 4: Add the First Clip to the Timeline

Figure 9.8 shows Premiere's control layout.

You want to add the La140.mov clip to your Timeline by dragging it from the Project window onto the Video 1 Track in the Timeline window. When you're finished, your timeline should look like Figure 9.9.

This is your background image, so we want it in the lowest track in the timeline. The other clip will be stacked on top of it.

If you look in the Program monitor window (that's the one on the right), you should see a weird green pattern. This monitor is displaying the contents of the timeline, the La140 movie.

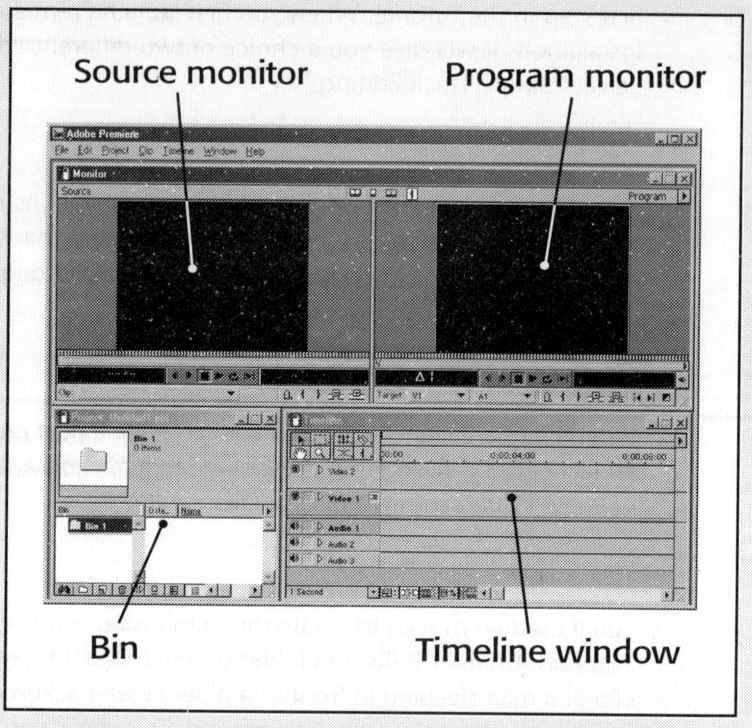

FIGURE 9.8 Adobe Premiere's window layout is similar to many other editing programs. You drag imported footage from a *bin* into the *timeline* to add it to your project. Clips can be previewed on the *Source* monitor, while the *Program* monitor displays your final, edited project.

Step 5: Add the Second Clip

Now, drag the Jay.mov clip to the Video 2 track in your timeline. Now, in the Program Monitor, you should see the footage of the guy sleeping in front of the blue screen (Figure 9.10).

Step 6: Open the Effects Controls

Before you can go any further, you need to open the Effects Controls window. First, select the jay.mov clip by clicking on it in the Timeline window. Then, choose Window>Show Effect Controls. This should open the Effect Controls palette.

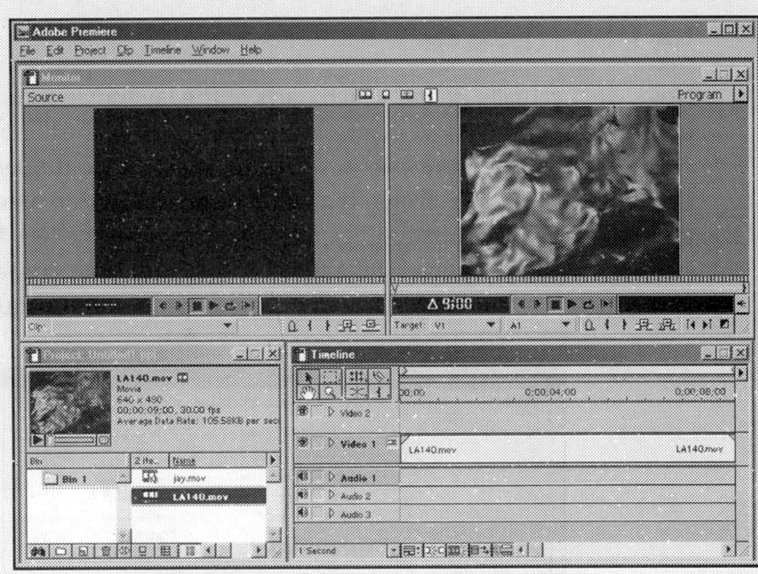

FIGURE 9.9 Timeline with first clip.

FIGURE 9.10 After you've dragged the second clip, your timeline should look like this.

Step 7: Add a Chroma Key

Now, we'll actually define which parts of the Jay movie should be transparent. In the Effect Controls palette, click the check box next to Transparency—the Transparency Settings dialog should open. In the Transparency Settings dialog is a video thumbnail called Sample. Below this are five small controls. Click the third one from the left, the one that looks like a peeling page. This activates the Composite Preview feature. Finally, select *Chroma* from the Key Type pop-up menu (Figure 9.11).

FIGURE 9.11 You use Premiere's Transparency Settings dialog to control what makes a layer transparent.

Step 8: Define Your Key

You should also see a small thumbnail labeled *Color*. This is where you define the color in your video that should be *keyed out*. Move the mouse over this small thumbnail and notice that it turns into an eyedropper. Click with the eyedropper somewhere near the man's head. You should see some black specs in the Sample window.

When you clicked, you selected one particular shade of blue as your key color. As you can plainly see, the background behind the man is not uniform, it's made up of varying shades of blue (this is because we didn't do a very good job of evenly lighting our background). Those black pixels you see in the sample window are the few pixels of that exact color on which you clicked. They're being keyed out and are revealing the underlying video clip.

Step 9: Refine Your Key

Obviously, just knocking out a few pixels is not really the effect we were hoping for. Fortunately, by tweaking a few controls, we can get things working a little better. With the *Similarity* slider, you can tell Premiere to key out pixels that are similar to the one you clicked on with the eyedropper.

Drag the *Similarity* slider to the right, and you'll see pixels in the Sample window begin to disappear. The trick is to select enough similar pixels to knock out the background, but not so many that you begin to key out the man. The correct Similarity value will vary depending on the original color you picked. In our key, a Similarity of about 26 worked well.

Step 10: Smooth Your Key

Unfortunately, as you knock out pixels, the edge of the man will get a little rough and jagged. You can use the Blend slider to blend and blur the edge of the key. Slide it to the right and, again, try to balance knocking out pixels with knocking out the man. In our key, a blend value of 4 worked well (Figure 9.12).

FIGURE 9.12 Using the Similarity and Blend sliders, you can refine your key to better blend the foreground and background.

Step 11: Finish Up

Press OK to accept your key settings and you're done! Choose Project>Preview to preview your movie. Note that you might have to save your project file and you'll have to wait a bit for the project to render.

Keying Tips

As you can see, getting a good key can be quite complicated. You need to make sure your background is lit properly, and you have to spend some time configuring your key effect. Here are some tips for getting good key results.

CREATING A GOOD BLUE SCREEN (OR GREEN SCREEN)

The one factor that will make or break your keying efforts is the quality of your colored backdrop. If it's not lit well, if it's not evenly colored, or if it's too close to your actors, then your editing program will have a hard time creating a clean composite.

You might be able to rent a blue-screen stage, if there are any good-sized video production facilities in your area, but this is usually pretty expensive. It's much more cost-effective to simply build your own. You'll need a good-sized area like a garage, and you'll need colored material. Whether to use blue or green depends on your actor's costumes and props. If they contain lots of blues, for example, then go for a green screen. If your costumes contain both blue and green, then you might need to alter them.

Your goal is to create a flat, uniform background that you can shoot in front of. Obviously, you'll need something flat and blue (or green). Fabric makes a good backdrop and is easy to hang from the ceiling. Alternatively, you can get large flat pieces of smooth wood and paint them. When selecting a color, bear in mind that you want something really bright and neon-like—a super-bright blue or green.

Make sure that you build a screen that's big enough for the types of shots you want to make. If you plan on really wide shots, you'll need a really big blue screen. Obviously, the bigger the screen, the more expensive and complicated to build, so you might want to think about lots of medium shots and close-ups when you shoot blue-screen footage.

LIGHTING YOUR SCREEN

Once you've built your blue or green screen, you have to light it. This is the tricky part because you want the lighting on the screen to be as even as possible. Your camera will see any variations in lighting as variations in color, and your editing program will have a harder time isolating a single color for keying. You also want to be sure that there's enough light on the screen so that its color looks very bright.

Unless it's a very small screen, you'll need to use a couple of big fill lights. If you've rented a lighting kit, you should have what you need to get even lighting across a fairly large screen. If you don't have any professional lights, you can use simple work lights that you might find at a hardware store.

It might take a lot of adjusting to get the lighting on your screen perfectly even. However, don't just judge by eye. Set up your camera and shoot some footage of your screen. Look very closely to be sure that there's no darkening of the screen from one part to another. Once you think you have your lighting set properly, shoot some footage and throw it into your editing program. There you can try a quick key to make sure it works.

PLACING AND LIGHTING YOUR ACTORS

Once you've got your screen lit, you need to start thinking about lighting the actors that will be performing in front of the screen. You'll want to follow the same lighting guidelines that you'd consider when lighting in any other situation. You also need to make sure that there's a good amount of space between the actors and the screen. If your actors are too close to the screen, blue light might reflect onto their hair and shoulders. These colored areas will get keyed out when you perform your composite, resulting in pieces of your actors disappearing!

After you've lit your actors, have them move around as they will during the scene. Watch your background very closely to see if the actors cast shadows or do anything else that might cause the lighting on your screen to change.

ADJUSTING YOUR CAMERA'S SHARPNESS

Unfortunately, most digital video cameras have a tendency to perform a lot of digital sharpening of their image. Although this can make for clearer, sharper-looking video, it can also play havoc with your color keying (Figure 9.13).

Check your manual to see if your camera has a sharpness control. If it does, try dialing it down to eliminate any halos like those shown in Figure 9.13. Obviously, you want to strike a balance between less sharpening and good key footage, and you should shoot some experiments to try out in your editing package.

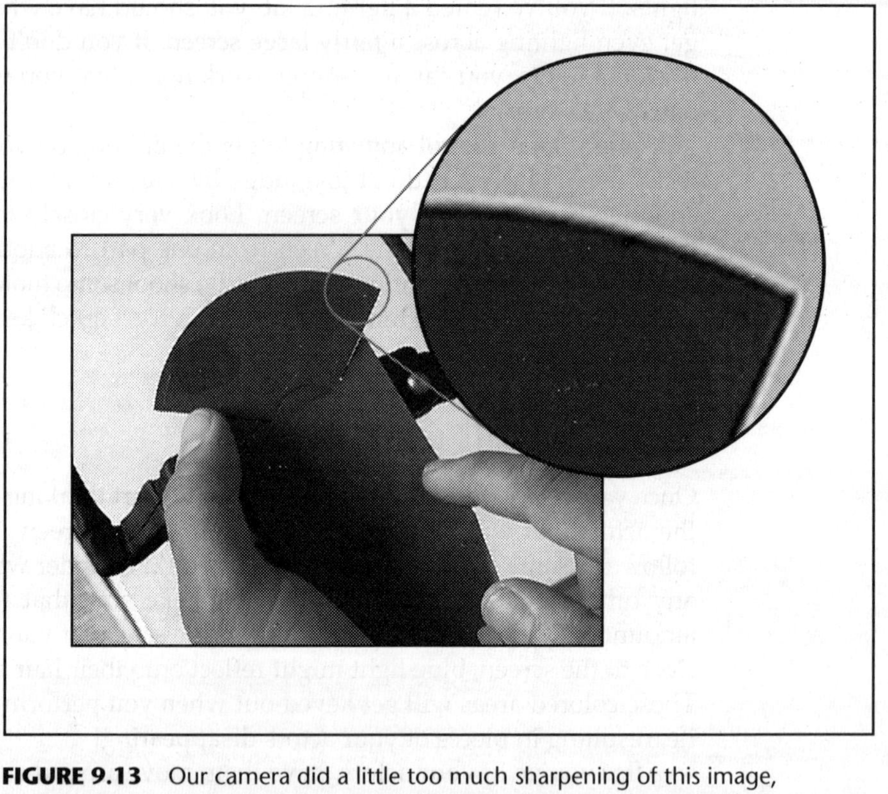

FIGURE 9.13 Our camera did a little too much sharpening of this image, resulting in the ugly white halo around the edge of the remote control. Unfortunately, this halo is still visible in the final composite (see page 207).

SET YOUR CAMERA'S IRIS

As you learned in Chapter 6, your camera constantly adjusts its exposure setting to ensure that you get the best image. This can really mess up a blue-screen shoot, though. If the camera irises down to better expose a performer's face, then your blue-screen color will change, and your key will get messed up. If your camera has a manual iris mode, activate it, and lock your exposure at something that's generally appropriate to your scene. Remember to put it back into auto mode when you head off to shoot somewhere else.

INFORM YOUR ACTORS

Your actors will need to know the boundaries of where they can and cannot move. Consider putting masking tape on the floor to mark the area that will work for your composite.

DON'T MOVE YOUR CAMERA!

Using a moving camera—*any* type of movement, even panning or zooming—can make compositing *much* more difficult, because your background plate will need to have the same sort of movement in it. Therefore, plan on keeping your camera locked down in a static shot when shooting blue screen.

COMPOSE YOUR SHOTS CAREFULLY

One of the trickiest things about blue-screen photography is composing scenes that don't look like an actor standing in front a blue screen that has an image on it. Remember, just because you have that huge screen, you don't have to shoot a huge, wide shot. Consider using medium shots and close-ups when you're shooting blue screen. Another good choice is to place props and set pieces in the foreground of your scene to create a sense of depth.

Alpha Channels

Let's say, for example, that you've created a computer-generated space ship or dinosaur in a 3D animation program, and you want to add it to some live footage. Or perhaps you've painted an image in a paint program and you want to have pieces of video showing through. For these types of effects, you'll need to learn about *alpha channels*.

An alpha channel is simply a piece of video that is inserted between two other pieces of video. It works like a stencil to control which parts of the top piece of video are visible (Figure 9.14).

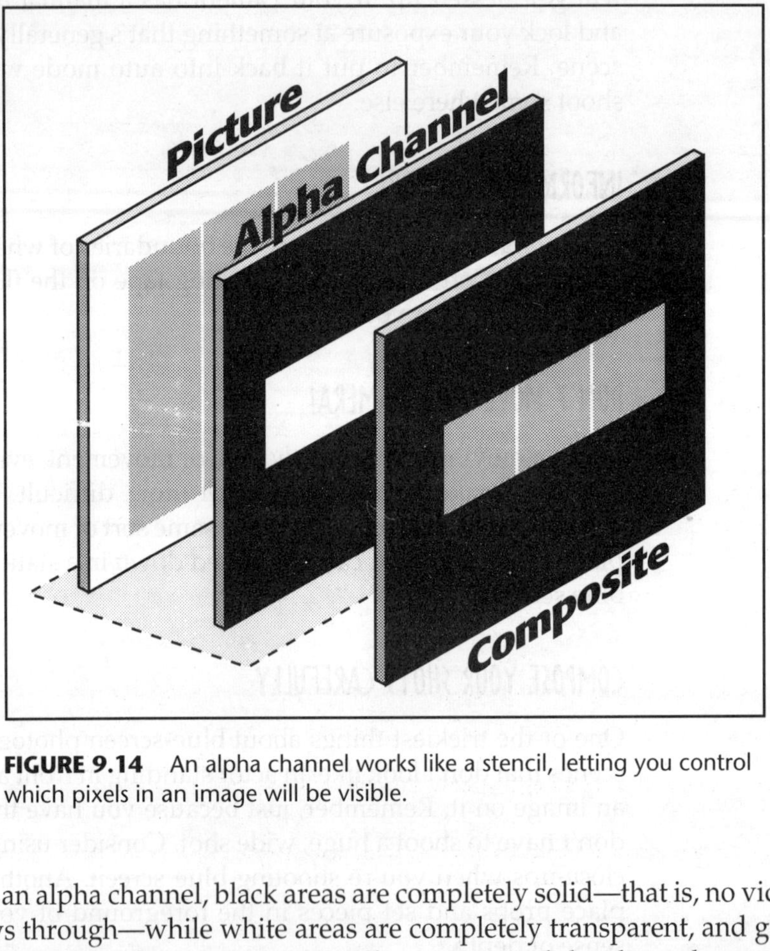

FIGURE 9.14 An alpha channel works like a stencil, letting you control which pixels in an image will be visible.

In an alpha channel, black areas are completely solid—that is, no video shows through—while white areas are completely transparent, and gray areas are somewhere in between. When creating alpha channel composites, your alpha channel can be a completely separate piece of video that you load into your project, or it can be stored inside the video that you're compositing.

Most 3D animation programs can automatically create an alpha channel when they render a final animation. Check your 3D program's documentation to learn more about how to create an alpha channel.

Most editing and effects programs will automatically recognize an alpha channel when you stack two pieces of video on top of each other. Some programs require you to activate the alpha channel using the same interface that you use to activate color keying.

Stacking Layers

Many editing programs let you simply stack layers of video on top of each other. Obviously, if one video clip fills the entire screen, you won't be able to see any clips that are lying below. However, any editing program that lets you stack video clips probably lets you change the size, or scaling, of any clip to reveal other layers below. You can also usually change or animate the position and scaling of a layer to create animated collages and composites.

In the *Consumer Electronics* video, I used layer stacking to put the sitcom and news programs onto the Consumer's TV screen. Actually shooting the TV with video playing on it was too difficult, because of reflections on the screen and the general hassle of trying to figure out what video needed to be playing during what shot.

Therefore, I took the video footage that I wanted to be showing the TV set, stacked it on top of my live plate in my editing program, scaled it down, positioned it over the TV set, and then lowered its opacity a bit to let some of the screen's normal texture and reflection show through (Figure 9.15).

You can also use layer stacking to create collages and composites like you might see at the beginning of a football game or in a music video.

ROTOSCOPING

Rotoscoping is the process of painting onto frames of film or video. Animators often use rotoscoping to create realistic motion. They'll shoot film footage of actors and then trace and paint over the frames to create a final animation with incredibly realistic motion. DV filmmakers use rotoscoping for everything from removing wires and rods, to creating mattes for compositing, to creating special effects such as laser blasts and explosions.

Rotoscoping can be very time-consuming, labor-intensive work but it's often the easiest—or only—way to achieve certain effects. If you're really serious about rotoscoping, you'll want to get some special

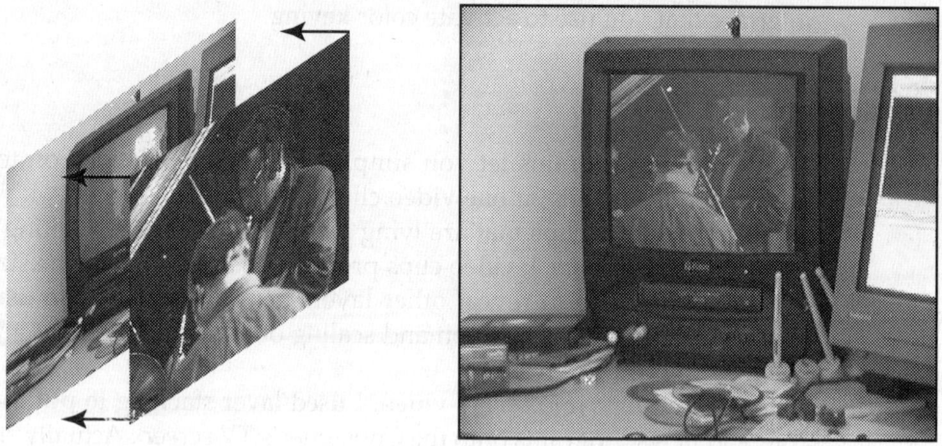

FIGURE 9.15 These two images were composited by simply stacking two layers on top of each other in an editing program. The upper layer was resized to fit on the TV screen, and then made slightly transparent to let some of the screen's reflections show through.

rotoscoping software. For many effects, though, you'll be able to get away with using your editing program and a simple paint program. In this section, you'll learn the basic steps that you need to follow to perform any type of rotoscoping.

Rotoscoping 101

Let's say you have a simple scene that needs some rotoscoping. For this example, we're going to use a scene from *Consumer Electronics*—the scene where the Consumer becomes rich.

When the Consumer hits the Rich button, the script describes his clothes changing, the Mona Lisa appearing on the wall behind him, and the walls turning a deep red color. To achieve the red walls, I decided to paint the walls behind the consumer using rotoscoping painting tools.

Fortunately, I had access to a program called Commotion, a professional rotoscoping tool that provides a lot of automatic rotoscoping features. If you're working on a small budget, you'll want a more affordable solution.

Whatever your rotoscoping task, here's the basic procedure that you'll need to follow:

1. **Choose a section of video.** As rotoscoping is very labor intensive, you don't want to do any more painting then you need to. Fortunately, most effects—laser blasts and so on—are very short, sometimes just a few frames. In your editing program, try to identify a very specific range of frames, so that you don't need to deal with any more video than necessary (Figure 9.16).

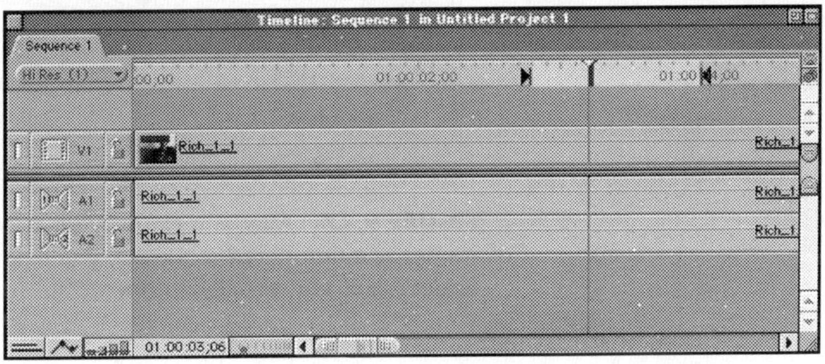

FIGURE 9.16 The rotoscoping process begins by identifying the range of frames you want to edit. Here, we've set in and out points around the frames that we want to edit.

2. **Export your footage.** Your goal is to export your footage in a format that can be read by a painting or image-editing program. Most mid-range and high-end image editors can export video as sequences of still image files. If your editor can't, you're not going to be able to rotoscope your footage using this technique. If you're using a program such as Premiere, you shouldn't have any problems.

Specify a starting and ending range that encompasses the frames you want to edit, and then export those frames as a sequence of still images. Most Mac editing programs can export PICT or TIFF stills, and most Windows programs can export BMP or TIFF files. You should end up with a series of files, one for each frame of video you exported, and all named and numbered sequentially (Figure 9.17).

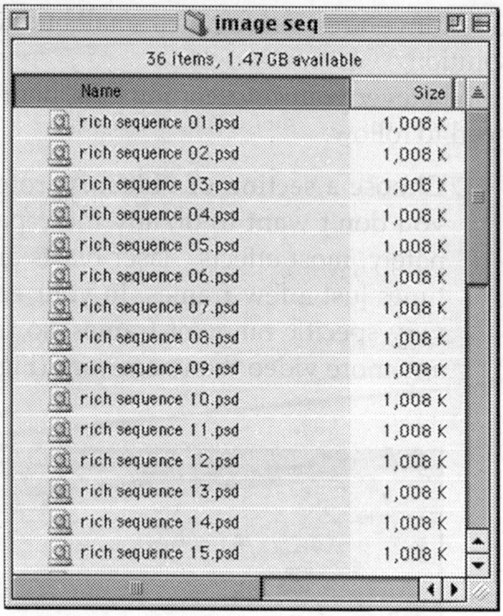

FIGURE 9.17 After you export your selected frames as a numbered sequence, you'll have a folder full of sequentially numbered still images.

3. **Edit your images.** Now, using a painting or image-editing program, open each file and do your rotoscoping. If you need to remove wires or rods, you'll want to use a clone or rubber-stamp tool to remove the offending wires and rods. For other effects, simply use the appropriate tool and start painting. As you finish modifying each frame, save it and move to the next document (Figure 9.18).
4. **Import your modified frames.** Now, import your modified frames back into your image editor. If your editor can export video as still frames, then it can probably import a sequence of numbered frames and treat them as a video clip. Check your manual for details.
5. **Splice your modified images back into your movie.** Now, replace the original section of your movie with your new, modified frames.

That's it, you're done.

In addition to adding new elements to a shot, you can use rotoscoping to correct problems such as drop-outs and static that might occur on frames of your movie. Just export the trouble areas and paint out the problems. Although rotoscoping gives you an incredible amount of power over your final footage, as with other effects, you shouldn't rely

FIGURE 9.18 You can open each image and paint on it to make the changes you want. Here, we begin painting on the wall with a semi-transparent brush.

on rotoscoping to solve all of your problems—it's just too labor intensive. Whenever possible, try to find a practical solution to your effects needs.

THE RIGHT TOOL FOR THE JOB: A QUICK GUIDE TO SPECIAL EFFECTS

Every special effects task is different, and each presents its own unique problems. In general, though, all effects work is built on the basic techniques listed previously. The following sections are a quick guide to how to create particular types of effects. Although these sections don't offer step-by-step solutions, they should give you an idea of how and where to start. As you progress, you can figure out the details on your own.

Laser Beams

If you're working on a science fiction epic and want to have plenty of ray guns and laser beams, then get ready for a lot of rotoscoping work. This is how the pros do it: they simply paint in laser blasts. Fortunately, laser beams travel quickly, so you'll only need to modify a few frames for each laser beam shot.

Storms and Lightning

Although you can always try to shoot a lightning storm, getting lightning to strike where and when you want it to is not easy. Fortunately, you can always add your own lightning bolts by painting them in by hand or by using special Lightning filters like the one included with Adobe After Effects (Figure 9.19).

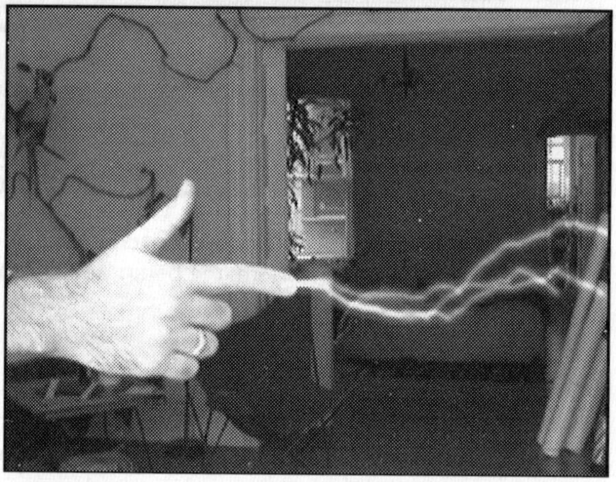

FIGURE 9.19 Using Adobe After Effects' Lightning filter, we quickly and easily added these animated lightning bolts.

For storm clouds and menacing skies, you'll want to find some stock footage of the right type of sky and then composite it in to your final shot. Companies such as ArtBeats (www.artbeats.com) sell high-quality movie footage of clouds, skies, and storms.

Explosions

Of course, the fun way to show something blowing up in a movie is to hire a demolitions expert and actually blow something up. This is expensive and very dangerous and is not recommended. Fortunately, there's an easier, safer way. Companies such as ArtBeats (www.artbeats.com)

sell stock footage of explosions that you can composite into your own videos. To make this work, you'll want to use a process called *luminance keying*, which is identical to the chroma key technique described previously, except that instead of keying out a particular color, luminance keying keys out a certain level of brightness. Therefore, if you have footage of an explosion on a black background, you can luminance key out the black to leave only the explosion (Figure 9.20, see next page). Check your editing program's manuals for more details.

Putting an Actor into a Computer-Generated Set

Often, the easiest way to show actors in an exotic location is to composite them into that location. See the *chroma key* explanation on page 204.

Putting Dinosaurs, Spaceships, or Other Objects into a Scene

If you want to add something to a scene—a prop, character, or set piece—your biggest job will be to create the footage of that object. For example, you might create photorealistic objects using a 3D animation and rendering program to make final shots that are very believable. In addition, you could create animated scenes to create a *Roger Rabbit*-like mix of real and fantasy. Either way, you're going to need to learn how to create computer-generated animation, or find someone who can do this work for you.

Once you've created your animated imagery, you'll most likely composite it into your scene using alpha channel compositing (see page 217).

SUMMARY

By now, you should be pretty comfortable with the concepts behind the most fundamental special effects procedures. Before you embark on any effects work, make sure you understand the following:

- **Practical effects.** When you should try to create your effects using real-world, practical techniques, and when you should try to create them digitally.
- **Filters.** What they're used for, and how you apply them.
- **Compositing.** What it's used for, and what types of compositing feature you can expect to find in an editing or effects program (keying, alpha channel compositing, layer stacking).

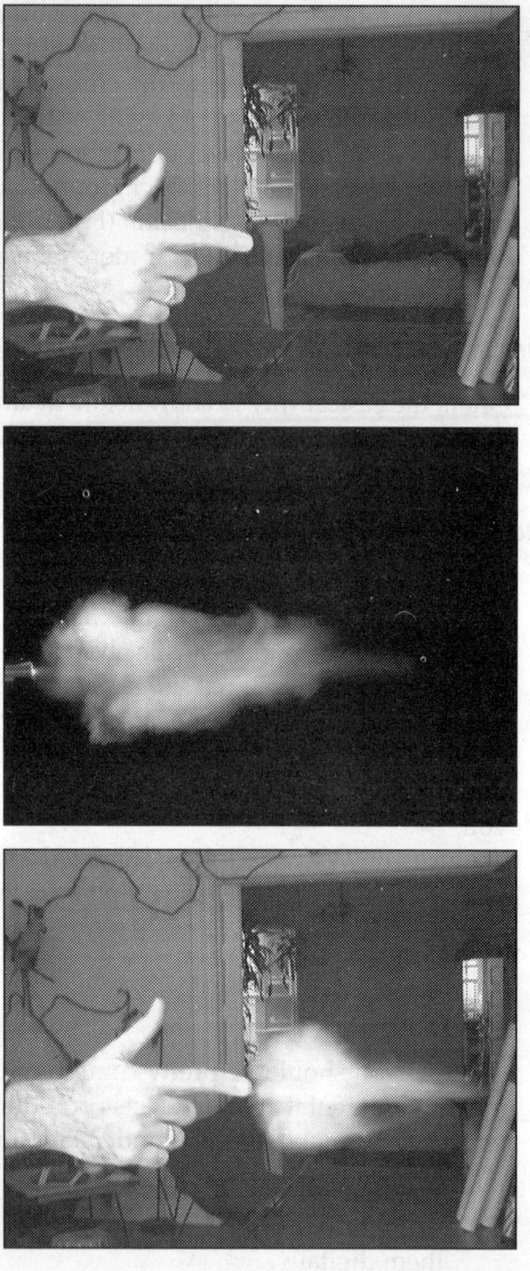

FIGURE 9.20 A luminance key works just like a chroma key, but instead of replacing a color, it replaces a certain level of brightness, or luminance. In this example, we used a luminance key to composite footage of the muzzle flash of a gun onto a shot of a hand. The luminance key was told to knock out the black, or the area of no luminance.

- **Rotoscoping.** What it is, and how you can do it using your current software.
- **The importance of planning your effects.** The pros spend months storyboarding and planning for their effects—you should, too.

Although we haven't talked about a lot of specific software packages, hopefully you now know what types of features to look for to achieve the effects you need.

CHAPTER

10

Output

IN THIS CHAPTER

- What to Do First
- Film School on a Disk
- Analog and Digital

Once your movie is edited, polished, and you've tacked on your end credits, you're ready for your big opening! You might not be able to swing a gala premiere at a fancy theater packed with limousines and reporters, but that's okay; there are still plenty of other ways to deliver your movie to your family and your friends. In this chapter, we look at all the ways you can output your movie for delivery via the Internet, CD, or videotape.

E-MAIL AND WEB DELIVERY

For short movies and scenes, you might want to consider e-mailing your finished product to your family and friends. Alternatively, if you want more people to be able to see your movie, you can put it on a Web page. Then, instead of having to send out lots of e-mails with big attachments, you can just send the Web page address. Finally, you can submit your movie to many Web-based film festivals and movie sites.

Before you can do any of these things, though, you have to get your movie into a form that's suitable for online delivery. As you already know, Web and e-mail access can be very slow, so you need to get your movie's file size as low as possible. For e-mail, you'll want your movie to come in around 2MB, as anything bigger might not fit through your mail server.

If you're going to post your video to a Web site, then it can be larger, but if you make too big a file, people with slow connections won't bother to download your movie. Obviously, this is less of a concern if you know your friends have fast connections.

Once you've identified your target file size, you're ready to try to shrink your movie. First, you need to pick a frame size. If you've been working with full-frame video, then your movie currently has a frame size of 720 × 540 pixels—*way* too big for Web delivery. If you used a capture device that grabs smaller video, then your movie might already be an appropriate frame size.

Unless you were using your camera's wide-screen option, then your video has an aspect ratio of 4:3 (see page 96 for more on aspect ratios). If you size your movie down to 320 × 240 pixels, you'll have an image that's one-quarter of its original size. Or, you can go all the way down to 160 × 120 for a movie that's really small.

Shrinking your movie's frame size will make your final file size much smaller, but to really get things ready for e-mail or the Web, you're going to want to compress your movie. DV footage is already compressed, but there are other compression schemes that work much better—that is, they make much smaller files—for Web delivery. Sorenson and MPEG compression are the best choices for e-mail or Web delivery. Your editing program should offer you a choice of compression options, including controls for image quality. Experiment with different settings to find the right balance between good image quality and small file size.

Compressing a Movie in iMovie for Web or E-Mail

Once you've finished editing in iMovie, you can export your movie for e-mail or the Web by simply choosing File>Export. iMovie provides special predefined export settings for creating small-frame, highly compressed movies. Just pick one of these, name your file, and iMovie will create your compressed movie (Figure 10.1).

Compressing a Movie in Pinnacle Studio

Pinnacle Studio lets you easily create Web-ready movies by simply clicking the Make Movie tab. Select the MPEG button, and then press the Set-

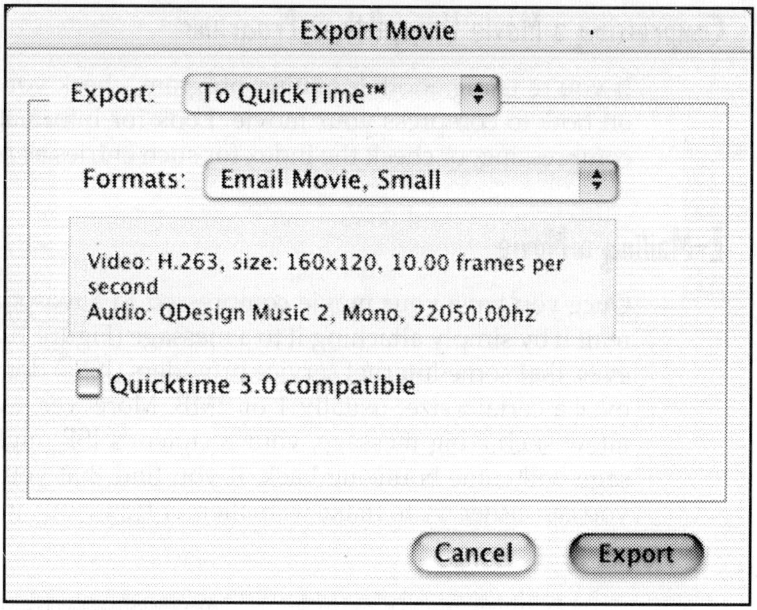

FIGURE 10.1 iMovie's Export command can automatically create small, compressed movies that are of an appropriate size for e-mail or Web posting.

tings button. From the Settings pop-up window, you can select low- or high-bandwidth Internet settings to automatically resize and compress your movie (Figure 10.2).

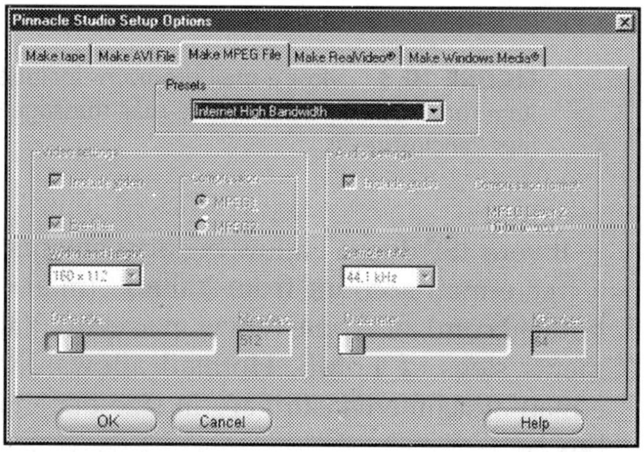

FIGURE 10.2 Pinnacle Studio provides predefined settings for compressing movies for Internet playback.

Compressing a Movie Using Other Programs

If you're using another editing program, check your manual for details on how to compress your movie. Look for information on exporting or compressing, or check the index for such entries as *MPEG* or *Sorenson*.

E-Mailing a Movie

Once you have your movie compressed to a reasonable size, you can e-mail it by simply attaching it to a message (Figure 10.3). Be warned, however, that some Internet service providers (ISPs) don't allow attachments over a certain size, usually 1 or 2MB. Moreover, even if your ISP does allow such a big message, your recipient's ISP might not, and the message will come bouncing back. If you find that you can't send a movie, you can either try to make it smaller, or figure out another way to send it.

FIGURE 10.3 Most e-mail programs include a special button or menu item for attaching a file to an e-mail message (some programs call these files "enclosures").

If your ISP doesn't allow big attachments, then you might want to get a free e-mail account from Yahoo!, (mail.yahoo.com) Hotmail (www.hotmail.com), or Apple (www.mac.com). Yahoo! currently allows attachments sizes of 1.5MB, Hotmail allows 1MB attachments, and Apple e-mail attachments can vary in size depending on how full your mailbox is.

If you can't get your movie to fit through your e-mail mailbox, you might want to consider posting it on the Web.

HINT

Sharing Movies through an iDisk

If you're a Mac user, you can also share movies through the free 20MB iDisk that Apple will give you. If you don't already have an iTools account, just go to www.mac.com and sign up. From the iDisk tab, you can mount your iDisk on your desktop, just as if it were another hard drive. It's actually stored on Apple's server and accessed via your Internet connection. Copy your movies to your Public folder. Any other Mac users can mount your Public folder on their desktop and copy your movies to their hard drive.

Putting a Movie on the Web

Although e-mailing videos is cool, putting videos on the Web is usually a far better way to distribute your videos online. When you put your video on the Web, you only have to upload it once (to your Web site). Then, you can e-mail the address to all your friends. They don't have to hassle with big e-mail downloads, and can view your movie when they're ready. In addition, if you build your page well and submit it to search engines, you might even develop an audience beyond your family and friends.

There are a number of ways to put your video on the Web, and which method is right for you depends largely on how experienced you are with creating Web sites. No matter how you intend to serve your movie, you'll need to go through the compression steps described previously to prepare your movie for posting. Once it's reduced to a nice small size, you can think about how to get it online.

USING A VIDEO-SHARING WEB SITE

The easiest way to get your movies online is to use a video-sharing Web site. These sites let you upload movies into albums. You can then mail the album address to your friends and they can view the videos online. Most sites give you a fixed amount of space—10 or 20MB—so you need to be sure you've done a good job in compressing your movies.

Once you have some movies to upload, take a look at these sites:

Pinnacle Studio On-Line. Pinnacle System's Studio On-Line site will give you a free account with 10MB of online storage. In addition to letting you create albums full of movies, Studio On-Line also lets you create online address books and online calendars (ideal for scheduling complicated video shoots!) (Figure 10.4).

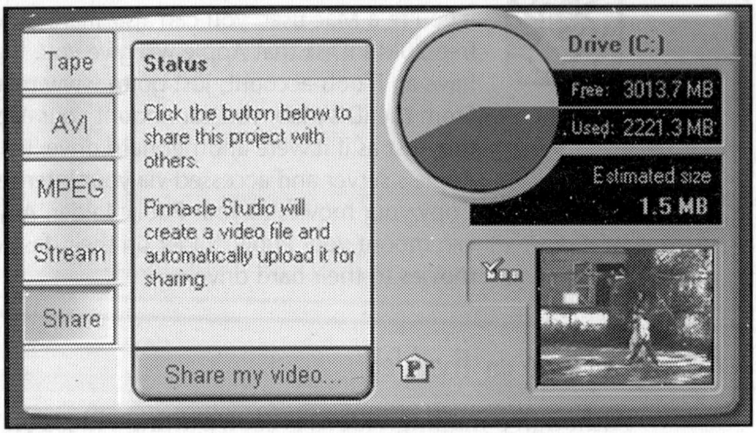

FIGURE 10.4 Pinnacle Studio can automatically upload your finished movies to Pinnacle's movie-sharing Web site, for sharing with your friends.

Apple iTools. The iTools section of Apple's Web site (www.apple.com/itools) provides a whole bunch of really cool features, including automatic Web page creation. As mentioned on page 233, you can sign up for a free Apple iDisk, 20MB of online storage, to which you can upload your movies.

Then, using the Home Page feature on the iTools Web site, you can automatically construct Web pages that include your movie (Figure 10.5). Apple provides a bunch of pre-built themes, or you can create your own. You can also include still images, MP3 files and, of course, text. If you've been wanting to build a Web page, iTools is definitely the easiest way to do it.

BUILDING A PAGE FROM SCRATCH

If you have some experience building Web sites, then you can build your own Web site from scratch. You will, of course, need a hosting service or Web server of your own. You can include your movie files (once they've been properly compressed) on your pages just as you would an image. If you're not sure how to do this, consult the documentation that came with your Web authoring software.

FIGURE 10.5 Apple's free iTools Web site provides everything you need to create your own cool-looking Web sites that feature videos, pictures, text, MP3 files, and more.

DELIVERING MOVIES ON VIDEOTAPE

All this digital stuff is cool, but the easiest way to deliver your movies is on plain old videotape. Videotape is great because it's cheap, almost everyone has a player, it doesn't require lots of fancy compression, and it can easily be watched on any size TV or even big projectors. On the downside, VHS video quality leaves a lot to be desired when compared to some digital formats, and you can only make copies in real-time.

If you want to deliver on video, your first choice is to pick a videotape format. If you shot using a DV camera, then you've probably printed your edited, finished video from your computer back out to DV tape to create a "master." If you want to make more DV copies, you can just stick more blank DV tapes into your camera and print to them from your computer.

If you have two DV cameras, you can attach them to each other using a FireWire cable and make digital dubs, or *clones*. Clones are great because they're exact duplicates of your original tape, with no loss in quality (Figure 10.6).

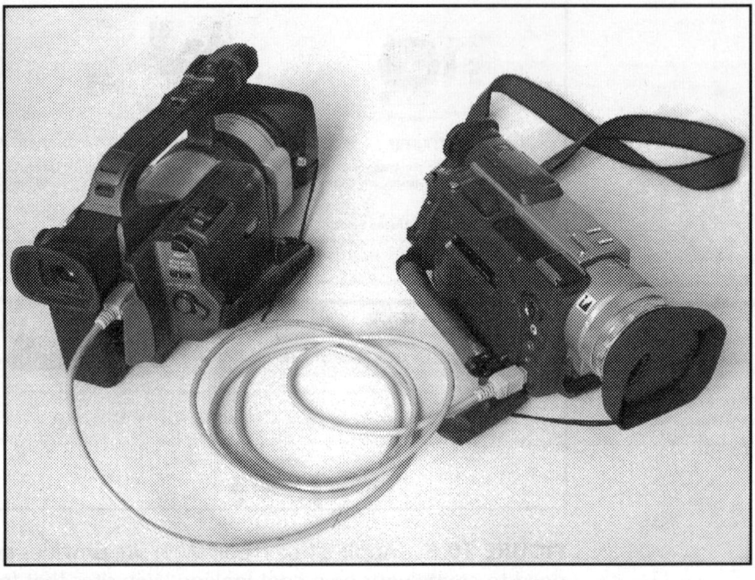

FIGURE 10.6 With a 4-pin to 4-pin FireWire cable, you can attach two cameras together to create perfect digital dubs, or *clones*.

The downside to making copies onto DV tape is that your friends will have to have a DV camera or deck to watch your movie. If they do, great—a cloned DV tape will be the best quality you can get. However, if they don't have a DV camera, you'll need to dub your footage to another format, usually VHS.

Attach your camera to your VHS deck by patching its audio and video outs (or S-video and audio out) to the audio and video in on the back of your VHS deck. Then, you can simply press Play on your camera, and record on your VHS deck to make a copy.

Be aware that the VHS copy will lose one *generation*. Colors will appear less saturated (and might even bleed and smear a little bit), and you might pick up some noise and static in the copy. If you copy this VHS tape again, you'll lose another generation and things will get even worse. Therefore, when making copies, you always want to use the best, earliest source that you can.

If you originally captured your video at a small size (320 × 240) using a Web-resolution capture device such as a Dazzle box, then you probably won't have much luck outputting to videotape. Some of these boxes can spit out a full-res image; others can't. Check your manual for details.

DELIVERING MOVIES ON CD-ROM

If you have a CD burner, you can put movies on CD-ROM. Since blank CDs are even cheaper than VHS tape, CD-ROM can be a very inexpensive way of distributing a bunch of copies of your movie. However, in most cases, you'll need to size your movie down, so distributing on CD doesn't always get you the nice, full-screen view that a VHS tape can provide. On the other hand, most computer monitors deliver much better color and image quality than a VHS tape does.

If you want to deliver on CD, you have a couple of options as to how to prepare your movie. First, just as with Web or e-mail delivery, you'll need to make your movie smaller. Since most computers can't handle full-size video, you'll need to shrink your frame size and compress your movie for smooth playback.

Again, Sorenson or MPEG compression are your best options. See the examples on page 230 for more about compressing your movie with these formats.

Once you have your movies resized and compressed, you can simply burn them to a disk just as you would with any other type of file. Be sure that your friends have the software (and computing power) that they need to play a movie file.

DELIVERING MOVIES ON DVD

DVD is probably your most expensive option, both in terms of DVD-burning hardware and blank media. However, nothing will deliver higher quality or a bigger "cool" factor than making your own DVDs. What's more, if you put your movie on DVD, it can be played in any DVD player—whether in a computer, or attached to a TV. Moreover, you can add cool things such as subtitles, chapter lists, and director's commentaries.

To make a DVD you'll need a very fast computer, a DVD burner, and DVD-authoring software. A burner alone will cost you somewhere between $600 and $1000. Check your DVD mastering software to find out what kind of computer you'll need for creating and mastering a disk.

If you're a Mac user, you're in luck, as there's no easier way to create a DVD than Apple's iDVD software, which is bundled with all Macs that ship with DVD drives. If you don't have a Mac, try to find a friend with a Mac equipped with a "SuperDrive" (this is what Apple calls their DVD burning drive).

Before you can put your video onto a DVD, it will have to be converted to MPEG-2 format, a procedure that is very processor-intensive and can take many hours. Your DVD mastering software should include instructions on how to perform this conversion.

Finally, you'll need blank DVDs. Again, your DVD burner's docs should explain exactly what type of media you need (there are two different kinds of DVD-Rs), and you should be able to find blank disks for about $10 each.

ONLINE FILM FESTIVALS

Finally, if you're particularly pleased with your movie, and you think it might appeal to more than just your friends and family, consider entering it in an online film festival. In a film festival, many people will get to see your movie. Be ready, though, because you'll also probably get some feedback—possibly good and bad. Hearing what other people think about your movie can be a great way to learn how to do a better job next time, but it can also be a difficult, humbling experience.

iFilm (www.ifilm.com) is the best-known, most popular online film festival. Their site includes detailed submission instructions, and they accept entries on videotape or electronically. Be sure to read their submission guidelines, and put your video into the proper size and format before you upload.

Other online film festivals include:

- **iFliks**—www.ifliks.com
- **Anarchy**—www.slamdance.com/anarchy/
- **FilmsOn**—www.filmson.com

SUMMARY

Hopefully, you now have a pretty clear idea of how to get your finished movie out of your computer and into the world. To sum up:

- Choose your delivery medium (online, videotape, CD).
- Resize your movie, and compress it as appropriate for your chosen medium.
- Transfer or dub your movie.

APPENDIX

A

Making It In Movie Making

One of the great things about digital video technology is that sophisticated movie-making tools are now available for very little money (well, "very little" compared to how much things used to cost). Therefore, you no longer need a huge movie studio to get a movie made. However, if your movie-making experiences have led you to believe that you might like to make movies for a living, then you might want to think about where to proceed from here.

Like many aspiring filmmakers, you might have fantasies about being a famous, big-name movie director, commanding high-powered stars and zillion-dollar budgets. Although such a job might (or might not) be an enviable one, it's very hard to achieve. Fortunately, there are many other career possibilities within the world of movie making. In this appendix, we'll look at a few of them, and discuss how to refine your career objectives.

WHAT DO YOU WANT TO BE?

It's a bit of a cliché to say that "movie making is always a collaborative effort," but hopefully your experience with this book has shown you that that cliché is very true. For example, in many of your projects, you'll probably find that, in addition to actors, you need extra people to help carry gear, set up lights, hold things, and so forth. Although having to find four or five people (in addition to your actors) might sound like a lot, it's nothing compared to what a big film crew requires.

Consider a 35mm film camera of the type that is used for most feature films. While one person can run a DV camera with no problem, a big film camera usually requires a mob of people, including:

- The director of photography, who decides (with the help of the director) how a scene will be lit and framed, and what camera moves will be performed.
- The camera operator, who actually runs the camera.
- The first assistant camera, who is responsible for loading the film camera, setting up the lenses and filters for each shot, and making sure the shot is in focus.
- The second assistant camera, who is responsible for keeping camera reports, slating each shot, and sometimes loading film.

Then there are the gaffers, best boys, and electricians who handle all of the electrical concerns for setting up lights and other equipment, as well as the grips who assist the gaffer and coordinate the placement of all of the electrical and lighting rigging. And that's just to run the camera!

The point is, you can't necessarily choose a career as a "movie maker"; you need to figure out what part of movie making you enjoy. You might already have some ideas based on your movie-making experience. For example, maybe you like shooting but can't stand editing. Or maybe you hate editing, but love creating special effects. Or maybe you've been having a predilection to building sets or making props. If so, you'll probably want to start focusing your practice and study in the area that interests you most.

However, just because you're more interested in one area of production doesn't mean you can ignore all of the other areas. To be good at *any* part of movie making, you need to be well versed in all movie-making technique, vocabulary, and practice. You'll make a better editor if you have some experience shooting, and you'll shoot more usable footage if you know something about the concerns of the editing room. Even if you're interested in costuming, prop building, or set design, you'll be well served by understanding the theoretical concerns of good story telling, as well as the technical concerns of what makes for a good picture.

If you want to be a director, you really need to know *everything*. Of course, you don't need to be as experienced or as capable as your individual crew members are. However, to make reasonable decisions about shots, edits, or effects, you need to know what shots, edits, or effects are reasonable. Directors also need to know a good amount about writing and acting so as to understand how to strengthen a story and how to get a good performance out of an actor.

So, as you begin to think of a particular movie-making career direction, you need to think about the specific area of movie making in which you're interested, while simultaneously trying to learn as much as you can about any part of the movie-making process. No one in the movie industry (or any industry, for that matter) ever feels like they've learned too much.

If you're not sure what it is you like about movie making, that's okay—maybe you like many different parts of it. Just keep making movies and see if you find your interest focusing. If not, you might want to try to study and practice many different disciplines.

If you haven't really thought about what it is about movie making that really interests you, then consider the following list of movie-related disciplines:

Cinematography. Cinematography is the art and science of shooting moving footage. Whether you're shooting video or film, cinematography obviously is very closely related to photography. As a cinematographer, you'll spend lots of time studying and considering lighting, exposure, film stock, camera techniques, composition, camera motion, and more. If you already have a background in photography or another visual art form, then you might find yourself drawn to the camera, and cinematography might be a good road for you to follow.

Editing. As discussed in Chapter 8, editing is almost an invisible art form. As an editor, your job is to manipulate the audience's perception of time and events by placing clips together in a particular order. Editing is a powerful cinematic tool, and a good editor can often fix everything from bad direction to bad acting. Editing can be a very solitary experience, and a good editor needs to be able to keep a lot of information in his or her head. If you enjoy "putting the pieces together" in a project, then editing is a good choice.

Special effects. Special effects work is largely a cross-disciplinary task, as you need to know a good deal about both cinematography and editing. As a special effects creator, you'll spend lots of time simulating or manipulating camera moves and performing simple edits, in addition to creating effects.

Special effects work is not always about building spaceships or animating dinosaurs. As you saw in Chapter 9, sometimes special effects can be used for nothing more than repainting the color of a wall. In fact, often times, the most interesting special effects jobs are the ones that require you to create something that looks completely normal—perhaps you need to add cars to an empty parking lot, or waving stalks of corn to an empty field. Every special effects job is unique. If you like creating images, solving problems, and you have a taste for maniacal detail, then special effects might be your calling.

Sound. Because it's so easy to focus on the picture in a movie, it's often possible to forget the importance of sound. In many instances, sound is *more* important than picture is. Very often, you'll see filmmakers intentionally degrade the quality of their images to create an effect or strike a tone, but *no one* ever degrades the quality of their audio. There are many different sound-related jobs in the movie industry. If you think that audio is your bag, then you'll want to think about whether you prefer recording audio, mixing and editing audio, creating audio effects, or maybe all of the above. Being a good sound recorder, engineer, or editor requires attentive ears, an understanding of the importance and use of audio in a movie, and many of the same skills that an editor needs.

Music. Although you might think that music would be included under *sound*, there are some differences. Perhaps you're already a musician and would like to apply that talent to movie making. As you might already have discovered from your movie-making experiences, music is often the element that ties a movie together and makes it seem complete. Oftentimes, directors will hire a composer to create a brand new, original score specifically for their movie. Other times, they'll hire a music supervisor to find existing, prerecorded music (usually called *source* music). Sometimes, a director will use a combination of source music and score. If you fancy yourself a composer, then it will be your job to watch and re-watch the movie, and to try to create music that underscores the action, helps create a mood, and drives the story. If you're a music supervisor, you'll try to find existing music that serves these same functions. Music supervisors are also often called upon to find music to be used as a "prop" within a scene. Perhaps a character is listening to the radio, for example. It's the music supervisor's job to choose the music that that character is listening to. It's also the music supervisor's job to obtain licenses for all of the music they choose.

Production designer. The production designer "designs" the look of the entire production. Think about movies that you've seen that have a very particular look and ambiance. *Blade Runner*, *Star Wars*, *The Royal Tennenbaums*, *Casablanca*, *The Wizard of Oz*, *The Godfather*, and so on and so on. The production designers for these movies worked with the directors (as well as the costumers, set designers, and prop masters) to create the "look" of props, costumes, sets—everything that appears on-screen. Production designers have to weigh many different elements when doing their job. They need to think about the colors that are appropriate to the mood and tone of the movie. They need to think about the styles that are appropriate to the era and venue of the movie, and they need to think of visual elements that reinforce the characters and storylines. If you already find that you have a knack for designing—designing anything—then you might be well suited to production design.

Props, costumes, sets. See "Production designer."

Directing. It's sometimes difficult to describe what, exactly, a director does, because it's other crew members who make many of the important decisions. For example, a good cinematographer will often know much more about getting a good shot, or have better ideas about how to shoot a particular scene or choreograph a particular camera move than will the director. Similarly, a good production designer will often be more responsible than the director for creating the "look" of a movie. So, what does the director do? Two things, really. First, it is the director who has the original "vision" of what the story is really about and how it should be told. Throughout the production, the director is usually the one person who has a clear view of how everything fits together, and whether each element is serving that original vision. Second, it is the director's task to get all of the individual performers and crew members to deliver the goods. In other words, it's the director's job to figure out how to get everyone involved in the movie to produce their best work, and to produce work that satisfies the original goal and vision. Sometimes, the director's work is something organizational ("go here, shoot that, edit this"), but at other times, it's inspirational. A director might have to work very hard to help an actor get to a particular emotional moment, or to help an editor understand what tone and pacing a particular scene is supposed to have. Directing is hard work that requires dedication and concentration.

Producing. In Hollywood, there are many different types of producers. There are executive producers and associate producers and just regular producers. Simply put: a producer puts the entire movie package together. It is their job to make sure that the project's writer, director, actors, and crew are all assembled, and that they can work together. Most importantly, it is the producer's job to find the money that will pay for everything. Being a producer involves everything from schmoozing people to getting potential crew members and actors interested in your project, to trying to find financing, loans, and financial support.

Of course, there are loads of other movie-related professions: title creators, animators, stunt people, accountants, electricians, choreographers, fight arrangers, armorers, construction workers, truck drivers, and on and on. Once you've picked some areas in which you think you're interested, it's time to start studying and practicing those disciplines by making more movies, going to film school, taking classes, reading books, watching movies, and so on. Once you feel confident in your abilities, there are a number of different places where you might be able to find work.

FINDING A MOVIE-MAKING JOB

Although you might have your sights set on producing big-budget movies, the reality is that such jobs are *very* hard to come by. Whether or not you want to work toward such a goal, in the meantime, you're going to have to pay your bills. Most film- and video-related jobs exist *outside* Hollywood and have little to do with the movie industry. They do, however, enable you to spend time in your chosen discipline.

When you think you're ready to start looking for work, there are a number of areas in which you can ply your trade. In the simplest terms, they break down into the following categories:

- **Industrial production.** *Lots* of people need films and videos for a lot of reasons besides entertaining. Corporations and businesses often need videos produced for training purposes, while schools and universities often need videos made for educational applications. Videos are used for marketing and sales, for trade shows, for presentations at meetings, and on and on. The term *industrial quality* usually denotes a level of video quality that is lower than what you expect to see on TV. However, with the advent of digital video, industrial quality is not nearly as low quality as it used to be. In fact, today's industrial quality is sometimes better than what used to be considered broadcast quality! Moreover, with the advent of the

Web, many people are satisfied with lower-quality Web delivery of their industrial videos. Your DV camera and editing setup are probably good enough for producing industrial-level work.

- **Commercial production.** "Commercial" film and video production is usually a step up from industrial production in terms of quality. Commercial productions include the production of everything from television commercials to music videos to television shows. Commercial jobs are often shot with film instead of video, and usually have substantially larger budgets than industrial productions do. A good, three-chip DV camera is suitable for many types of commercial work.
- **Feature production.** At the extreme end of the production continuum is movie production. Whether it's an independent film that you're trying to put together yourself, or a big-budget Hollywood film that you've landed a contract for, few productions are as competitive as full-length feature work. Of course, few productions have the potential to be as exotic, exciting, and lucrative.

If your ultimate goal is feature production, there's a good chance that you'll have to work your way up the production ladder, cutting your teeth on industrials until you can find some commercial work, and then trying to parlay that into a feature job.

So, how do you find industrial or commercial work? There are a couple of different approaches. You can apply to existing video production facilities or television stations—your phone book might list a few—or you can create your own production company and take a stab at being a freelancer.

Whatever tack you take for job-hunting, you'll need a demo reel to show off your work. Demo reels are typically short—three to five minutes—and are simply a "video portfolio" of your ability. Find some of your best work, edit it together, add some music if necessary, and you're on your way. Obviously, what "best work" means depends largely on the type of work you're looking for. If you're a cinematographer, you'll want to include examples of your camera work, while a writer will probably want to show scenes that he or she has written. Some people create a single reel to show off multiple talents.

Spec Work

Many aspiring commercial filmmakers will create projects "on spec" with the hope of landing a real job or account later. For example, filmmakers who are interested in making commercials will often shoot entire, polished commercials for real products without ever contacting the company that makes the product. The filmmaker pays for everything out of his or her own pocket, and hopes to use the resulting ad as an example of his or her ability to make commercials. Very rarely does the company end up buying the spot, but such productions can often lead to more work.

WHERE TO LEARN MORE

Of course, it's absolutely fine if you simply enjoy movie making as a hobby. You don't have to have any "career goals" to want to learn more and to continue to shoot your ideas. Whatever your goals, if you want to be a better movie maker, you need to keep learning. Practice is a good way to learn, but educated practice is even better. In addition to taking classes and working with other filmmakers, there are a number of other resources for learning about movie making.

There are many great books out there about movie making. Here are a few of them; all of them guaranteed to be fun, interesting reading whether or not you're interested in a movie-making career. Spend some time reading these books, and you'll know a lot more about what goes into good movie making.

On Writing

Story: Substance, Structure, Style, and the Principles of Screenwriting by Robert McKee. *Story* is an excellent book for any writer, and a fascinating look into what makes many great movies work. One of McKee's strengths is his lack of formula. In his telling, there's no one single trick to making a good script, so his theories apply well to any type of project.

Making a Good Script Great by Linda Segar. A great book with a lot of fine tips on polishing your script. Offers very good advice on how to hunt down and solve the problems that most screenwriters face.

Adventures in the Screen Trade: A Personal View of Hollywood and Screenwriting by William Goldman. A fascinating, funny book about personal Hollywood experience written by the writer of *Butch Cassidy and the Sundance Kid* and *The Princess Bride,* among others.

Monster: Living Off the Big Screen by John Gregory Dunne. A hilarious look at the writing of the Robert Redford movie *Up Close, and Personal.*

If you want a clear view of what can be involved in writing for Hollywood, this book is one of the best, and an entertaining read no matter what your interests.

Screenplays

One of the best ways to learn how to write good screenplays is to read good screenplays. Reading actual screenplays and shooting scripts is also a good way to learn what a screenplay should actually look like, and how to format tricky descriptions and situations. Fortunately, screenplays are easier to find than ever before. A number of Web sites provide electronic versions of screenplays. Check out homepage.mac.com/cyberrookies/screenplays.html.

The problem with online screenplays is that they're not necessarily paginated and formatted as a real screenplay would be. Fortunately, Newmarket has begun publishing shooting scripts for actual movies, and they have meticulously preserved all correct paginating and formatting. You can order copies at homepage.mac.com/cyberrookies/suggestedreading.html.

Finally, if you live somewhere with a good film and theatre bookstore, you might find that they have copies of actual studio scripts. These are the best types of scripts to find, as they are copies of the scripts that were actually used to shoot with. Check out homepage.mac.com/cyberrookies/screenplays.html for a list of bookstores that sell scripts.

On Editing

Digital Non-Linear Desktop Editing by Sonja Schenk. Provides detailed tutorials and extensive discussions of all aspects of editing. Because the book is not specific to any particular editing program, it's an ideal tutorial for any DV editor. Written by a professional editor who's worked on many TV and film projects.

On Producing

Wannabe: A Would-Be Player's Misadventures in Hollywood by Everett Weinberger. A funny account by a guy who simply decided that he'd go to Hollywood and make it as a producer. A good look at what the general Hollywood environment can be like for a newcomer.

On Filmmaking in General

The Battle of Brazil by Jack Mathews. A detailed account of the making of Terry Gilliam's *Brazil*, this book is both funny and infuriating and gives one of the clearest views of how producers, studios, and directors frequently battle for creative control of a project.

Final Cut: Art, Money, and Ego in the Making of Heaven's Gate, the Film That Sank United Artists by Stephen Bach. An incredible account of the making of Michael Cimino's *Heaven's Gate*, the movie that drove United Artists—then the oldest movie studio in existence—out of business. Written by the man who was a vice president of production at the time, *Final Cut* does a better job than just about any other book of showing the boardroom end of the movie business. Fascinating for anyone who goes to the movies.

Thinking in Pictures: The Making of the Movie Matewan by John Sayles. This book details not only the making of John Sayles' masterpiece *Matewan*, but also explains his entire approach to movie making. Getting to hear the perspective of one of the original "independent" filmmakers is great for anyone who wants to get started making movies.

Woody Allen on Location by Thierry De Navacelle. During the making of Woody Allen's *Radio Days* in 1986, the author was allowed to stay on the set and keep a diary of the progress of the entire production. Few books provide such a detailed, up-close view of the day-to-day process of feature filmmaking. What's more, this is as close as most of us will ever come to seeing up-close, the process of a filmmaker as gifted as Woody Allen. This book is out of print, but if you can find a copy, it's definitely worth reading.

You can order these books online, at homepage.mac.com/cyberrookies/suggestedreading.html.

APPENDIX

B

About the CD-ROM

The CD-ROM included with this book includes all of the footage and data that you need to complete the book's tutorials and activities. It also includes a lot of additional reading that will help you become a better movie maker. The CD-ROM is organized into the following folders, each of which is divided into subfolders, by chapter:

- **Activities**: In this folder, you'll find all of the support files for the book's activities, including QuickTime movies and further reading.
- **Tutorials**: The Tutorials folder contains all of the source material for the book's tutorials.
- **Filmschool**: This folder contains a number of essays that will teach you more about the history and theory of filmmaking in general. Many of these essays are designed to accompany movies that you can rent at your local video store or library.

- **Software**: This folder contains demo versions of Adobe *Premiere* for Macintosh and Windows. If you don't already have editing software, you can use Premiere for the book's tutorials.

All of the video on the CD-ROM is stored in QuickTime format. If you don't have QuickTime 5, you can get it on the Web at www.apple.com/QuickTime.

All of the essays are in PDF format. To read them, you'll need a copy of Adobe Acrobat Reader. If you don't already have it, it's available for download at www.adobe.com/acrobat.

System Requirements

A digital video camera with a FireWire interface; a video editing application such as *iMovie*, *Pinnacle Studio*, or *Adobe Premiere* (demo included), and the following minimum computer configurations:

Mac: 300MHz G3 or better; minimum 128MB of RAM; minimum 6GB hard drive; OS 9.1 or higher.

Windows: 300MHz Pentium II or better; minimum 128MB of RAM; minimum 6GB hard drive space; Windows 98 or newer; DirectX 6-compatible video card capable of displaying millions of colors; DirectX 6-compatible sound card; FireWire port, if you plan to attach a DV camera.

Glossary

Included here is a glossary of many video and film production terms that are discussed in this book, and many that are not. As you continue to learn about and research video production, you'll most likely run into these terms and concepts. Hopefully, these definitions will help you on your way.

accelerator cards—Custom hardware that can accelerate certain features, such as 3D rendering, rendering of plug-in filters, or display of complex video.

action safe—The area of your image that will most likely be visible on any video monitor. Essential action should be kept within the action-safe area, as action that falls outside this area might be lost due to *overscan*.

aliasing—The "jaggies," those stair-stepping patterns that occur on a diagonal or curved line on a computer or video display. Can be smoothed or corrected through *anti-aliasing* processes.

alpha channel—An 8-bit color channel (see *channels*) used to specify the transparency of each pixel in an image. An alpha channel works like a sophisticated stencil, and is the digital equivalent of a matte (see *matte*).

analog—Information represented electronically as a continuous, varying signal. (See also *digital*.)

anti-aliasing—The process of eliminating "jagged" edges on computer-generated text and graphics. Anti-aliased graphics have their edges slightly blurred and mixed with background colors to eliminate the jagged, stair-stepping patterns that can occur on diagonal or curved lines.

aperture—In any type of camera, light is focused by the lens, through an *aperture* and onto the focal plane. The size of the aperture controls how much light passes through to the focal plane. In addition to controlling the brightness of the exposure, the aperture controls the *depth of field* in the image. By balancing the size of the aperture (as measured in *f-stops*) with the *shutter speed*, you can trade off between varying depth of field and/or the ability to better resolve fast motion.

art director—The person in charge of the execution of the production designer's vision who manages set construction, set dressing, props, and scenic painting.

aspect ratio—The ratio of the width of the picture to the height. Aspect ratios can be expressed as ratios, such as 4:3, or as numbers, such as 1.33.

ATA—A type of hard drive interface. Not as fast as SCSI, but fast enough for DV.

audio compressor—A filter (or piece of hardware) that reduces the dynamic range of a sound to accommodate loud peaks.

audio mixer—A piece of hardware that takes several audio signals and mixes them together, allowing for the mixing of different sources. Mixers usually include some type of equalization control.

audio sampling rate—The number of samples per second that are used to digitize a particular sound. Most DV cameras can record at several audio sampling rates. Higher rates yield better results. Measured in kilohertz, 44.1 kHz is considered audio CD quality, and 48 kHz is considered DAT quality.

balanced audio—A type of microphone connector that provides extra power. Sometimes needed if you want to have microphone cable lengths of 25 feet or longer.

bandwidth—The amount of digital information that can be passed through a connection at a given time. High bandwidth is needed for high-quality images.

barn doors—A set of hinged, door-like flaps that attach to the front of a light and serve to control where the light falls.

bars and tone—A combination of *color bars* and *60 Hz audio reference tone*, usually recorded onto the head of each videotape. Used for calibrating video and audio levels.

bin—A film-editing term that refers to the place in which the shots for a scene are stored. In software editing systems, bins can also be referred to as folders, galleries, or libraries.

binary—A system for encoded digital information using two components, 0 and 1.

blue spill—A bluish light that is cast onto the back of a foreground subject because of a reflection from a blue screen.

blue screen—A special screen, usually comprised of blue cloth or backdrops painted with special blue paint that is placed behind a foreground element. Blue-screen shots are those shots that you intend to later composite with other elements using a chroma key function. Blue is used because most living animals have little naturally occurring blue colors.

BNC connector—A connector used to carry composite video, component video, timecode, and AES/EBU audio signals.

boom—A long (sometimes up to 100' long) pole with a microphone at the end. Technically, a boom is a large, sometimes hydraulically controlled device, as opposed to a *fishpole*, which is a smaller, handheld pole. Increasingly, the term *boom* is used to refer to any stick with a mic at the end.

bounce card—A piece of white material, such as foam core, used to create soft, indirect lighting.

broadcast colors—Your computer monitor can display many more colors than can NTSC video. Broadcast colors are those colors that are safe—that is, they will display properly—for use in broadcast video. Many programs, such as Adobe Photoshop and Adobe After Effects, include special filters that will convert the colors in an image to their nearest broadcast safe equivalent. (See also *NTSC legal*.)

broadcast quality—A somewhat vague term referring to the minimum quality considered acceptable for broadcast television. Until the 1980s, 3/4" Umatic tape was considered broadcast quality, and then Betacam SP was introduced and became the standard for broadcast quality. Today, Hi8 and MiniDV are often considered broadcast quality because the final master is usually Digital Betacam.

bumping up—The process of transferring a videotape from a lower-quality format to a higher-quality format; for example, bumping up MiniDV tapes to DVCPro.

byte—A unit of computer storage. How much 1 byte equates to depends on what you are storing. If you're just storing text, then a single byte can hold one character. For video or audio, what a byte holds depends on how your video is compressed and stored.

candelas—A measurement of the intensity of light.

capturing—The process of moving video data from a DV camera into a computer. Because the camera has already digitized the data, the computer does not have to perform any digitizing.

CCD—(See *charge-coupled device*.)

CDR—CD Recordable. A special type of compact disc that can be recorded by the end user using a special drive. Standard audio or data formats are supported by most recording programs, along with Video CD, a special format that can store 70 minutes of full-screen, full-motion MPEG1-compressed video.

CG—Character generator. A special machine for creating titles and other text characters for inclusion in a video. Most editing packages include CG features.

CGI—Computer generated imagery. Used to refer to any effect that is created digitally, be it a composite or a fully digital image such as a walking dinosaur. CGI is often used as a noun: "we'll fill that spot with some CGI of a duck."

channel—The color in an RGB image is divided into channels, one each for the red, green, and blue information in the image. When these channels are combined, a full-color image results. Certain effects are easier to achieve by manipulating individual color channels. Additional *alpha channels* can also be added for specifying transparency and selections. (See *alpha channel*.)

charge-coupled device (CCD)—A special type of chip that can convert light into electronic signals. A DV camera focuses light through a lens and onto a CCD, where it is converted into electronic signals that can be stored on tape.

chroma key—A special key function that will render a specific color in a layer transparent. For example, if you shoot someone in front of an evenly lit blue screen, you can use a chroma key function to render the blue completely transparent, thus revealing underlying video layers.

chroma—The part of the video signal that contains the color information.

chromatic aberration—Color shifts and color artifacts in an image caused by faults in a lens, or by the camera's inability to register all three channels of color information. Single-chip video cameras are especially prone to chromatic aberration.

chrominance—The *saturation* and *hue* of a video signal. Although slightly different in meaning, this term is often used interchangeably with the term *chroma* to refer to color.

cinematographer—(See *director of photography*.)

Cinepak—A QuickTime CODEC. Very *lossy*, but good for delivery mediums with low data rates such as CD-ROM or the Web.

close-up—A shot where the subject fills the majority of the frame. If the subject is a person, the shot will consist primarily of that person's head and shoulders.

CODEC—COmpressor/DECompressor. An algorithm for compressing and decompressing video and audio.

color bars—A test pattern used to check whether a video system is calibrated correctly. A waveform monitor and vectorscope are used, in conjunction with color bars, to check the brightness, hue, and saturation.

color depth—The number of colors that a given video system can display. The greater the number of bits per pixel that are used to store color, the higher the color depth.

color spectrum—The range of visible light that extends from violet to red.

color temperature—Light sources have different color temperatures, which are measured in degrees Kelvin. The color temperature of tungsten light is 3200°K, and the color temperature of daylight is about 5500°K.

color correction—A post-production process to correct the overall color of a videotape master in order to get the best quality image, with an emphasis on enhancing skin tones.

composite video—A video signal that contains all the luminance, chroma, and timing (or sync) information in one composite signal.

compositing—The process of layering media elements on top of one another to create collages or special effects.

condensor—A type of mic that records sounds through a "capacitance" mechanism. Condensor mics require a power supply (usually in the form of a small battery). Because of the nature of their pickup mechanism, condensor mics can be very small.

continuity—During a shoot, the process of keeping track of dialogue changes, actors' positions, wardrobe, and props so that the footage from shot to shot, and day to day, will cut together. Usually, the person in charge of continuity makes notes on a copy of the script and takes Polaroids of the set.

co-processors—Extra processors that are used to speed up a computer, or to perform special functions. (See *accelerator cards*.)

coverage—Shooting all of the footage that will be needed to properly *cover* an event or scene.

CPU—Central processing unit. The box that contains the motherboard, peripheral cards, and some storage drives. Also used to refer to the main processing chip that the system uses.

cross-platform—Programs or hardware that come in different versions for different platforms. Ideally, the program's interface and features are identical from one platform to the next.

CRT monitor—The monitor attached to your computer. Short for *cathode ray tube*.

cut-away—A shot of something other than the main action or dialogue in a scene that is used to build the story and smooth rough edits.

D.P.—(See *director of photography.*)

data rate—The amount of data that a particular connection can sustain over time. Usually measured in bytes per second.

daylight—Daylight is the combination of sunlight and skylight.

decibel—The standard unit for measuring sound. A subjective scale where one unit equals one increment of "loudness."

degauss—To completely erase all the information on a magnetic video or audio tape, using a demagnetizing device.

depth of field—A measure of how much, and at what depth, of the image is in focus.

destination monitor—The monitor or window that displays an edited sequence as it plays, as opposed to the source monitor, which plays unedited source footage. Also called the *record monitor*.

destructive editing—Any form of editing (either video or audio) that physically alters your original source material.

device control—The ability of a piece of hardware, such as an edit controller or a CPU, to control a peripheral device, such as a VTR, via a remote control cable.

diffuse light—Light from a soft, undirected source, such as an typical household bulb.

diffusion gel—A semitransparent piece of white plastic used to make a light softer.

digital—Information recorded electronically as a series of discrete pulses, or *samples,* usually using a *binary* system.

digital zoom—A "fake" zoom that creates a zooming effect by enlarging the image on-the-fly. Unfortunately, when enlarging, the image is severely degraded.

digitizing—The process of taking analog video information from a camera or deck and turning it into digital information that can be used by a computer.

diopter—An adjustment on the eyepiece of a camera that allows you to correct the focus of the eyepiece to match your vision.

director of photography—The film lighting and camera specialist responsible for the look of the photography and in charge of the camera and lighting crews.

dissolve—A transition in which the first shot is partially or completely replaced by gradually superimposing the next shot.

distressing—A process of making objects on a set look aged or weathered.

drag-and-drop editing—A two-step editing method in which the user selects a shot, and drags it from one position and drops it in another position; for example, from a bin to the timeline, or from one position in the timeline to another.

drop-outs—A weak portion of the video signal that results in a problem in playback. *Hits* are small drop-outs that are only one or two horizontal lines in size. *Glitches* are larger, where 5 percent or more of the image drops out. Large analog drop-outs can result in a few rolling video frames, and large digital drop-outs can result in random "holes" across the screen.

dub—A copy of a videotape, also known as a *dupe*.

DVD—Digital video disc (sometimes called "digital versatile disc"). An optical storage medium that is the same physical size as a compact disc. There are several different DVD standards and formats, including DVD-RAM (a rewritable format), DVD-ROM (a read-only format), and DVD-video (the format that is used for video releases).

dynamic—A mic that derives its power from the pressure of the sound that is being recorded. Handheld mics are usually dynamic.

edit controller—A piece of hardware used in linear editing systems to control and synchronize multiple video decks.

edit decision list—A list of all the edits in a project, identified by a chronological *event* number, source name, source in-point, source out-point, master in-point, and master-out point.

EDL—(See *edit decision list*.)

EIDE—A type of hard drive interface. Not as fast as SCSI, but fast enough for DV.

EIS—(See *electronic image stabilization*.)

EISA slots—A type of expansion slot used in Windows-based computers.

electret condensor—A cheaper, lower-quality version of the condensor mechanism.

electronic image stabilization—Special circuitry in a camera that attempts to compensate for shaking and vibrating by electronically shifting the image to compensate for camera movement. Electronic image stabilization frequently results in a slightly blurred image.

electronic zoom—Electronic controls that are used to zoom the lens in and out. These are the only zoom controls found on most prosumer camcorders.

EQ—(See *equalization*.)

equalization—The process of adjusting the volume of individual *frequency* ranges within a sound. Equalization can be used to correct problems in a sound, or to "sweeten" or enhance the sound to bring out particular qualities.

Ethernet—A standard networking protocol for connecting computers together through one of several types of networking cable.

exposure—The process of allowing light to enter the camera, exposing the film or video stock to light, which results in a recorded image.

fade out—A dissolve from full video to black video, or from audio to silence.

field dominance—Hardware and software that play the field of video containing the odd-numbered scan lines first are known as *field one dominant*. Those that play the field of video containing the even-numbered scan lines first are known as *field two dominant*. Field one dominance is the norm.

fields—Each frame of interlaced video consists of two fields: one field contains the odd-numbered scan lines, and the other contains the even-numbered scan lines. In NTSC video, each field has 262.5 horizontal lines.

film grain—Images are recorded on film by exposing the film's light-sensitive emulsion. Comprised of chemical particles, the film's emulsion has a visible grain when projected. Many video producers try to mimic this grainy look to produce an image that looks more film-like.

filters—Special glass attachments that can be added to a camera lens to change the optical properties of the lens. Or, special pieces of software that can be added to a host application to perform special image processing functions.

FireWire—Apple Computer's name for the IEEE-1394 specification.

fluid head tripod—A special type of tripod head that is filled with hydraulic fluid that smoothes the motion of the camera head.

focal length—The size of the angle of view of the lens, measured in millimeters. The smaller the number, the wider the lens. Zoom lenses have a range of focal lengths.

focal plane—The area in a camera onto which light is focused. In a film camera, the film rests on the focal plane; in a digital video camera, the CCD rests on the focal plane.

focus ring—A rotatable ring on the lens of a camera that allows for manual focusing. Ideally, you want a focus ring with distance markings so that you can perform more complicated manual focus effects such as *pulling* or *racking* focus.

Foley—The process of creating and recording ambient sound effects in real time while watching the attendant video or film. Foley work is usually performed on a Foley stage equipped with special surfaces and props. Named for Jack Foley, the originator of the technique.

fps—Fps, or frames per second, is used to describe the speed at which film and video play. Film plays at 24fps, PAL video at 25fps, and NTSC video at 29.97 fps.

fragmentation—When a hard drive has had many files deleted and replaced, it can become fragmented, which can slow its performance. At this point, it might need to be defragmented, or optimized.

frame—One complete film or video picture, each frame of video contains two fields. Moving images need at least 18 frames per second to appear as full-motion, and 24fps to allow for sync sound. NTSC video plays at 29.97fps, and PAL video plays at 25fps.

frame rate—When speaking of video or film recording, the number of frames per second that are recorded (and then played back).

frequency—An audio signal is made up of different frequencies, or wavelengths, which yield the high (or treble), mid, and low (or bass) tones. The human voice resides mostly in the mid-tones.

Fresnel lens—A lens attached to a light that allows for focusing of the beam of light.

f-stop—A measure of the size of a camera's aperture. The higher the f-stop, the smaller the aperture.

gain—The strength (or amplitude) of an audio or video signal.

garbage matte—A special matte used to knock out extraneous objects in a compositing shot. Garbage mattes are usually applied to a blue-screen shot before chroma keying. They can be used to eliminate props, mic booms, and other objects that can't be eliminated through keying.

gate—A special type of audio filter that only allows a specific range of frequencies to pass.

gel frame—A metal frame that holds lighting gels in front of the light.

globes—The professional term for light bulb.

green spill—The same as blue spill, except that it occurs with a green screen as a backdrop, rather than a blue screen.

green screen—Same as blue screen, but used for those occasions when you need to have blue elements in your foreground.

handheld—The typical handheld mic used by rock stars, comedians, and wandering talk show hosts. Usually an omnidirectional, dynamic microphone.

handles—Extra footage at the head and tail of each shot to allow the editor room to add dissolves and manipulate the pacing of a scene.

hard cut—An edit from one shot to another without any sort of transition in between, such as a dissolve.

hard light—Light from a direct, focused light source.

HDTV—High-definition television, a subgroup of the new DTV digital television broadcast standard that has a 16:9 aspect ratio; a resolution of either 1280 × 720 or 1920 × 1080; a frame rate of 23.96, 24, 29.97, 30, 59.95, or 60fps; and either interlaced or progressive scanning.

HMI lights—High-powered arc lights used to simulate daylight. The lights at a baseball stadium are HMI lights.

hot-swapping—Replacing a peripheral without shutting off the computer's power. Note: not all peripherals are hot-swappable!

HSB—Just as colors can be defined by specifying RGB (red, green, and blue) values, colors can also be defined by specifying hue, saturation, and brightness. Many color pickers allow you to switch to an HSB mode. For some operations, selecting a color is easier in one mode than in another.

hue—The shade of a color.

IDE drives—Hard drives that adhere to the IDE interface specification.

IE1394—(See *FireWire.*)

IEEE-1394—A high-speed serial interface that can be used to attach DV cameras, storage devices, printers, or networks to a computer.

iLink—Sony's name for the IEEE-1394 specification.

illumination—The amount of light cast on a subject.

inbetweening—The process of calculation (or interpolation) that is required to generate all of the frames between two *keyframes* in an animation.

incident light—Light coming from a direct source, such as the sun, a light, etc.

in-point—The starting point of an edit.

insert mode—In most NLEs, a method of editing in the timeline that allows the placement of a shot between two shots without covering up what's already there. Instead, the second shot (and all the shots following it) move down to accommodate the new shot. (See also *overwrite mode.*)

intensity (of light)—The strength of a light source, measured in candelas.

interface—The controls and windows that you use to operate a program.

interleaving—The process of alternating data across multiple discs, as in an array.

iris—Synonymous with aperture. The iris is the physical mechanism that can be opened or closed to change the size of the aperture. "Irising down," for example, means to close down the iris (go to a higher f-stop).

IRQ—Special addressing information used by peripherals attached to a Windows-based computer. Each peripheral must have its own IRQ.

ISA slots—A type of expansion slot used in Windows-based computers.

ISO-9660—A format for writing CD-ROMs. Can be read by either Mac or Windows-based computers.

JKL—A way of editing using the J, K, and L keys on computer keyboard specifically programmed to allow for fast shuttling through clips in an NLE.

Kelvin scale—A temperature scale used by scientists, similar to Celsius. Light temperature is usually measured in degrees Kelvin (°K).

key effect—Different types of "keys" can be used to remove the background from a video clip to expose underlying video. (See *chroma key* and *luminance key*.)

keyframe interval—When compressing video, the frequency at which a keyframe will occur.

keyframe—When animating, you will explicitly define the parameters of an animated element by creating a keyframe. The computer will automatically calculate the changes that occur between keyframes. (See *inbetweening*.)

LANC (or Control-L)—A device control protocol most commonly found on consumer equipment and incapable of frame accuracy. (See also *RS-422* and *RS-232*.)

latitude—The size of the grayscale ranging from darkest black to brightest white. The human eye sees more latitude than can be recorded on film or video.

lavalier—A small, clip-on mic. Usually an omnidirectional, condensor microphone.

LCD—Liquid crystal display. The type of display used as a viewfinder on most cameras. In terms of cameras, LCD usually refers to a small, flip-out screen, as opposed to the optical viewfinder.

lens—Usually a series of separate glass lenses, the lens on a camera is what focuses light onto the *focal plane* to create an image.

letterboxing —The process of putting black bars at the top and bottom of the screen to change a 4:3 aspect ratio image to a wider aspect ratio image.

light kit —A set of professional lights, light stands, and lighting accessories, usually contained in a heavy-duty carrying case.

light meter—A small, handheld device used to record the illumination at a particular location, usually measured in footcandles or lux, which can then be translated to f-stops.

lighting gel—Translucent pieces of special colored plastic used to change the brightness and color of a light source.

linear editing—Editing using linear media (e.g., tape to tape), as opposed to using random access media stored on a computer hard drive. All tape is linear, so linear media can be either digital or analog.

locking picture—The process of formally finalizing the editing of a film for story, so that the sound editors can start working without have to deal with any changes in timing.

logging—The process of recording the contents of each field tape using timecode, shot names, and descriptions. The first step in the editing process.

long shot—A shot that plays out over a long period of time.

looping—The process of re-recording dialog in a studio. Called "looping" because the actor sometimes watches a continuous loop of the scene that is being re-recorded. Also known as ADR, for automatic dialogue replacement.

lossless—Used to denote a form of compression that does not degrade the quality of the image being compressed.

lossy—Used to denote a form of compression that degrades the quality of the image being compressed.

luma key—(See *luminance key*.)

luminance key—A special key function that will use the luminance values in a layer to determine the transparency of that layer. For example, a luminance key could be set to render the darkest areas of the layer transparent.

luminance—The strength (or amplitude) of the *grayscale* (or brightness) portion of a video signal.

lux—A measurement for the amount of illumination on a subject, using the metric scale. (See also *footcandles*.)

master shot—A wide shot that contains all the action in particular scene. Used as the basis for building the scene.

M-JPEG—(See *MJPEG*.)

MJPEG—A lossy, high-quality CODEC that can deliver full-motion, full-frame video. Almost always requires special compression hardware.

montage—In editing, the process of juxtaposing two shots against each other to arrive at an effect different from what each shot would imply on its own.

motherboard—The main circuit board inside a computer.

motion blur—When an object moves quickly, it will be look blurrier. Individual frames of video or film should show a certain amount of blur around moving objects. Motion blur is usually the result of average shutter speeds (1/60th to 1/125th of a second). Faster shutter speeds will result in less motion blur; slower shutter speeds will result in more. A lack of motion blur will result in stuttery, stroboscopic motion.

MPEG—A lossy, high-quality CODEC. Comes in several flavors: MPEG1 is used for the VCD format, and MPEG2 is used for DVD format video. Both flavors are suitable for distribution of full-motion, full-frame video.

ND—(See *neutral density*.)

negative cutter—The person who physically cuts the film negative to conform to the final cut.

neon light—A light consisting of a glass tube filled with neon gas, which varies in color.

Kino-flo tubes—Color-corrected fluorescent light tubes used to replace normal fluorescent light tubes when shooting at a location that will have fluorescent lights visible in the shot.

net—A large screen used to decrease the strength of the light falling on the subject, usually used for exterior shoots.

neutral density—A lens filter or lighting gel that tones down brightness without changing the color temperature.

NLE—(See *non-linear editing system*.)

non-destructive editing—Any form of editing (either video or audio) that leaves your original source material unaltered.

non-linear editing system—A digital editing system that uses a software interface and digitized audio and video stored on a hard drive, which allows for random access, non-linearity, and non-destructive editing.

notch—A special type of audio filter that can eliminate a specific, defined frequency of sound.

NTSC—Acronym for National Television Standards Committee, NTSC is the broadcast video standard for North America and Japan, with a frame rate of 29.97 fps and 525 horizontal scan lines.

NTSC legal—Refers to colors that fit within the NTSC guidelines for broadcast television. A vectorscope is used to determine if an image is within the NTSC legal color boundaries.

NTSC monitor—(See *NTSC/PAL monitor*.)

NTSC/PAL monitor—The monitor attached to your camera, video deck, or NTSC outputs of your video digitizing system. Used to display the video you are editing.

omnidirectional—A mic that picks up sounds from all directions.

off-line clip—An off-line clip is one that has been logged but does not have any audio or video media attached to it, whether because it hasn't been captured yet, or because the media has been deleted.

off-line editing—Off-line editing means working in a draft mode with the intention to eventually take the project to a better resolution, and possibly better videotape format, in order to do a final pass that will improve its look, quality, and polish.

OIS—(See *optical image stabilization*.)

one-light print—A one-light print is a film print created from the film negative that uses a single, constant, optimized light setting (i.e., one light) for the red, green, and blue lights used to create the print.

onion-skinning—Some animation programs can display semi-opaque overlays of previous frames. These "onion-skin" frames can be used as a reference for drawing or retouching the current frame.

on-line editing—Creation of the final master videotape, whatever the means or format involved, usually conformed from the original production footage using an EDL.

operating system—The low-level program that controls the communication between all of the subsystems (storage, memory, video, peripherals, etc.) in your computer.

optical image stabilization—A special optical apparatus in a camera that attempts to compensate for shaking and vibrating by altering the camera's optical properties on-the-fly to compensate for camera movement. Because OIS doesn't alter your image data, there is no image degradation.

optical viewfinder—The eyepiece on a camera that you look through to frame your shot, as opposed to the flip-out LCD viewfinder present on some cameras.

opticals—Special effects that are traditionally added by an "optical" department. Usually, these are effects that are added through a separate optical printing pass. Lightning bolts, light flares, glows, and halos are all traditional optical effects that can now be performed through rotoscoping, or with the application of custom filters.

out-point—The end point of an edit.

overexposure—Refers to video or film that was shot with too much light or at the wrong camera settings, resulting in a whitish, washed-out, faded-looking image.

overlapping edit—An edit where the picture ends before or after the sound ends. Also called an *L-cut* or a *split-edit*.

overscan—All video formats scan more image than they need, to compensate for the fact that not all monitors and televisions display images at exactly the same size. To keep your action and titles within the visible area, you'll want to pay attention to the *action* and *title safe* areas of the screen.

overwrite mode—In most NLEs, a method of editing that allows the placement of a shot in the timeline that covers up anything that was previously occupying that space. (See also *insert mode.*)

PAL—Acronym for Phase Alternate by Line, a television standard used in most of Europe and Asia, with a frame rate of 25fps and 625 horizontal scan lines, resulting in somewhat higher-quality video than NTSC.

PAL monitor—(See *NTSC/PAL monitor.*)

pan—To rotate the camera left and right around the camera's vertical axis.

parabolic—A special type of mic that can be used to record sounds from great distances.

partitions—Logical divisions in a hard drive that make the drive appear to be more than a single drive.

patch bay—A rack of video and audio input and output connectors that makes it easier to reconfigure the hardware in an editing system.

pedestal—To raise the camera up or down.

phono connector—A medium-sized single prong connector used primarily for analog audio, especially headphones. Also known as *1/4" connector.*

pistol-grip tripod—A tripod with a head that is controlled by a single pistol-grip mechanism. Such heads can be freely rotated around all axes simultaneously, making it very difficult to perform a smooth motion along a single axis.

pixel—Short for *pic*ture *el*ement.—A single point on your screen.

platform—The computer hardware/OS combination on which you have chosen to work.

plug-ins—Special effects and add-ons that can be added to a host application. (See *filters.*)

polarizer—A lens filter that polarizes the light coming into the lens. Can be used to increase saturation and to eliminate reflections in glass or water.

practical light—A light source that is both part of the scenery and a source of light for the camera.

preroll—The process of rewinding the videotape to a cue point several seconds before the in-point so that playback of the tape is stabilized and up to full speed when the tape reaches the in-point.

prime lens—A lens with fixed focal length.

production designer—The designer who is responsible for the look of the entire production. They will supervise the set decorators, costumes, and other visual artists.

progressive scan—A type of video display where each horizontal line is scanned consecutively from top to bottom, resulting in a full frame of video without the need for *fields*.

prop—Short for property, a prop is any object on the set that is used by the actors, such as a knife, as opposed to set dressing and scenery, which provide a backdrop for the action.

proxy—A placeholder. Usually used in editing programs to take the place of video that has yet to be shot, or has yet to be digitized at the highest quality.

pull focus—Pull (or pulling) focus is a technique used to change focal lengths during a large camera or subject move, such as a dolly. The camera assistant literally moves the lens to compensate for the camera/subject movement so that the subject remains in focus throughout the shot.

QuickTime—A software architecture for displaying and manipulating time-based data (such as video and audio) on a computer.

rack focus—A shot where the focus is set on an object in the background, and then the focus is pulled, or racked, to an object in the foreground (or vice versa). Exemplified by a shot of a billiard ball, and then a rack focus to reveal the person holding the cue stick.

radio cut—An edit of a scene based on dialogue only, disregarding whether the picture works or not, the idea being that the result should play like an old-fashioned radio show.

RAM—Random access memory. The electronic memory inside your computer that is used to hold programs and data when working.

RCA connector—A small, single-prong connector most commonly used to carry composite video and unbalanced audio signals.

reaction—A shot of a person in a scene as he or she reacts to the dialogue or action of the scene.

real media—A special streaming video and audio architecture created by Real, Inc.

realtime—A function, such as playback or recording, that occurs immediately and in real time, without the need for rendering and without any speeding up of the process, such as 4x (quadruple speed) recording.

real-time editing—Editing that can happen in real time. That is, effects and edits do not have to be calculated or rendered before they can be seen.

reflective light—Light coming from an indirect source, such as a bounce card, the sky (but not the sun), etc. (See also *incident light*.)

reflector—A shiny board or fabric used to redirect a bright light source, such as the sun.

RGB color space—The range of colors that can be displayed and recorded by your computer.

room tone—The sound of the room in which a scene was recorded. During a shoot, the sound recorder will record roughly a minute's worth of the quieted location to create an "empty" sound with the right atmosphere. This sound will be used by the sound editor to correct audio problems.

rotoscoping—The process of painting over existing frames of video or film. In DV production, rotoscoping is used for everything from painting in special effects, to painting custom-made mattes for compositing.

rough cut—An early edit of a project, as opposed to the final cut.

router—An electronic patching system for audio and video equipment.

RS-232—A serial device control protocol that allows for computers to control video decks and other hardware. RS-232 is most commonly used for low-end professional and consumer equipment.

RS-422—A serial device control protocol that allows for computers to control video decks and other hardware. RS-422 is the standard for professional equipment, uses SMPTE timecode, and is capable of frame accuracy.

SAG—Acronym for the Screen Actors' Guild.

saturated colors—The technical term for bright, bold colors is *saturated.* For example, a true red is saturated, while pink and maroon are *desaturated* reds.

saturation—The amount of color in the video signal.

screen correction shot—A shot of a blue-screen or green-screen stage that has no actors in it and is used by compositing software to help create the matte.

scrim—A lighting accessory used to tone down the brightness of a light. Single scrim dim the light by 1/2 f-stop, and double scrims dim the light by a full f-stop. Half scrims are a half-moon shape, to allow for further manipulation of the light.

SCSI IDs—When using SCSI devices, each device on the SCSI chain must have its own, unique SCSI ID. A SCSI port can support up to seven devices.

SCSI—Small Computer Systems Interface. An interface standard for connecting hard drives and other peripherals. Comes in many different flavors, including SCSI-2, Ultra-SCSI, and Ultrawide-SCSI.

seamless edit—A style of editing where the edits appear natural and do not call attention to themselves. A traditional Hollywood movie dialogue scene is usually seamlessly edited.

SECAM—Acronym for *Sequential Colour a Memoire,* SECAM is the broadcast television standard for France, Russia, and much of eastern Europe (just as NTSC is the broadcast standard for the United States).

sequence—An assembly of shots edited together.

sharpening—In a video camera, a special algorithm that is applied to the video image to make it sharper. With too much sharpening, strange artifacts will appear in the image.

shooting ratio—The ratio of the length of footage shot to the length of the final film. For example, a project with a 5:1 ratio would have shot five hours of footage for a one-hour-long final project.

shot list—A list of the shots a director plans to shoot on a particular day of filming or taping. Usually, a shot list is derived by carefully going over the script, the storyboard, and blocking the scene with the actors in rehearsals.

shotgun—A very directional mic that is often affixed to the front of the camera or to a boom or fishpole.

shutter speed—The speed of the rotation of the *shutter* inside the lens, measured in rotations per second.

shutter—In a camera, the shutter opens and closes to control how long the focal plane is exposed to light. There is no physical shutter in a video camera; instead, the camera's CCD samples light for an appropriate length of time, and then shuts off.

sides—A dialogue-only version of a script, used to make readings easier for actors.

signal—Electronic information (video or audio) that is passed from one device to another.

single-chip—A camera that uses a single CCD to gather all three (red, green, and blue) of the signals that will be used to create a full-color image.

skylight—The ambient light from the sky, which consists of the reflected light of the sun. On a cloudy day, there is no sunlight, but there is still skylight.

slating —When, recording the sound separately from the video or film, the process of holding a slate in front of the camera. On the slate are written the scene and take numbers. The top of the slate can be clapped to produce a distinct sound that will be used for syncing the audio and video.

slow reveal —A moving shot—often a pan or dolly—that reveals something slowly, such as a slow pan of a bathroom that reveals a dead person in the bathtub.

slow-motion—A shot that plays at a slower speed than full-motion film or video. Usually described as a percentage of full motion.

slugline—The first line of a scene in a screenplay that identifies whether the scene is interior or exterior, the location, and the time of day, all in uppercase letters.

snow—The image of a video signal that has no control track, also known as *noise.*

soft light—Light from a diffuse, often indirect light source.

Sorenson compressor—A lossy QuickTime CODEC with very good quality. Sorenson is the ideal compression choice for Internet- and CD-ROM-based video distribution.

source monitor—The monitor or window that displays the unedited source footage, as opposed to the destination (or record) monitor, which plays the edited sequence.

SP-DIF—Short for Sony/Phillips Digital Interface, a digital audio format used for consumer equipment.

spin rate—Measured in revolutions per minute, the speed at which a hard drive spins.

spotting—Watching a locked-picture edit of your project with the intent of identifying all of the sound effects and music cues that will be needed.

storage—Nonvolatile storage that is used for long-term holding of programs and data. Usually magnetic or optical.

storyboard editing—A method of editing using thumbnails of each shot and organizing them in a bin, prior to drag-and-drop editing them into a sequence.

streaming video—Video that is downloaded, on demand, iteratively to the viewer's computer.

striped drives—Hard drives that have been indexed with special information so that they can be used as an array.

strobing—The odd, stuttery motion caused by fast shutter speeds. Strobing appears because of a lack of motion blur.

sunlight—The light from the sun.

super—To superimpose. Usually used to refer to the process of superimposing a title over an image.

S-video—(See *Y/C video.*)

S-video connector—A proprietary cable that is used to carry the Y/C video signal.

sweetening—The process of polishing the audio on a project by adding effects, equalizing, and fine-tuning edits.

switcher—(See *router.*)

sync—Short for synchronization, the electronic pulses used to coordinate the operation of several interconnected pieces of video hardware. Also, the electronic pulses used to regulate the playback of the videotape in the VTR. (See also *sync sound.*)

sync sound—Recording sound and video that are synchronized together, whether onto the same tape or by two or more separate recording devices.

telecine—The process of transferring film to videotape.

telephoto lens—A lens with a very narrow field of view (and, therefore, a long focal length). Telephoto lenses magnify objects in their field of view. Typically, lenses with focal lengths greater than 70 mm (equivalent to a 35mm film camera) are considered wide angle.

termination—The last device in a SCSI chain must have a terminator—a connector that signifies the end of the chain—placed on it. Bad termination can result in the entire SCSI chain malfunctioning.

three-chip—A camera that uses three separate CCDs to gather separate red, green, and blue data.

three-point editing—A method of editing where each edit is performed using an in- and an out-point on both the source footage and the edited sequence. Once the editor enters three of the four in- and out-points, the NLE or edit controller will automatically calculate the fourth in- or out-point.

three-point lighting—The standard way to light a person using a strong directed key light, a diffuse, less intense fill light, and a strong backlight.

throughput—A measure of the speed at which data can be moved through a computer or storage system.

tilt—To rotate the camera up and down around its horizontal axis.

timecode—A numbering system encoded in the video tape itself. It measures time in the format hh:mm:ss:ff, where h= hours, m=minutes, s=seconds, and f=frames.

timeline—A chronological display of an edited sequence in a non-linear editing system.

title safe—Another guide similar to the action safe area, the title safe area is slightly smaller. To ensure that your titles are visible on any monitor, always make certain that they fall within the title safe area.

transcoder—A device that changes the video signal from one format to another, such as from component to composite or from analog to digital.

travelling matte—A matte (see *matte*) that changes over time to follow the action of a moving element. Travelling mattes are used to composite a moving element into a scene. In the digital world, an animated alpha channel serves the same function as a travelling matte.

trim mode—The process of adjusting, or fine-tuning, an existing edit in an NLE.

tungsten light—Light from an incandescent source, such as a household light bulb. Tungsten light is weaker than daylight and tends to have a warm cast.

turnkey system—A video editing system that is preconfigured and assembled, and provides everything you need to start working.

tweening—(See *inbetweening*.)

UltraATA—A type of hard drive interface. Not as fast as SCSI, but fast enough for DV.

uncompressed video—Video that has not had any compression applied to it, either by the camera or by a computer.

unidirectional—A mic that picks up sounds from a particular direction.

USB—Universal serial bus. A standard for attaching serial devices such as keyboards, disk drives, and some types of storage. At the time of this writing, USB video capture devices were just becoming available.

UV filter—A filter that can be attached to the front of the lens. Filters out excess ultraviolet light and serves to protect the lens from scratching and breaking.

vacuum tubes—Before the invention of the CCD, video cameras used vacuum tubes to convert light into electronic signals.

VCD—Video compact disc. A format for storing 70 minutes of full-frame, full-motion, MPEG1 compressed video on a normal compact disc or recordable compact disc.

vectorscope—A special monitor for calibrating the hue, or color information, in a video signal.

vertical banding—Bright vertical smears that can occur in some video cameras when the camera is pointed at a very bright source.

VGA monitor—The monitor attached to your computer.

Video for Windows—A software architecture for displaying and manipulating time-based data (such as video and audio) on a computer.

virtual memory—A process by which the disk space can be used as a substitute for RAM.

VTR—Video tape recorder, the professional term for VCR.

VU meter— Volume unit meter. The volume meters on a sound recording device. VU meters help you gauge whether you are recording acceptable audio levels.

wattage—A measurement of the amount of electrical power used by a light, which determines the light's intensity.

white balance—When a camera has been calibrated to correctly display white, the camera is *white balanced*. Once it is calibrated for white, other colors should display properly.

widescreen—Standard NTSC or PAL video uses an aspect ratio of 4:3. Most film features are shot in a wider-screen aspect ratio. Some cameras include an option for shooting in a 16:9 aspect ratio. However, these modes are not actually any wider; rather, they are just cropped 4:3 images.

wild sounds—Non-sync sounds recorded by hand "in the wild" using a portable recording system.

wipe—A type of transition in which one image is wiped over another.

XLR cable—(See *XLR connector*.)

XLR connectors—Three-pronged, balanced audio connectors for connecting mics and other recording equipment.

Y/C video—Also called S-video (short for separate video), Y/C video has separate luma (Y) and chroma (C) video signals. (See also *component video* and *composite video*.)

YUV color space—The range of colors that can be displayed and recorded on digital video.

zebra—Special lines that can be displayed in a viewfinder that indicate areas of overexposure in an image.

zoom lens—A lens with variable focal lengths.

zoom ring—Similar to a focus ring, but used for manually zooming the camera.

Index

FIREWALL MEDIA

(An imprint of Laxmi Publications Pvt. Ltd.)

Computer Books *for School, BCA, MCA, IGNOU, DOEACC and Engineering Students and Professionals*

ISBN	TITLE	AUTHOR	PRICE	PAGES
	.NET			
8170087155	**Building Business Intelligence Applications with .Net**	Robert Ericsson	Rs. 295.00	404
8170083567	**Learning VB.Net Through Applications**	Clayton Crooks	Rs. 295.00	450
8131800865	**Magic of C# with .Net Frame Work**	Shibi Panikkar, Kumar Sanjeev	Rs. 495.00	950
8170082471	**Magic of ASP.Net with C#**	Shibi Panikkar, Kumar Sanjeev	Rs. 395.00	828
8170089662	**ASP.Net Interview Questions and Answers**	J. Rajaram	Rs. 95.00	175
	A TO Z SERIES			
8170083214	**Access 2002 from A to Z**	Julia Kelly, Stephen L. Nelson	Rs. 75.00	185
8170083222	**Excel 2002 from A to Z**	Stephen L. Nelson	Rs. 75.00	193
8170083230	**Front Page 2002 from A to Z**	Heather Williamson	Rs. 85.00	219
8170083249	**Outlook 2002 from A to Z**	Stephen L. Nelson	Rs. 75.00	202
8170083257	**Page Maker 7 from A to Z**	Marc Campbell	Rs. 75.00	202
8170083265	**PowerPoint 2002 from A to Z**	Stephen L. Nelson	Rs. 75.00	202
8170083273	**Windows XP from A to Z**	Pat Coleman	Rs. 95.00	249
8170083281	**Word 2002 from A to Z**	Stephen L. Nelson	Rs. 75.00	199
817008329X	**XML from A to Z**	Heather Williamson	Rs. 75.00	200
8170083303	**Dreamweaver 4 from A to Z**	Heather Williamson	Rs. 85.00	215
	BEGINNERS & GENERAL INTEREST			
817008248X	**Shortcuts to Success in Computing**	Dheeraj Mehrotra	Rs. 55.00	110
8170083311	**Pictorial Computer Dictionary**	Dheeraj Mehrotra	Rs. 45.00	156
8170083486	**Pocket Net Browser**	Dheeraj Mehrotra	Rs. 95.00	302
8170084261	**1000 IT Quizzes**	Dheeraj Mehrotra	Rs. 75.00	120
8131800679	**Information Technology Bible**	Remesh Bangia	Rs. 295.00	567
8131800377	**Fundamentals of Information Technology Including MS Office**	Dinesh Maidasani, Jai Narayan Yadav	Rs. 175.00	356
813180089X	**Fundamentals of Information Technology Including MS Office (Hindi Medium)**	Dinesh Maidasani, Jai Narayan Yadav	Rs. 175.00	425
8170089719	**Foundations of Computer Science**	Ashok Arora	Rs. 250.00	386

ISBN	TITLE	AUTHOR	PRICE	PAGES
	CALL CENTERS			
8170082196	**Call Centers Made Easy**	Stephen Medcroft	Rs. 195.00	310
	CISCO			
8170087481	**Enabling IP Routing with Cisco Routers**	R. Das, K. Chakrabarty	Rs. 295.00	486
817008749X	**Designing Networks with Cisco**	H. Pasricha, D. Jagu	Rs. 195.00	316
8170087503	**Cisco IP Routing Protocols: Troubleshooting Techniques**	V. Anand, K. Chakrabarty	Rs. 295.00	409
	DATABASES			
8170089530	**DBMS—Complete Practical Approach**	Sharad Maheshwari, Ruchin Jain	Rs. 350.00	656
8170082404	**Learn to Program Visual Basic-Examples**	John Smiley	Rs. 295.00	482
8170082412	**Learn to Program Visual Basic-Databases**	John Smiley	Rs. 325.00	653
8170082420	**Learn to Program Visual Basic-Objects**	John Smiley	Rs. 325.00	670
817008475X	**IT Resources-Access 2002 VBA Programming Access**	Michele Amelot	Rs. 195.00	424
8170084512	**The Power of Oracle 9i**	Rajiv Parida, Vinod Sharma	Rs. 475.00	1035
8170088518	**Principles and Implementation of Data Warehousing**	Rajiv A. Parida	Rs. 295.00	487
817008864X	**DBA Study Guide OCP Prep Guide**	Nazar Abdul	Rs. 295.00	474
8170088658	**Oracle 11i—The Complete Reference**	Rashmi Anandi	Rs. 495.00	975
8131800067	**Toxonomy of Database Management System**	Aditya Kumar Gupta	Rs. 75.00	146
8131800385	**Introduction to SQL and PL/SQL**	Sharad Maheshwari, Ruchin Jain	Rs. 200.00	389
	DOEACC 'O' LEVEL			
8170088089	**DOEACC 'O' Level Model Test Papers**	Ramesh Bangia	Rs. 175.00	296
8170089115	**DOEACC 'O' & 'A' Level Programming & Problem Solving Through 'C' Language (Model Test Paper with Solutions)**	Mukesh Sharma	Rs. 95.00	213
8170089069	**DOEACC 'O' & 'A' Level Business Systems (Model Test Paper with Solutions)**	Mukesh Sharma	Rs. 100.00	252
8170085640	**Programming and Problem Solving Through "C" Language**	Harsha Priya, R. Ranjeet	Rs. 95.00	306

ISBN	TITLE	AUTHOR	PRICE	PAGES
8170084474	**IT Tools and Applications**	Ramesh Bangia	Rs. 145.00	370
8170085594	**Business Systems**	Ramesh Bangia	Rs. 175.00	452
8170089514	**Internet & Web Design**	Ramesh Bangia	Rs. 150.00	300

ELECTRONIC COMMERCE

ISBN	TITLE	AUTHOR	PRICE	PAGES
8170085497	**Electronic Commerce**	Pete Loshin, John Vacca	Rs. 295.00	472
817008119X	**E-Commerce**	Mamta Bhusry	Rs. 95.00	215
8170083524	**Marketing in the Cyber Age**	Kurt Rohner	Rs. 295.00	223

HARDWARE/EMBEDDED SYSTEMS

ISBN	TITLE	AUTHOR	PRICE	PAGES
8170087473	**Essential Electronics for PC Technicians**	John W. Farber	Rs. 295.00	546
8170086264	**Grid Computing: A Practical Guide to Technology and Applications**	Ahmar Abbas	Rs. 295.00	408
8170088186	**CD Cracking Uncovered Protection Against Unsanctioned CD Copy**	Kris Kaspersky	Rs. 295.00	422
8170083435	**Practical Linux Programming: Device Drivers, Embedded Systems and the Internet**	Ashfaq A. Khan	Rs. 295.00	420
8170083575	**TCP/IP Application Layer Protocols for Embedded Systems**	M. Tim Jones	Rs. 295.00	460
8131800520	**PC Repair and Maintenance : A Practical Guide**	Joel Rosenthal, Kevin Irwin	Rs. 195.00	362
8131800768	**The A+ Certification and PC Repair Handbook**	Christopher A Crayton, Joel Z. Rosenthal	Rs. 495.00	888

INTERNET & WEB TECHNOLOGY

ISBN	TITLE	AUTHOR	PRICE	PAGES
8170083206	**The Internet Handbook for Writers, Students and Teachers**	Mary McGuire, Linda Stilborne	Rs. 195.00	276
8170084776	**Way in-Internet Getting Started**	Elizabeth Bramire	Rs. 95.00	165
8170088976	**Web Technology**	Ramesh Bangia	Rs. 250.00	560
8170087163	**Web Design with Macromedia Studio MX 2004**	Eric Hunley	Rs. 295.00	558
8170083400	**Professional Web Design (Techniques and Templates)**	Clint Eccher	Rs. 295.00	425
8170088046	**HTML, XHTML, CSS and XML**	Teodoru Gugoiu	Rs. 195.00	355
8170083583	**FrontPage 2000 for Visual Learners**	Chris Charuhas	Rs. 95.00	200
8170083591	**HTML & Java Script for Visual Learners**	Chris Charuhas	Rs. 95.00	200

ISBN	TITLE	AUTHOR	PRICE	PAGES
8170083605	**The Visual Learners Guide to Managing Web Projects**	Chris Charuhas	Rs. 95.00	130
8170083613	**Dreamweaver 4 for Visual Learners**	Chris Charuhas	Rs. 95.00	200
8170084768	**IT Resource-Implementing XML: Managing and Formatting Data**	Johhny Brochard	Rs. 125.00	279
8170089476	**Design Your Web World**	Sunil Jalota	Rs. 75.00	146

KEEPING AHEAD SERIES

ISBN	TITLE	AUTHOR	PRICE	PAGES
8170084652	**Keeping Ahead-Exchange 2000 Server**	Philippe Levesque	Rs. 145.00	285
8170084660	**Keeping Ahead-Windows 2000 Professional**	Jose Dardoigne	Rs. 175.00	388
8170084679	**Keeping Ahead-Windows 2000 Server**	Philippe Mathon	Rs. 175.00	360
8170084687	**Keeping Ahead-Linux Administration Kernel Version 2.0 to 2.2**	Bruno Guèrin	Rs. 125.00	240
8170084695	**Keeping Ahead-Using Linux Kernel Version 2.0 to 2.2**	Bruno Guèrin	Rs. 125.00	258
8170084709	**Keeping Ahead-Java 2**	Benjamin Aumaille	Rs. 145.00	284
8170084717	**Keeping Ahead-SQL Server 7**	Joelle Mosset	Rs. 145.00	329
8170084725	**Keeping Ahead-JavaScript and VBScript**	Benjamin Aumaille	Rs. 145.00	313
8170084733	**Keeping Ahead-C++ Programming Language**	Bruno Dubois	Rs. 125.00	234
8170084741	**Keeping Ahead-TCP/IP in the NT Environment**	Bruno Ferec	Rs. 125.00	230

MCSE

ISBN	TITLE	AUTHOR	PRICE	PAGES
817008489X	**MCSE-Administering SQL Server 7.0**	Jerome Gabillaud	Rs. 295.00	580
8170084903	**MCSE-Networking Essentials**	Jose Dordoigne	Rs. 245.00	453
8170084911	**MCSE-Windows 2000 Professional**	Jose Dordoigne	Rs. 325.00	665
817008492X	**MCSE-Windows 2000 Server**	Phillippe Mathon	Rs. 345.00	712

MULTIMEDIA AND ANIMATION

ISBN	TITLE	AUTHOR	PRICE	PAGES
8170088208	**3DS Max 6 Animation with Character Studio 4 and Plug-Ins**	Boris Kulagin, Dmitry Morozov	Rs. 175.00	216

Please write for a free color Firewall Media Catalog for details on the above books.

ISBN	TITLE	AUTHOR	PRICE	PAGES
8170088216	**Adobe Audition: Soundtracks for Digital Video**	Roman Petelin, Yury Petelin	Rs. 195.00	278
8170086205	**Building A Digital Human**	Ken Brilliant	Rs. 295.00	380
8170086213	**Making Digital Videos**	Ben Long	Rs. 295.00	284
8170087171	**Illustrating with Macromedia Flash ™ MX2004**	Robert Firbaugh	Rs. 245.00	366
8170082439	**Multimedia Basics-Technology (Vol. I)**	Andreas Holzinger	Rs. 195.00	312
8170082447	**Multimedia Basics-Learning (Vol. II)**	Andreas Holzinger	Rs. 195.00	326
8170082455	**Multimedia Basics-Design (Vol. III)**	Andreas Holzinger	Rs. 195.00	280
8170083532	**Maya Feature Creature Creations**	Todd Palamar	Rs. 295.00	376
8170083540	**Sound Forge Power**	Scott R. Garrigus	Rs. 195.00	344
8131800288	**Multimedia and Web Technology**	Ramesh Bangia	Rs. 395.00	878
813180044X	**Photoshop CS**	Shruti Lal	Rs. 195.00	434

NETWORKING

ISBN	TITLE	AUTHOR	PRICE	PAGES
817008721X	**Networking Essentials**	Jose Dordoigne	Rs. 195.00	453
8170089328	**TCP/IP Distributed System**	Vivek Acharya	Rs. 250.00	474
8170087023	**Computer Networks**	Ajit Kumar Singh	Rs. 95.00	181
8131800148	**The Real—world Network Troubleshooting Manual**	Alan Sugano	Rs. 295.00	396
817008203X	**Telecom & Networking Glossary**	Robert Mastin	Rs. 300.00	250
8170082048	**Data Networking Made Easy**	Karen Patten	Rs. 360.00	350
8170082056	**Digital Convergence**	Andy Covell	Rs. 300.00	234

OFFICE AUTOMATION

ISBN	TITLE	AUTHOR	PRICE	PAGES
8170089891	**Desk Top Publishing**	Dinesh Maidasani	Rs. 150.00	311
8170087805	**Learning Computer Fundamentals, MS Office and Internet & Web Technology**	Dinesh Maidasani	Rs. 95.00	301
8170087686	**MS-Word 2000 Thumb-Rules and Details**	Snigdha Banerjee	Rs. 175.00	390
8170089239	**Computer Accounting with Tally 7.2**	Firewall Media	Rs. 195.00	330

ON YOUR SIDE SERIES

ISBN	TITLE	AUTHOR	PRICE	PAGES
8170084830	**On your Side-Powerpoint 2002**	Andrew Blackburn	Rs. 145.00	282
8170084849	**On your Side-Excel 2002**	Adrienne Tommy	Rs. 125.00	275

ISBN	TITLE	AUTHOR	PRICE	PAGES
8170084857	**On your Side-Word 2002**	Adrienne Tommy	Rs. 125.00	289
8170084865	**On your Side-Access 2002**	Adrienne Tommy	Rs. 125.00	303
8170084873	**On your Side-Frontpage 2002**	Andrew Blackburn	Rs. 95.00	245
8170084881	**On your Side-Windows XP**	Adrienne Tommy	Rs. 125.00	310

OPERATING SYSTEMS

ISBN	TITLE	AUTHOR	PRICE	PAGES
8170087236	**Linux—A Practical Approach**	B. Mohamed Ibrahim	Rs. 95.00	187
8170088623	**Red Hat Linux Study Guide**	Vijay Shekhar	Rs. 350.00	635
8170088631	**Red Hat Linux-The Complete Bible**	Vijay Shekhar	Rs. 545.00	1176
8170089581	**Unix and Shell Programming**	Archana Verma	Rs. 80.00	137
8170089131	**Operating System Concepts**	P.S. Gill	Rs. 95.00	181
8170083427	**The MS-Windows XP Professional Handbook**	Louis Columbus	Rs. 295.00	330
8170084784	**Way in-Windows XP Home Edition**	Andrew Blackburn	Rs. 95.00	183
8170086221	**Cyber Rookies—Operating System Fundamentals**	D. Irtegov	Rs. 295.00	498

PROGRAMMING

ISBN	TITLE	AUTHOR	PRICE	PAGES
8170087791	**The Art of Programming Through Flowcharts & Algorithms**	Anil Bikas Chaudhuri	Rs. 95.00	160
8170086248	**Preventative Programming Techniques: Avoid and Correct Common Mistakes**	Brian Hawkins	Rs. 295.00	322
8170083443	**Learning Computer Programming : It's not about Languages**	Mary Farrell	Rs. 295.00	375
8170086256	**Object-Oriented Programming: From Problem Solving to Java**	José M. Garrido	Rs. 295.00	360
817008931X	**Object-Oriented Programming-Concept and Implementation**	A. Rajesh	Rs. 95.00	182
8170089107	**Java: J2SE-5 A Practical Approach**	B. Mohammad Ibrahim	Rs. 175.00	332
8170089409	**Advance Java**	Gajendra Gupta	Rs. 175.00	305
8170088038	**Assembly Language Programming for Intel Processors Family**	Vasile Lungu	Rs. 295.00	577
8170088178	**The Assembly Programming Master Book**	Vlad Pirogov	Rs. 395.00	726
813180075X	**Java Messaging**	Eric Bruno	Rs. 295.00	480

ISBN	TITLE	AUTHOR	PRICE	PAGES

PROGRAMMING - C#, C, C++

ISBN	TITLE	AUTHOR	PRICE	PAGES
8170083702	**The Power of C#**	Rajiv Parida	Rs. 295.00	576
8170085632	**Mastering Graphics Programming in 'C'**	Sudhir Dawra	Rs. 145.00	286
8170088879	**Programming in C and Numerical Analysis**	J.B. Dixit	Rs. 350.00	355
8170087074	**Mastering C Programs**	J.B. Dixit	Rs. 195.00	434
8170081262	**Programming in C**	J.B. Dixit	Rs. 295.00	506
8170087619	**Unix and C Programming**	Ashok Arora, Shefali Bansal	Rs. 295.00	606
817008878X	**C Interview Questions and Answers**	J. Rajaram	Rs. 75.00	139
8170089034	**Pragmatic C**	R.K. Jangda	Rs. 150.00	258
8170086140	**Data Structure for 'C' Programming**	Ajay Kumar	Rs. 145.00	290
8170081270	**Programming in C++**	J.B. Dixit	Rs. 260.00	602
8170088194	**Hackish C++ Pranks & Tricks**	Michael Flenov	Rs. 245.00	326
8170082889	**Basics of C++ Programming**	Nishant Kundalia	Rs. 95.00	168
8170083648	**Mastering C++ Programs**	J.B. Dixit	Rs. 295.00	598
817008623X	**Cyber Rookies—C++ Programming Fundamentals**	Chuck Easttom	Rs. 295.00	417
8131800202	**Data Structure using C++**	N. Jayalakshmi	Rs. 65.00	126
8170089123	**C++ Made Easy**	T.D. Malhotra	Rs. 250.00	449
8131800393	**C++ & Introduction to C#**	T.D. Malhotra, Rajeev A. Parida, A. Rajesh	Rs. 200.00	440
8131800350	**OOPS with C++**	M. Jaya Prasad	Rs. 150.00	317

SECURITY

ISBN	TITLE	AUTHOR	PRICE	PAGES
8170083419	**Computer Forensics : Computer Crime Scene Investigation**	John Vacca	Rs. 445.00	731
8131800156	**Computer Evidence (Collection and Preservation)**	Christopher L.T. Brown	Rs. 295.00	394
8170083494	**Firewall Architecture for the Enterprise**	Norbert Pohlmann, Tim Crothers	Rs. 295.00	480
8170086272	**Net Spies**	Andrew Gauntlett	Rs. 195.00	210
3826607546	**Firewall Systems**	Norbert Pohlmann	Rs. 1630.00	544
8131800504	**Homeland Security Techniques and Technologies**	Jesus Mena	Rs. 295.00	346

Please write for a free color Firewall Media Catalog for details on the above books.

ISBN	TITLE	AUTHOR	PRICE	PAGES

ENGINEERING AND TECHNOLOGY

ISBN	TITLE	AUTHOR	PRICE	PAGES
817008718X	**Human Aspects of Software Engineering**	James E. Tomayko, Orit Hazzan	Rs. 195.00	338
8131800032	**Management Information Systems**	Avdhesh Gupta, Anurag Malik	Rs. 195.00	400
8170087953	**Human Computer Interaction**	Rajendra Ranjan Kumar	Rs. 95.00	210
8170088097	**Structured System Analysis and Design**	Preeti Gupta	Rs. 125.00	192
817008802X	**Autocad 2005 for Engineers**	Ionel Simion	Rs. 175.00	271
8170088054	**Digital Signal Processing Fundamentals**	Ashfaq A. Khan	Rs. 295.00	391
8131800164	**Digital Communication System Using System VUE**	Dennis Silage	Rs. 295.00	365
8170089719	**Foundations of Computer Science**	Ashok Arora	Rs. 250.00	386
817008363X	**Practical Project Management**	Ivan Bayross	Rs. 195.00	342
8131800806	**Digital Signal Processing using MATLAB and Wavelets**	Michael Weeks	Rs. 350.00	452
8131800792	**Classical Electrodynamics**	Hans C. Dhanian	Rs. 395.00	620
8131800512	**The Software Vulnerability Guide**	Herbert H. Thompson, Scott G. Chase	Rs. 195.00	368
8131800776	**Robot Modelling and Kinematics**	Rachid Manseur	Rs. 295.00	380
8131800369	**System Software**	M. Joseph	Rs. 95.00	185

STRAIGHT TO THE POINT SERIES

ISBN	TITLE	AUTHOR	PRICE	PAGES
8170084601	**STTP : Word 2002**	Corinne Hervo	Rs. 45.00	154
817008461X	**STTP : Excel 2002**	Corinne Hervo	Rs. 45.00	153
8170084628	**STTP : Dreamweaver 4**	Corinne Hervo	Rs. 45.00	135
8170084636	**STTP : Flash 5**	Corinne Hervo	Rs. 45.00	183
8170084644	**STTP : Photoshop 6**	Corinne Hervo	Rs. 45.00	152
817008881X	**STTP : MS Office 2000**	Dinesh Maidasani	Rs. 125.00	290
8170086100	**STTP : MS Office 2003**	Dinesh Maidasani	Rs. 145.00	288
8170087651	**STTP : MS Word 2003**	Firewall Media	Rs. 60.00	150
8170088011	**STTP : Photoshop CS**	Firewall Media	Rs. 60.00	150
8170088143	**STTP : MS Excel 2003**	Firewall Media	Rs. 60.00	150
8170088151	**STTP : CorelDraw 12**	Firewall Media	Rs. 60.00	150
8131800105	**STTP : 3ds MAX 7**	Dinesh Maidasani	Rs. 95.00	182
8131800083	**STTP : Auto CAD 2006**	Dinesh Maidasani	Rs. 95.00	190
8131800245	**STTP : CorelDraw X3**	Dinesh Maidasani	Rs. 75.00	188

Please write for a free color Firewall Media Catalog for details on the above books.

ISBN	TITLE	AUTHOR	PRICE	PAGES
8131800253	**STTP : Dreamweaver 8**	Dinesh Maidasani	Rs. 75.00	148
8131800237	**STTP : Photoshop CS2**	Dinesh Maidasani	Rs. 75.00	172
8170088380	**STTP : Tally 7.2**	Firewall Media	Rs. 175.00	322
8131800091	**STTP : Flash 8**	Dinesh Maidasani	Rs. 95.00	180
8131800407	**STTP : My SQL 5.0**	Dinesh Maidasani	Rs. 85.00	166
8131800458	**STTP : Microsoft Power Point 2003**	Dinesh Maidasani	Rs. 75.00	142

STUDIO FACTORY

ISBN	TITLE	AUTHOR	PRICE	PAGES
8170084792	**Studio Factory—Photoshop 6**	Christophe Aubry	Rs. 175.00	364
8170084806	**Studio Factory—Flash 5**	Sami Ben Yahiya	Rs. 145.00	314
8170084814	**Studio Factory—Dreamweaver Ultradev 4**	Phillippe Chatellier	Rs. 95.00	240
8170084822	**Studio Factory—Dreamweaver 4**	Christophe Aubry	Rs. 175.00	373
8170087643	**Studio Factory—Dreamweaver MX**	Christophe Aubry	Rs. 195.00	407
8170087627	**Studio Factory—Flash MX**	Arnaud Blanche	Rs. 145.00	337
817008766X	**Studio Factory—Photoshop 7**	Cyril Guerin	Rs. 195.00	420

LAXMI PUBLICATIONS (P) LTD

113, Golden House, Daryaganj, New Delhi-110002
Phone : **011 - 43 53 25 00**
Fax : **011 - 43 53 25 28**
EMAIL : info@laxmipublications.com
Website : www.laxmipublications.com

BRANCHES

- 129/1, IIIrd Main Road, IX Cross, Chamrajpet, **Bangalore** (*Phone* : 080-26 61 15 61)
- 26, Damodaran Street, T. Nagar, **Chennai** (*Phone* : 044-24 34 47 26)
- 43/1394D, St. Benedict's Road, Ernakulam North, **Cochin** (*Phone* : 0484-239 70 04)
- Pan Bazar, Rani Bari, **Guwahati** (*Phones* : 0361-254 36 69, 251 38 81)
- 4-2-453, Ist Floor, Ramkote, **Hyderabad** (*Phone* : 040-24 75 02 47)
- Adda Tanda Chowk, N.D. 365, **Jalandhar City** (*Phone* : 0181-222 12 72)
- 106/A, Ist Floor, S.N. Banerjee Road, **Kolkata** (*Phones* : 033-22 27 37 73, 22 27 52 47)
- 18, Madan Mohan Malviya Marg, **Lucknow** (*Phone* : 0522-220 95 78)
- 142-C, Victor House, Ground Floor, N.M. Joshi Marg, Lower Parel (W), **Mumbai** (*Phones* : 022-24 91 54 15, 24 92 78 69)
- Radha Govind Street, Tharpagna, **Ranchi** (*Phone* : 0651-230 77 64)